D1715385

Italian Politics

ITALIAN POLITICS:
A REVIEW

Books in This Series

Italian Politics: The Year of the Tycoon, edited by Richard S. Katz and Piero Ignazi

Italian Politics: Ending the First Republic, edited by Carol Mershon and Gianfranco Pasquino

Italian Politics

The Year of the Tycoon

EDITED BY

Richard S. Katz
and Piero Ignazi

A Publication of the Istituto Cattaneo

WestviewPress

A Division of HarperCollins*Publishers*

Italian Politics: A Review, Volume 10

Published in 1996 in the United States of America by Westview Press, Inc., 5500 Central Avenue, Boulder, Colorado 80301-2877, and in the United Kingdom by Westview Press, 12 Hid's Copse Road, Cumnor Hill, Oxford OX2 9JJ

A CIP catalog for this book is available from the Library of Congress.
ISBN 0-8133-8972-0 (hc)—ISBN 0-8133-2976-0 (pbk)

The Istituto Cattaneo, founded in 1965, is a private, nonprofit organization. It aims to promote, finance, and conduct research, studies, and other activities that contribute to the knowledge of contemporary Italian society and, especially, of the Italian political system.

Istituto Carlo Cattaneo, Via Santo Stefano 11, 40125 Bologna, Italy

10   9   8   7   6   5   4   3   2   1

Contents

Chronology of Italian Political Events, 1994

January

3   Ciampi defends himself against Berlusconi's accusation that he raised taxes, reconfirming a 1.2 percent tax cut.

4   At the Cusani trial, Carlo Sama's former right hand man, Marcello Portesi, accuses Bossi of having asked for and obtained 200 million *lire* from Montedison to finance the Northern League.

5   Bossi admits to having contact with Carlo Sama, but denies charges of kickbacks paid by the League's ex-treasurer, Alessandro Patelli.
New dissension within the DC: Martinazzoli parts with neo-centrists Mastella, Casini, and D'Onofrio, who are accused of having independent contacts with the other parties.

8   Ciampi refuses the resignation of police chief Parisi, accused in the SISDE scandal.

9   A bomb explodes in Rome, in front of the NATO offices in EUR.

10 The Pope appeals for Catholic unity in a letter to Italian bishops.

11 Indro Montanelli, the founder of the *Giornale*, resigns over political dissension with Berlusconi, the daily paper's publisher.

12 Ciampi resigns.
As the judicial year begins, Vittorio Sgroi, Procurator General for the Court of Cassation, criticizes the activism (protagonism) of the *Mani pulite* judges and the excessive presence of Public Prosecutors in the trials.

13 Carlo Azeglio Ciampi returns his mandate to President Scalfaro, who sets new elections for March 27.

Luigi Abete, president of *Confindustria*, distances himself from Berlusconi, declaring the business world's neutrality until the presentation of programs and candidates.

14 Rabbi Toaff, head of the Italian Jewish community, asks Scalfaro to change the date of the March 27 election, which falls on Passover.
Negotiations between FIAT and labor leaders over the 1994-96 industrial plan fail.

16 Scalfaro refuses Ciampi's resignation.

17 Protests by Jewish citizens are greeted by the government with an exceptional decree which extends the vote to Monday, March 28.
1,800 workers and technicians at FIAT go on unemployment benefits at midnight.

18 The DC is dissolved and two new parties are formed: the Italian Popular Party (PPI), headed by Martinazzoli, and the Christian Democratic Center (CCD), by neo-centrists Casini, D'Onofrio, and Mastella.

19 Following the opening of an investigation of Gioia Tauro's ENEL plant jobs, top business managers are arrested.
Silvio Berlusconi gives an ultimatum to the moderate forces: if there is no alliance agreement in a week, his entry into politics will be inevitable.

21 Minister of the Interior Nicola Mancino resigns following his direct involvement in the investigations of SISDE slush funds. Ciampi refuses his resignation.

22 Giorgio La Malfa is re-elected secretary of the PRI.
Fausto Bertinotti takes Armando Cossutta's place as secretary of the Communist Refoundation, and MSI secretary Gianfranco Fini launches his National Alliance project, while Martinazzoli illustrates PPI policy by shutting out the PDS and entering into a dialogue with the League.

24 Segni and Maroni initial an accord for an electoral alliance.

26 Silvio Berlusconi resigns as president of Fininvest and announces his plans to enter into politics and form a coalition to oppose the Left.
The accord between Segni and the League falls through.

27 The CSM allows certain judges, including Tiziana Parenti of the *Mani pulite* investigating team, to be candidates in the parliamentary elections.

28 The MSI convention opens and adopts the symbol of the National Alliance for future elections.

30 The PRI is divided over electoral coalitions: with only six "no" votes, La Malfa's proposal of an alliance with Segni and Martinazzoli passes, against those who supported an alliance with the Left.

31 Bossi declares that he is against an accord with the MSI-AN.

February

1 A Progressive electoral accord is formed, including the PDS, the Greens, the Network, Communist Refoundation, AD, PSI, *Rinascita Socialista*, and the Social Christians.

3 A Doxa poll reveals that 26 percent of Italians consider Berlusconi the most trustworthy man in politics, followed by Ciampi with 10 percent and Occhetto and Segni with 7 percent.
Disagreements over candidacies arise in the newly-formed Progressive line-up: AD and the Greens refuse to participate in the public introduction of the symbol.

4 At the League congress in Bologna, Bossi says yes to an alliance with *Forza Italia* and no to Fini and Segni.

6 In Rome, Berlusconi announces his principle electoral program based on the fight against unemployment, the reduction of taxes, and *laissez-faire* economics.

7 Berlusconi and Fini conclude an accord for the nomination of candidates common to *Forza Italia* and the National Alliance in the Center and the South.

10 Bossi and Berlusconi reach an agreement for common lists in the North.

11 Silvio Berlusconi's brother Paolo is arrested on charges that he paid a kickback for the sale of three Milano 3 buildings. By evening, house arrest is granted.

13 Two Italian volunteer workers, Sergio Passadore and Gianfranco Stefani, are kidnapped in Somalia.

16 Massimo D'Alema, second-in-charge of the PDS, is included on the list of those being investigated for payments to the ex-PCI, after Craxi's denunciation.

17 The *Banca d'Italia* reduces the discount rate by half a point, bringing it to 7.5 percent.
Mario Sarcinelli is named president of the BNL.

19 Achille Occhetto is also listed as being investigated following accusations by Craxi, who himself is accused of slander.

21 FIAT and union leaders sign an agreement allowing early retirement for more than 6,000 workers and unemployment compensation for 4,000.

22 Certain electoral lists are disallowed for irregularities according to the new electoral law: Mario Segni's Pact is excluded from the proportional vote in 8 districts (*circoscrizioni*) and in all the senatorial constituencies in Lazio. The League, AD, the Greens, Communist Refoundation, Pannella's List, and the Network are also excluded in certain constituencies.

23 Other exclusions are effected by the Court of Appeals, including Segni's Pact (10 constituencies), *Forza Italia* in Puglia and in the Marches, and the League in Umbria.

26 With the privatization of 51 percent of the *Banca Commerciale Italiana*, IRI definitively exits the credit sector. The selling price of the shares is fixed at 5,400 *lire*, 5.3 percent less than the Bourse quote.

28 Shares of COMIT sell out on the first day of sale.
   At a convention in Rome, Scalfaro incites disagreement by claiming the parity of public and private schools.

March

2 Berlusconi proposes a single rate personal income tax (IRPEF) of 30 percent.

5 The Pope intervenes in the argument over private and public schools in favor of Scalfaro's views of a few days before.

7 The revelations of a witness who turned state's evidence lead to the arrest of two Neapolitan magistrates (Alessandro Cono Lancuba, Prosecutor of Melfi, and Vito Masi, of the Naples court) and the request to arrest two members of Parliament (MPs).

8 The Milan prosecutor's office investigates Fininvest and searches the offices of Publitalia to ascertain the possible use of a slush fund in the acquisition of soccer player Gianluigi Lentini by A.C. Milan.

10 Berlusconi reacts to the Fininvest investigations by accusing the Milanese investigative team of political maneuvering against *Forza Italia*.

11 Paolo Berlusconi verifies that he paid 1.3 billion *lire* to Pieve Emanuele's PCI-PSI junta to obtain concessions to construct a golf course.

13 The names of the journalists involved in the kickbacks made by the Montedison group are released: Giuseppe Turani of *La Repubblica*, Ugo Bertone of *La Stampa*, and Osvaldo De Paolini of *Il Sole 24 Ore*.

19 Don Giuseppe Diana, Anti-Mafia priest and witness in the ongoing trials in Napoli against bosses and tainted politicians, is killed in a mob ambush.

20 In Somalia two RAI journalists are killed: Ilaria Alpi of Tg3 and Milan Hrovatin, a cameraman from Trieste.

22 President of the Anti-Mafia Commission Luciano Violante's declaration, leading to the investigation of president of Publitalia Dell'Utri in Catania, was denied by MP who questioned the journalist.

23 La Digos searches the Rome offices of *Forza Italia*, following a warrant signed by the Palmi attorney's office.
Anti-Mafia president Violante resigns.

27 First day of parliamentary elections: the turnout is 57.3 percent.

28 The electoral results give 46 percent of the vote to the Right: *Forza Italia* comes in first and the Freedom Alliance (*Polo della Libertà*) (FI, AN, League, and CCD) wins an absolute majority in the Chamber with 366 seats and a relative majority in the Senate with 154 seats.

29 In the first negotiations to form a new government, Bossi asserts the primary role of the League as first-place party in number of elected parliamentarians (118 deputies and 58 senators).

30 Martinazzoli resigns as secretary of the PPI.

April

1 Bossi walks out on the League-*Forza Italia* meeting, thus slowing the formation of a government.

4 New dissension between Bossi and Berlusconi, who appeals to the League MPs against the declarations of their leader.

5 The Catholic Church, through Cardinal Ruini, sends a conciliatory message to *Forza Italia*, arousing the objections of PPI president Rosa Russo Jervolino.

6 Bossi proposes the formation of a government that will change the Constitution in favor of federalism and then hand over to an executive led by Berlusconi.

8   On Ciampi's last day in *Palazzo Chigi*, Bossi meets Scalfaro to reconfirm the condition of federalism for the formation of a new government.

9   At the *Riformatori* convention Pannella reconfirms his support of the Freedom Alliance.

10 In Pontida before 30,000 supporters Bossi confirms that the League will only enter into a government that approves federalism as soon as possible.

12 Tiziana Parenti, a former judge of the *Mani pulite* investigative team and newly-elected *Forza Italia* MP, denies the possibility of Mafia infiltration within her party's "clubs."

15 Installation of the new Parliament of the Twelfth Legislature. Contrary to common practice, the presidency of both Chambers is determined by the majority.

16 By a margin of only one vote over outgoing president Spadolini, *Forza Italia* senator Carlo Scognamiglio is elected to the presidency of *Palazzo Madama*. Irene Pivetti, League deputy, is elected president of the Chamber by an ample margin of 347 votes.
    Giulio di Donato (PSI) is arrested: he is the first former member of Parliament to be arrested.
    Licio Gelli is sentenced to 17 years in prison.

19 Following Antonio Galasso's turning state's evidence, ex-solicitor Matteo Cinque is arrested in Naples, accused of favoring crime boss Carmine Alfieri.

20 Five deputies favoring an understanding with *Forza Italia* leave Mario Segni's Pact: Michelini, Tremonti, Milio, Siciliani, and Stajano.

23 Fini and Bossi travel to the *Quirinale* to affirm their consent to the nomination of Berlusconi as the head of government.

25 A large demonstration in Milan for the April 25 celebrations; confrontations with Bossi, who attends.

26 Scalfaro declares that he will personally act as guarantor in the conflict of interests between Berlusconi as businessman and as future prime minister.

29 Judge Piercamillo Davigo of the *Mani pulite* investigative team refuses offers made by the AN to be minister of Justice. Meanwhile, Milan Magistrate for Preliminary Investigations Italo Ghitti leaves his position in order to be nominated for the July elections for the renewal of the CSM.

May

2 The possibility of neo-fascist ministers, raising a vast echo heard among the international press, hampers the formation of the new government. Berlusconi says he is turning to the experts of the AN, and not to the old members of the MSI.

4 A motion by the socialist group in Strasbourg, approved with only one dissenting vote, asks that fascist ministers not enter the Italian government. Scalfaro reacts by asserting government autonomy and Berlusconi declares that he wants to proceed without interference.

7 Di Pietro refuses the Ministry of the Interior, after a meeting with Berlusconi.

10 The Berlusconi government is formed. It includes five ministers from the National Alliance, three of whom were past leaders of the MSI.

12 Former Minister of Health Francesco De Lorenzo is arrested in Naples after inquests into corruption in the health care system.

13 Thirty-seven undersecretaries are nominated. All of them are members of Parliament except for Gianni Letta, the undersecretary to the Prime Minister.

14 After his exclusion from the government, League ideologue Gianfranco Miglio breaks with Bossi and signs on with the mixed group.

16 Debates in Vicenza over a skinhead demonstration: Maroni removes the *questore* and prefect who had authorized the parade.
The Court of Appeals of Bologna confirms the prison sentence for Valerio Fioravanti, Francesca Mambro, and Sergio Picciafuoco for the Bologna "massacre."

18 A vote of investiture passes in the Senate with 159 votes against 153. The absences of four PPI senators are decisive: Cecchi Gori, Grillo, Zanoletti, and Cusumano, who are expelled from the group.

20 The Chamber also approves the vote of investiture with 366 votes "for" and 245 "against."

21 The Palermo attorney's office requests an adjournment in the case of Giulio Andreotti, accused of complicity with Mafia bosses.

25 The presidents of the parliamentary commissions are named: in the Chamber none are assigned to members of the opposition.
Rumors in the Bourse of an *avviso di garanzia* against Silvio Berlusconi cause the collapse of the MIB index by 2.6 percent.

28 Scalfaro is challenged by the *Autonomi* in Brescia during the celebrations for the twentieth anniversary of the *Piazza della Loggia* massacre.

30 *Avvisi di garanzia* by the Ravenna attorney's office for the heads of Mediobanca.

31 Romano Prodi, president of IRI, resigns.

June

1 United States president Bill Clinton visits Italy in preparation for the G-7 meeting in Naples.
   In the Senate, opposition groups claim the presidencies of numerous commissions.

3 Marco Taradash, president of the supervisory commission of the RAI, requests investigations by the magistrates on party patronage and on the former management of the RAI.

4 Berlusconi dissociates himself from Taradash's statements, which had sparked dissension within the majority.

7 Berlusconi attacks RAI, accusing it of bleeding the public with accounts strongly in the red and of continuing to side with those who had been defeated in the elections.

8 The first provisions of the Council of Ministers foreseeing tax relief (25 percent less for IRPEF) on the new hires at an undetermined date at a 50 percent discount on the profits reinvested by businesses.

12 At the election for the European Parliament, *Forza Italia* reaches 30 percent, the National Alliance holds, and the League falls back a bit. The PDS, PPI, and the Pact lose.

13 After the electoral defeat of the PDS (down 1.2 percent from the parliamentary elections) Achille Occhetto resigns as secretary, as does Del Turco (PSI) and Bordon (AD).

19 Bossi confronts the differences within the League, re-establishing the party's unity in the Pontida assembly and re-affirming the rejection of a single party with Fini and Berlusconi.

23 To counter leaks from certain ministers, Berlusconi names Giuliano Ferrara, Minister for Parliamentary Relations, official government spokesperson.

26 6.5 million voters in the first round for the administrative elections: the Progressives surprisingly win the Sardinian Council presidency and earn increase their vote relative to the European elections, aided by the clashes in the second round between League candidates and *Forza Italia* candidates.

29 The Council of Ministers decides to reiterate the decree for the financial reconstruction of RAI, but opposes the plan presented by the board of directors of the "professors."
Sergio Cofferati replaces Bruno Trentin as secretary of the CGIL.

30 The RAI board of directors and the general manager of the RAI, Gianni Locatelli, resign.

July

1 The national council of the PDS elects a new secretary: Massimo d'Alema, with 249 against 173 for Walter Veltroni.

4 The first spending cuts are approved, hitting mostly Health and Social Security.

8 The G-7 summit begins in Naples.

11 A new board of directors is named for the RAI. The directors are Ennio Presutti, Letizia Moratti, Franco Cardini, Alfio Marchini, and Mauro Miccio.

12 New heads of the secret service are named: Gaetano Marino at the head of SISDE, Sergio Siracusa for SISMI, and Umberto Pierantoni for CESIS.

13 The Council of Ministers approves the Biondi decree, calling for strong restrictions on the judges' power to arrest and returning to freedom those awaiting justice as a result of the *Mani pulite* investigations.
Letizia Moratti is unanimously elected president of RAI.

14 The judges in the Milan investigative team threaten to quit, following the approval of the Biondi decree. Bossi also voices strong doubts.
The board of directors nominates Gianni Billia, former manager of INPS, as general director of RAI.

16 Maroni declares he is ready to resign if the Biondi decree is not withdrawn.

17 Berlusconi gives Maroni an ultimatum: either he withdraws his accusations or he resigns. Bossi reaffirms his support of Maroni.

Italy is defeated by Brazil, by a penalty kick, in the finals for the World Soccer Championship.

19 The government abandons the Biondi decree.
Borrelli freezes the transfer request for the judges of the Milan investigative team, who return to the investigations.

21 The Chamber rejects the Biondi decree: 418 no, 33 yes, and 41 abstentions.

22 The government approves a decree for reduced fines in exchange for admission of building violations (*condono edilizio*).

23 Former Defense Minister Salvatore Andò (PSI) and former regional president Rino Nicolosi (DC) are arrested in Catania.

25 Salvatore Sciascia, responsible for Fininvest accounting, is arrested.

29 Berlusconi introduces his blind trust plan to separate his business interests from his political activities.
After fleeing from justice for a few days, Paolo Berlusconi gives himself up, to be placed under house arrest.
Rocco Buttiglione is elected secretary of Italian Popular Party.

30 Bossi rejects Berlusconi's plan and announces a League anti-trust proposal.

August

4   Giovanni Spadolini, former president of the Senate, dies. He had been the first non-Christian Democratic prime minister, minister with various portfolios and Senator for Life.

5   Tiziana Parenti is nominated by the Chamber presidents to the presidency of the Anti-Mafia Commission.

11 The *Banca d'Italia* raises the prime lending rate by half a point, bringing it to 7.5 percent.

13 After days of debate, Berlusconi and Bossi meet at Arcore and "make peace."

15 Debate over Berlusconi's declaration that: "If this government falls, disorder will reign."

16 The Minister of the Interior announces De Gennaro's transfer from the Anti-Mafia Investigations Division and Parisi's from head of the police, starting in 1995.

19 The National Alliance attacks Bankitalia, accusing governor Fazio of abuse of office.

22 Scalfaro defends the autonomy of the *Banca d'Italia*.

24 Minister of Labor Mastella and his undersecretary Letta declare that acquired rights on pensions will not be touched.

26 Fernando Masone, Roman questore, is named chief of Police, following the resignation of Vincenzo Parisi.

27 From the CL (*Comunione e Liberazione*) meeting in Rimini, chamber president Irene Pivetti invites Catholics to political unity and scolds former DC members for their vote in favor of abortion.

31 Bossi declares that Berlusconi asked Scalfaro for early elections. The prime minister and the president refute each other's claims.

September

2 Dissension within the government after the German Christian Democrats' proposal to create a two-tiered Europe, in which Italy would occupy the second tier.

3 At a convention on Italian economics, Di Pietro reveals a proposal to withdraw from *Mani pulite* with a judicial solution for the crimes committed and a legislative program for the future.

8 Minister of the Treasury Dini affirms that vested rights will not be touched in the pension reform plan.

10 Bitter encounters in the piazzas in Milan between Leoncavallo's *Autonomi* and the police, with injuries on both sides. Debates between Maroni and Formentini, the mayor.

13 First agreement between the government and the unions on the budget.

15 Minister of Finance Tremonti intervenes in the debates over budget cuts, affirming that the Treasury will have to provide 2,500 billion *lire* more in revenue in order to lessen the cuts to pensions.

17 The RAI board of directors names new network directors and heads of the news departments, eliciting complaints from the League and the opposition.

20 Antonio Gava, former Minister of the Interior and leader of the Neapolitan DC, is arrested under charges of complicity with the mob.

24 The *Mani pulite* inquest involves the world of fashion, with *avvisi di garanzia* for Giorgio Armani and Gianfranco Ferrè.

26 The RAI nominees are frozen, and the debate is passed to Parliament.

27 Government and labor unions break over pensions.

28 The government launches the 1995 budget, foreseeing 50 thousand billion *lire* in cuts and earnings tax amnesty, with hiring freezes for six months in the public sector and a shift in age limits for pensions, starting in 1995.

30 The Brescia attorney's office lists Di Pietro among those to be investigated, following accusations by Cusani, suggesting abuses of office and defamation.

October

1 Scalfaro signs the budget act after asking that the social security reform be removed.

4 Berlusconi accuses the judges of making "use of justice for distorted ends."

5 In an interview with the *Corriere della Sera*, Borrelli declares that the "Telepiù" investigation is reaching "very high levels" and attacks Biondi. Biondi resigns (refused by the government), and Ferrara announces the government's exposé of Borrelli at CSM.

6 The Council of Ministers unanimously approves an open letter against Borrelli addressed to Attorney General of the Court of Cassation Vittorio Sgroi.

7 Scalfaro sends the open letter against Borrelli to the CSM, together with a second letter in which the government reduces the accusatory tone of the first letter.

8 In response to stories of conflicts of interest between Berlusconi as corporate head and Berlusconi as politician, articles propose leaving the

Prime Minister possession of his assets, as long as their management is conceded to a blind trust.

9   Bossi and the opposition parties reject the proposals for a blind trust.

14 Over 3 million people take part in the general strike called by the labor unions against the budget. From Moscow, Berlusconi minimizes the event, declaring that it will not influence the government's economic decisions.

15 Labor leaders proclaim a new national strike with a demonstration in Rome on November 19.

17 The CSM proposes the shelving of the Borrelli case and Minister of Justice Biondi arranges for a ministerial inspection of the Milan investigative team in order to assess charges of abuse made by those implicated in *Tangentopoli*.

18 Vincenzo Desario is named director general of the *Banca d'Italia*.

20 Controversy in the Chamber: AN deputies attack Green deputy Mauro Paissan, rapporteur of the "save the RAI" decree.
    The CSM votes against the transfer of Chief Procurator of Milan, Borrelli.

23 A new effort, led by Maroni, arises in the League, harshly attacking the National Alliance.

24 The Palermo attorney's office opens an investigation on the red cooperatives and their relationship with the PDS in Sicily.

25 Scalfaro rejects Previti's proposal for a commission of inquiry on *Tangentopoli*, reaffirming the judges' autonomy.

28 Italian members of the Commission of the European Union are nominated: economist Mario Monti and radical MP Emma Bonino.

30 Former PSI financier Ferdinando Mach di Palmstein is arrested in Paris on charges of being Bettino Craxi's secret treasurer.

November

1   The RAI board of directors votes on the new appointments of heads of the new departments. Alfio Marchini resigns in protest of the decisions.

3   Maroni opens an investigation of speculators who spread unfounded rumors about the financial markets.

Minister of Finance Tremonti is added to the list of those to be investigated by the attorney's office in Rome, with accusations of abuse of office in the Secit case.

4 The Council of Ministers approves a document proposed by *leghista* Speroni, providing for the adoption of a run-off vote for regional elections. The AN and the CCD abstain.

6 Flooding in Piedmont and Liguria: more than 60 dead and 10,000 billion *lire* in damages.

8 The government allocates 3,000 billion *lire* for the regions hit by flooding.

9 Giuliano Amato is nominated by the presidents of both Chambers to head the Anti-trust office.

10 A no-confidence motion on the RAI board of directors presented by the opposition is passed in the Senate.

12 More than a million people show up for a demonstration in Rome to protest the budget.
An investigation is opened on the delays in aid: Mario Palmerio, prefect of Asti, receives an *avviso di garanzia* for malicious malfeasance.

14 The government receives a vote of confidence in the Chamber (321 yes, 134 no) on amnesty for the construction industry.

15 New rupture between the government and labor unions on pensions: CGIL, CISL, and UIL call another general strike for December 2.

19 Maroni denounces Berlusconi for failing to reach accord with the labor unions: "He wants social unrest." In the evening he denies directing his accusations toward the other members of the majority.

20 In the first round of voting for 242 communal administrations and the provincial council of Massa, *Forza Italia* and the AN lose ground; PDS and the *Popolari*, whose alliances are often rewarded by the electorate, gain.

21 The Chamber approves the 1995 budget.

22 Berlusconi receives an *avviso di garanzia* for participation in corruption. The Prime Minister declares that he will remain in office, denying every accusation.

23 Berlusconi asks for a confidence vote within a week.

25 Summit meeting at the Quirinale between Scalfaro and Berlusconi to avoid a crisis in the government.

27 Demonstration in Turin in support of Berlusconi.

29 The Court of Cassation withdraws the investigation of the Financial Police at the Milan attorney's office, sending the proceedings to the Brescia office.

December

1 After twenty-four hours of negotiations, an accord on pensions between the government and the labor unions is signed: the principle points of the understanding regard the cancellation of penalties for old-age pensions and the release of pensions starting June 1995 for laborers with 35 years of wage-earning. CGIL, CISL, and UIL cancel the strike called for December 2.

2 Head prosecutor Borrelli sends two letters of protest to Catelani and Scalfaro for inspections ordered by Biondi.
Student demonstrations all over Italy for the reform of secondary schools.

4 The second round in the local elections confirms the success of the Center-Left alliance of the *Popolari* and the *Progressisti*. Martinazzoli wins in Brescia, as well as Molteni in Sondrio, Pucci in Massa, and Errico in Brindisi. Gentilini, supported by the Northern League and a mixed centrist coalition, is elected in Treviso.
Only in Pescara did the candidate of the government area (FI, AN, CCD), Pace, surpass (by a few hundred votes) the candidate of the *Progressisti*, former mayor Collevecchio.

6 Antonio Di Pietro, symbol of the *Mani pulite* investigative team, resigns and leaves the magistrature. In his resignation letter to Borrelli, he claims to have become annoyed by the increasing accusations of politicization.

10 From Loreto Pope John Paul II releases a call for political unity among Catholics.

13 Berlusconi is interrogated for more than seven hours by the Milanese investigative team regarding Fininvest kickbacks to the Financial Police. Eleven inspectors from the Ministry of Justice resign.

14 In the vote to institute a special commission for television reform, the *leghista* deputies vote with the PPI-PDS opposition.
Berlusconi asks for a vote of confidence for December 21.

15 Berlusconi meets Scalfaro for reassurance on the future of the government.

16 Biondi's inspectors take back their resignations and return to the investigations.

17 A crisis in government is initiated with the announcement of two no-confidence motions, one by the PDS, and the other by the *leghisti* and the *popolari*. The motions are signed by a majority of deputies.

21 In the Chamber debate on no-confidence, Berlusconi attacks Bossi harshly, accusing him of betraying the majority, and calls for elections as a way out of the crisis.

22 Berlusconi visits the Quirinale and resigns from the premiership.
The Northern League is divided over the no confidence vote for the outgoing government.

23 Scalfaro begins consultations for forming a new government.
Ugo Dinacci, Biondi's leading inspector, is listed among those being investigated by the Salerno attorney's office for accusations of collusion with the *camorra*.

28 After initial overtures by Chamber group leader Dotti toward an institutional solution to the crisis, *Forza Italia* throws its support behind Berlusconi again: either Berlusconi is reinstalled or new elections are called.

30 After a television interview in which Berlusconi declares that Parliament is delegitimated, contention is sparked between Scalfaro and Berlusconi over the issue of new elections.

31 In his traditional year end message, Scalfaro addresses Berlusconi directly, calling on him to cooperate with the transition and to respect the constitution, with the goal of a rapid solution to the government crisis.

Translated by Sara L. Brann

1

Introduction

Richard S. Katz and Piero Ignazi

Institutional Changes and New Political Actors

The political life of Italy in 1994 was dominated by two major themes. The first is institutional. 1994 saw the implementation of the new parliamentary electoral law; the collapse of the Christian Democratic Party; the formation and the rise to power of *Forza Italia* along with the transformation of the MSI (a permanently excluded anti-system party that was rarely mentioned without the prefix "neo-Fascist") into the *Alleanza Nazionale* and its entry into government; and a Parliament and a government that are radically renewed in their composition. Altogether, these developments at least make it reasonable to ask whether 1993 was not, in fact, the final year of the First Republic, and 1994 the first year of the Second, or at least the first year of the period of transition leading to a new political system for Italy. On the other side, of course, it must be remembered that far-reaching though these changes may be, the Constitution of the Italian Republic was not amended, let alone replaced.

The second, and intimately intertwined, theme focuses on the meteoric rise, and perhaps ultimately the beginning of the equally meteoric decline, of Silvio Berlusconi as the dominating personality in Italian politics of the past year. Berlusconi was already an important personality in politics, based on his monopoly control of the commercial television networks and his friendship with Bettino Craxi. Nonetheless, his announcement, in November 1993, that the "categorical imperative" (*"imperativo categorico"*) of forming a center alliance to oppose the Left had led him to decide to enter politics was greeted with some skepticism. Although in recent polls 13 percent of interview respondents had answered the question "Do you have confidence in Silvio Berlusconi?" by saying, "Definitely yes", and 43 percent answered "Probably yes," Mario Segni described Berlusconi's entry into politics as "an inopportune initiative," while the *Lega* showed no enthusiasm. By mid-February, however, Berlusconi's newly formed *Forza Italia* had concluded electoral pacts with both the MSI (which agreed to present itself as the *Alleanza Nazionale*) and the *Lega Nord*. By the time of the parliamentary elections in March, it was clear to all (except perhaps *Lega* leader Umberto Bossi) that Berlusconi was *the* prime ministerial candidate of the right alliance, and on April 28, President of the Republic Oscar Luigi Scalfaro asked the *Cavaliere* to form a government. With an apparently firm majority in the Chamber of Deputies, and nearly a majority in the Senate, early speculation concerned whether the Berlusconi government would last the full parliamentary term. But by Christmas, Berlusconi had resigned rather than face three motions of no confidence in Parliament, one of them tabled by his erstwhile ally, the *Lega Nord*.

All that has happened under the Berlusconi government suggests that the First Republic was not only reasserting itself even before the government fell, but that indeed it had never really disappeared. On the other hand, regime transitions inevitably take time; a regime transition is a process, not a single event. It is also possible as parties and politicians adapt to the realities of the new electoral institutions (perhaps making further reforms) and to changes in the international system and in public opinion, that 1994, and the Berlusconi government, will be seen as the first steps in the evolution to a fundamentally altered political system. Similarly, it is possible that the fall of Berlusconi's government will allow the long discussed reforms of the Mammì law, potentially destroying the Fininvest broadcasting empire, the collapse of *Forza Italia*, and the disappearance of Berlusconi himself from the political scene; indeed, short of all this, Berlusconi may simply decide that politics is not as much fun as he hoped and withdraw. But it is also possible that the Dini government will be no more than a brief interregnum, after which Berlusconi will emerge triumphant from a new election, more securely in power than ever before. Perhaps indeed the Second Republic will prove to be a "Second Kingdom," even if an elective one.

A Second Italian Republic?

The passage of the reformed parliamentary electoral law in August 1993 was widely hailed as marking the inauguration of the Second Republic, and allusions to the Second Republic were common in political reporting throughout 1993 and into 1994. Indeed, the English edition of the last volume of this yearbook was subtitled "Ending the First Republic," and the concluding section of its introductory chapter was "The Transition to the Second Republic."[1] Much of what happened in 1994 only can be understood in the light of the expectations raised or reflected by the use of that phrase.

The Second Republic was short hand for changes in institutions and in behavior, not all of which were realized, and whose permanence has yet to be seen. In a fundamental sense, the term was a hyperbole. In contrast to the French or German use of adjectives to identify republics (e.g., the Fifth Republic or the Weimar Republic) the Second Italian republic was not taken to involve any fundamental institutional rupture or constitutional discontinuity. The changes made in the parliamentary electoral system were initiated by the ordinary process of referendum used many times before under the First Republic, and were completed by ordinary legislation. Although they qualify as "major" changes, they still were less far reaching than the French substitution of proportional representation for the two-ballot majority system in 1985 (or the change back in 1986) yet no one identified 1986 as the beginning of the Sixth French Republic.

If the Italian reforms were, on the surface, less drastic than the French, the expectations they raised were more far reaching. In the French case, the reformers (i.e., the Socialists in power) merely hoped to limit the short term consequences of their unpopularity; it was widely expected that the conservatives would restore the *status quo ante* if (when) they won the parliamentary election. In the Italian case, however, reform was forced on the ruling coalition against its will, and with the intention of bringing about permanent change to the working of the political system. Implementation of the electoral reform raised hopes that the old system of government by "center" coalitions which, while individually short lived, were always dominated by the same parties and generally by the same politicians, would be replaced by a system of governments which were more stable, more effective, and based on electoral choice rather than inter- and intraparty negotiations. This was seen to require a simpler party system, in which a single party or coalition of the Left would compete with a single party or coalition of the Right. The result would be transparency, *alternanza* and *governabilità*.

One of the hallmarks of the Second Republic was to be popular choice of the Prime Minister. Although proposals to implement this directly in a way analogous to that in which mayors were elected in 1993 were not enacted for the national level, it was assumed that the predominance of single-member seats in the new parliamentary electoral system would force the formation of electoral alliances, the leaders of which would be their prime ministerial candidates. Thus, the people would choose not only a government formula, but also a head of government, who by virtue of his (or, perhaps at some time in the future, her) personal mandate would have the authority to impose discipline within the coalition. In the view of many, the expected substitution of bi-polarity for center dominated fragmentation, of alternation for permanent government by the DC and PSI, of effective electoral choice for a situation in which nothing the electorate could do would produce substantial change, would so fundamentally alter the political system as to be worthy of the title Second Republic, even if the legal/constitutional order were unchanged.

Although the movement for electoral reform, with its objectives of increased popular control over both individual representatives and governments, reducing the fragmentation of the Italian party system, and reining in corruption predated the *tangentopoli* scandals, the overwhelming success of the April 1993 referendum on electoral law, supported by Mario Segni, was aided by public revulsion (and astonishment) over the scope of political corruption and the arrogance of the ruling parties in the face of its revelation. A tidal wave of indignation focused iconoclastic and punitive fury against the old parties and the old politicians. If there were a wholesale renewal of the political class, and especially if the members of the new political élite were to be fundamentally different in their origins and orientations rather than merely being new faces in old suits, this would be another justification for talk of a Second Republic.

The anticipated changes of institutional logic and of personnel were also expected to produce changes in behavior and political activity. One change would be an end to the political colonization of the public administration and of semi-state agencies, and of the system of *lottizzazione*, whereby positions were allotted to the governing parties and their factions (and, indeed, to the PCI and then the PDS as well), in proportion to their political strength. Presumably, the result would be a politically neutral and more efficient public service, in which not all interactions between citizens or businesses and the state would require the intermediation of political parties.

A second change would be increased fiscal responsibility in the government. On one side, it was hoped that once a clearly identifiable group of parties and politicians were both clearly in charge and liable to be ejected from office if they failed to behave responsibly, the government would no longer overstep its institutional bounds and would impose restraints on itself. In particular, it was hoped that if the government were made up of parties and politicians that did not owe their power to the distribution of political largess, the size of the bureaucracy would be reduced and less would be spent on projects and programs that were simply political payoffs. On the other side, it was also hoped that once government was perceived to be more efficient, the widespread evasion of taxes also would be reduced.

While these would be major changes in the character of Italian government and politics, they require changes not only in the government, but also in civil society. *Tangentopoli* was built not only by politicians demanding payments, but also by businesses generously offering them. If favors were offered in exchange for political support, it is also true that political support was given in exchange for favors. As Mershon and Pasquino observed last year,

> all the major social and political actors, willingly or not, to a greater or lesser degree (and the differences are crucial) have been involved in the degeneration of the preceding system and of the First Republic. In other words, the distinction between politics and civil society, which is so often drawn, had vanished in Italy. Politics had penetrated deep into society, and society had carved comfortable niches in politics, often simply for survival, at times to acquire political privileges.[2]

The slogan "Second Republic" also refers to the expectation that the separation of politics and civil society will reopen.

How much progress was made towards the realization of these aspirations? On the surface, the goal of installing a government whose composition and leadership were the direct consequence of electoral choice was realized in the victory of the *Poli* and the installation of Silvio Berlusconi as *Presidente del Consiglio*. In a deeper sense, however, the change was less clear cut. First, the *Poli* was not one alliance, but two: in the north Berlusconi's *Forza Italia* was allied with the *Lega* in the *Polo della Libertà*, which was opposed by the *Alleanza Nazionale*, but in the south and center, the Berlusconi coalition was the *Polo del Buon Governo* formed in alliance with the *Alleanza Nazionale*; in neither region could voters unambiguously vote either for or against the full coalition that ultimately formed the government. On many points, the allies were not in agreement; on March 6, it was reported that *Lega* leader Umberto Bossi had ordered his party not to support *Forza Italia* candidates in the 30 percent of northern constituencies allotted to them. Moreover, although Berlusconi was generally accepted as the leader and prime ministerial candidate of the *Poli* in both of its manifestations, once the election had made the *Lega* the largest single party in Parliament, Bossi did not immediately accept as unproblematic Berlusconi's claim of the right to be Prime Minister.

Second, the idea of a clear electoral choice requires an equally credible alternative that could have been chosen instead, but this clearly was lacking. The *Progressisti* had no clear leader; as Martin Bull observes in his chapter[3], although Achille Occhetto was leader of the predominant party in the alliance, out-going Prime Minister Carlo Azeglio Ciampi was the preferred choice of *Progressisti* supporters even though he was not himself a *Progressista* at all. The alliance was sufficiently fissiparous that it could not present common lists of candidates for the PR seats in the Chamber of Deputies; not only did this cost them roughly 10 seats when only the PDS and *Rifondazione Comunista* managed to clear the 4 percent threshold for sharing in the distribution of PR seats, but it also reinforced the perception that the *Progressisti* were merely an electoral alliance of convenience, and not a potential government.

Third, there were not two alliances, but three: the Pact for Italy, composed of Mario Segni's *pattisti* and Martinazzoli's *popolari* (with the support of some who are not from the *laici*, like former Socialist Prime Minister Giuliano Amato and former Liberal Secretary Valerio Zanone) received almost 16 percent of the vote. Given the unlikelihood of a coalition including such disparate parties as the PPI and *Rifondazione*, one could well see the choice confronting the electorate as the *Poli* or chaos— in many ways the equivalent of the non-choice confronting voters under the First Republic.

The similarity with the First Republic continued through the life of the Berlusconi government. The Alliance between Berlusconi and the *Lega* was never comfortable. In particular, Bossi was highly, and publicly, critical of Berlusconi's continued control of his Fininvest empire and of his (failed) attempt to abolish pretrial detention in cases of corruption and bribery. The *Lega* and *Forza Italia* generally opposed one another in the various subnational and European elections held during 1994. And, of course, the government ultimately resigned in the face of a no confidence motion tabled by Bossi himself after having served only seven months—significantly less than the average for the First Republic.

Greatest progress was made toward replacement of the political class, at least as indicated by parliamentary turnover. More than one third of the members of the Chamber of Deputies elected in 1992 had then served three or more terms in the Parliament, and the overall turnover rate was about 44 percent; the corresponding figures for the Parliament elected in 1994 were 12 percent with three or more previous terms and over 71 percent having no parliamentary experience. Indeed, upwards of one third of the members of the new Parliament report no previous experience in party or electoral politics at all. Naturally, the proportion of members lacking in parliamentary experience is highest for those parties that made great gains (the *Lega*, with 69.5 percent new members; *Alleanza Nazionale*, with 77.5 percent new members; and especially *Forza Italia*, with 90.4 percent with no previous parliamentary experience), but even for the PDS, the PPI, and *Rifondazione Comunista*, over half the deputies elected in 1994 are new. Somewhat fewer senators (about 60 percent) are without previous experience in Parliament, with the partisan distribution of the inexperienced roughly the same as it is for the Chamber.[4] Previous service in Parliament is not, of course, the only kind of political experience a member might have. Generally under one third of the members of each of the major groups report themselves to be political neophytes, a position which is least common among members of *Alleanza Nazionale* (under 20 percent); in contrast, over 80 percent of deputies and senators of *Forza Italia* report, with some apparent pride, that they had never been involved in party or electoral politics before entering the lists in 1994.

As the chapter by Stephen Gundle shows[5], at least as far as RAI is concerned, the system of politically motivated appointments to positions in semi-state agencies continued under the new government; although concentration of appointments in the ruling block did represent a change from the "consociationalism" (i.e., inclusion of the communists in the division of the "goodies" even though they were in opposition) of the First Republic. Moreover, although one of Bossi's complaints about the government was that the *Lega* had not received its fair share of RAI appointments, a contributing factor was the refusal of the *leghista* President of the Chamber of Deputies, Irene Pivetti, to use her appointment powers in a purely partisan way.

Finally, in terms of policy and efficiency, one can ask whether there has been a significant change. Several big issues confronted Italy at the beginning of 1994, and particularly at the beginning of the Berlusconi government's term of office. One was "completion" of the process of electoral reform. (Although there was no consensus regarding what needed to be done, there was widespread feeling that the reforms of 1993 were the beginning, and not the end, of the revision of the electoral law.) A second was reform of the Mammì law, and the better regulation of broadcasting in both the public and private sectors. A third was fiscal reform and reduction of the national budget deficit.

At the end of 1994, all these problems remained on the agenda. No action had been taken on electoral reform. Although widespread demands for the restructuring of broadcasting had been advanced, including by the *Lega* and the *Alleanza Nazionale*, Berlusconi had successfully prevented action by Parliament; only the December ruling of the Constitutional Court that sections of the Mammì law violated the constitution suggested any movement was likely.

Finally, Berlusconi's attempt to reduce the budget deficit turned out to be built in part of "smoke and mirrors" (e.g., one time increases in revenue from settling pending cases at a discount) and in part on cuts in pensions and social services. The optimism on which Berlusconi had built his image even before entering politics and which had brought him effective slogans as well as unfortunate ones like "one million more jobs" kept him from launching rigorous budget cuts. The taboo on imposing new taxes was maintained with accounting tricks and plea bargains until the monetary crisis forced the government to launch more serious provisions. But the interference on the pensions has been introduced in take it or leave it terms. And the even more worthy method has instigated the mobilization.

Confronted by Italy's largest demonstrations of the post-war era (between 1.2 and 1.5 million protesters in Rome) and a threatened general strike, the government backed down on spending cuts, with the result that the budget approved by Parliament two days before Berlusconi resigned had a projected deficit for 1995 of 156 million billion lire, or 9.07 percent of GDP.

In conclusion, the expectations arising from electoral reform and the overturning of the political landscape and the expectations for the formation of a new practice of politics—more transparent, more responsible, more honest, and more effective—have for the most part been disappointed.

If there has been a significant change, it involves the political actors and the political class: here renewal has been momentous. But those "responsible" for government through the continuance of the governing coalitions have not been clearly identified, nor has governing stability increased, nor has a new political practice been launched.

This diagnosis can be better understood by looking more closely at the second factor characterizing 1994, that is, the Berlusconi's entrance into the political arena.

The Electoral Victory of Berlusconi:
Premises and Effects

When, on the evening of March 28, the first projections of the electoral results were released, it was clear to everyone, even to the unshakable optimists on the Left, that there was a new player in Italian politics. The party established by Silvio Berlusconi within the space of a few weeks (although prepared with many months of covert activity) overcame the PDS in an instant, winning for itself the role of leading political party. All those who had considered Berlusconi's "descent into the field" to be merely the extravagant act of a billionaire in search of excitement were forced to change their minds. In fact, as McCarthy points out,[6] Berlusconi had discreetly cultivated his plan to enter politics since the summer of 1993, when the Milanese businessman's allies in politics began to fall. In particular, Bettino Craxi's exit from the scene denied Berlusconi of the political leader with whom he had woven a very tight political and personal partnership, to the point that Craxi had served as witness at Berlusconi's wedding.

The plan to affect political events in the most direct manner possible first assumed the cultural-theoretical cloak of the sponsorship of the *Associazione per il Buon Governo*, created by intellectuals with clear attach-

ments to the Liberal area like political scientist Giuliano Urbani; then, only when the imperative to create a rightist front in order to "avoiding handing the country over to a minority on the Left" did not take shape because of the reciprocal vetoes among the various parties, did *Forza Italia* enter the field as a genuine political party. Thus, Berlusconi's direct participation in electoral competition, although prepared for some time (the party's forma-tion had been under way since the summer) was the result of the failure of his activity as mediator among the various political leaders in the Center (from Bossi to Martinazzoli, from Segni to Pannella) all invited to Berlusco-ni's Arcore villa from late December to early January. Berlusconi's entry into the political arena after having made numerous attempts at *rassemble-ment* lends him the aura of a "Savior of the Fatherland," forced to abandon the comforts of a millionaire for the good of the country (as he himself has asserted again and again). And, most of all, his capacity to form coalitions stands out since in a few days he launched two of them, one with the Northern League (*il Polo della Libertà*) and one with the MSI in the South and in the Center (*il Polo del Buon Governo*): a political miracle considering the incompatibility of the two parties, which for the entire electoral campaign continued to insult each other ferociously. Only a new leader could break up the old games of the old politics and enter into the political market with a virginity that the anti-party sentiment following *Tangentopoli* required.[7] This is the source of the image of the newcomer and of the outsider to the old regime that Berlusconi immediately acquired in spite of his close relationship with the Socialist leadership.[8]

Even if the decision to present himself at the elections was more circumstantial than "autonomous," that is, influenced more by the choices of other political actors than by a decision that was precisely defined right from the beginning, the new political leader rapidly penetrated into the collective imagination. As Segatti shows,[9] by late January-early February, just fifteen days after the announcement of *Forza Italia*'s presentation, the electorate's appraisal had already reached the level that would be shown in the eventual outcome at the ballot box. The solid television campaign by the Fininvest channels in support of their owner as well as the coverage given by public television rapidly pushed Silvio Berlusconi to the center of the contest. He was aided by two factors: the "propaganda against" launched by the Left with some lapses in style, and the irrelevance of the other players in the electoral campaign: Bossi was by then a known personality, Martinazzoli avoided television by choice, Fini grew but still remained an obscure figure, Segni was in a free fall. On the other hand, Occhetto, overwhelmed by the delirium of omnipotence which the Left had enjoyed after the electoral triumphs at the December 1993 communal elections, had lost communicative effectiveness by cloaking himself in praise for Ciampi, for the City, for the financial markets, and by ignoring

the dead weight of the Communist Refoundation that was hammering the fickle electorate with its "enticing" proposals of taxation of Treasury Bonds. Obliged to appear as the reliable potential leader instead of as innovator, the leader of the PDS increasingly acquired a Gorbachev-like appearance (that of a leader who innovates and then sinks his creation). None of the other members of the progressive alliance distinguished themselves as potential leaders, aside from the incendiary but smooth Bertinotti and, in the initial phase, the "Oak's" second-in-command, D'Alema, who was quite effective in the televised debates.

The 1994 elections saw a meaningful leap in the personalization of politics. The introduction of the plurality system had no influence on this change because even in the past the encounter between the parties had been focused on the personalities of Craxi and De Mita or Craxi and Berlinguer. There was now however a maturation of the general tendency in industrialized societies for the person to overshadow the impersonal party. Moreover, this time, the earth-shaking change of the party system along with the disappearance of old denominations and the appearance of new ones required the physical identification of a leader; *Forza Italia's* formation was the quintessence of personalization, that is, a party created by and for a leader. Finally, the increased prominence of politics on television—from 4,925 minutes for the 1987 campaign to 7,066 in 1992, and 7,830 in 1994 (plus 14,052 minutes of pre-campaigning, from January 25 to February 24)[10]—ultimately stimulated this tendency; and whoever is better at using the medium gains a great advantage over the rest.

Thus, access to the media, communicative ability, "novelty" and centrality of political proposals, all made Berlusconi the magnet of the electoral campaign. Moreover, through his double accord with the League and the MSI-AN, Berlusconi was at the center of a system of alliances for the line-up on the Right. Inevitably, notwithstanding the reluctance which he declared at various times ("I am not a candidate for Prime Minister"), the day after the vote he was unanimously heralded as the natural *Presidente del Consiglio*. Occhetto himself, in an unexpected show of fairplay, declared that the Right had won the elections and that it was up to its leader to govern (although in the Senate the line-up on the Right did not have an absolute majority). In fact the decision by some senators elected on the lists of the *Popolari* and by the Segni's Pact to vote in favor of a Berlusconi government did not cause a stir. Common wisdom regarding the days following the elections is that the winners should not have to face too many obstacles. And if the numbers are lacking, the strength of the Government's attraction will provide. This is just what happened with the majority's recruitment of some members of the PPI and Segni's Pact, such as PPI Senator Grillo, later nominated undersecretary, and *pattista* Tremonti, future Minister of Finance.

This accommodating style of the Left and the Center after their electoral defeat was not matched by an analogous openness of the majority to accords with the opposition on the nomination of presidents of the two Chambers and of parliamentary commission chairpersons. Breaking a twenty-year tradition, the new majority refused to concede one of the two Chamber presidencies to someone from the opposition camp, or even to a member *super-partes*. In the Senate, where the *Poli* did not have a majority adequate simply to impose a president of the Right, and the opposition supported such a prestigious figure as out-going Senate president and former PRI leader Giovanni Spadolini, Carlo Scognamiglio prevailed by one vote. This victory in *Forza Italia*'s first parliamentary encounter reinforced and spread the interpretation of "to the victors belong the spoils": in other words, those who have won, even without arriving at an absolute majority, have the right to occupy every post, even those of the supervisory committees. And in fact in the Chamber all committees went to members of the majority; in the Senate, however, thanks to a smaller proportion on the Right and to different internal rules, the opposition parties managed to obtain nine chairmanships.[11]

An Inexperienced Government

The formation of the government was nonetheless problematic, both because of the composition of the coalition and because of the characteristics of the governing framework. As far as party participation in government goes, the coalitional logic of "the preemptory division of hypothetical electoral spoils"[12] adopted by Berlusconi imposed itself on the League's repeated skittishness (even immediately after the election) about collaborating with "the Fascists" (to use Bossi's term). So, the unusually long negotiation to please the numerous components of the majority composed of six different formations (the highest number of government groups since 1947)—12 days compared to Ciampi's 48 hours—reminds one of the extenuating compromises of the First Republic. Particularly disconcerting was the nomination of Minister of the Interior. After Berlusconi's final and sibylline declarations ("there will never be a *leghista* in Interior") and talk of a nomination for Di Pietro, the Italians' most loved magistrate, in the end it was the *Lega*'s second-in-command Roberto Maroni, who took office at the Viminale. But even more disconcerting was the completed list of ministers handed into the Quirinale. There were very few high profile personalities of political or professional experience, limited to Minister of the Treasury Lamberto Dini and Minister of Finance Giulio Tremonti, while greater sensation was caused by the inclusion in Government of friends and employees of the Fininvest group, that is, those economically connected to the Prime Minister: Giuliano Ferrara to the Ministry of Parliamentary Relations, Cesare Previti to the Ministry of Defense, Gianni Letta as undersecretary to the Prime Minister. The final surprise was ranking *Forza Italia* economist Antonio Martino's hi-jacking of the Ministry of Foreign Affairs, once occupied by his father. In any case, the truly new development of the Berlusconi government was the inclusion, for the first time in Europe, of a party directly descending from the fascist tradition.[13] The parliamentary group elected under the National Alliance banner is none other than the old MSI plus a few others.[14] Thus the protests and bad blood expressed at the international level in various ways and various venues were inevitable.[15] And the successive process of the National Alliance's evolution will not completely eliminate its heritage of the past and ideological ambiguities.[16]

The government's first steps aroused as much, if not more, perplexity. While the electoral campaign and *Forza Italia*'s own program were centered on a neo-laissez-faire approach—reduction of the income tax to a flat tax of 30 percent (later changed to 33 percent), support for private enterprise, privatization of the public sector, deregulation—the government made no moves in this direction. Except for some of Minister of Finance Tremonti's innovative measures—of particular significance are those that tie tax breaks to new hires—incompetence and inexperience and, above all, a marked continuation of the past were very much in evidence.

In the first place, the politics of pardons returned; in both construction and tax evasion, provisions typical of the former governing style were passed: immunity for violations and the possibility of ending a case by paying a modest fine.

In the second place, some ministers showed, at least, a certain tendency toward improvisation. For example, the Minister of Defense declared he was ready to send a contingent of the Italian army to Rwanda to protect the civilian population without having first informed the appropriate international organizations, raising questions in the international community (and in fact the minister changed his story a few days later).

In the same way, the Minister for the Environment Altero Matteoli, the former organizational director of the MSI (who never in his whole career made it to the headlines for any political initiatives), proposed abolishing the erosion walls on the Italian coasts, re-thinking the nuclear industry, and re-launching the *cementizio* plan for the highways. There were some innovations in the field of foreign policy.[17] Minister Martino immediately announced a turnaround on the Franco-German axis of support for European integration and the Maastricht Treaty and placed himself in line with the "euroskeptics." However, if some of the new ministers' "quips" could indicate the level of incompetence or inexperience, more significant was the government's action in two key sectors: broadcasting and justice.

Conflict of Interests

Decisions of great importance were made regarding broadcasting, a very delicate theme considering the particular position of the head of the government. After having demonized the RAI during the entire electoral campaign, defining it even as "a nest of communists"—while the data on the amount of time dedicated to the different lists belied any partiality in favor of the Left by the public service[18]—and after a series of strongly polemical declarations by numerous members of the majority and Berlusconi himself ("it is anomalous that the public television service is hostile to the government"), the plan for reorganization presented to the RAI board of directors was rejected, and the board was compelled to resign. As a consequence, a new board of directors was named, with Berlusconi directly intervening in the selection process, in spite of the fact that it was the responsibility of the Chamber presidents alone. The new board immediately showed its alignment with the government with the board president's shocking declaration on the "complementarity" of the RAI with Fininvest and with the "expulsion" of the network directors and ranking television news journalists (and in fact two of the three directors of televisions news came from Fininvest).

To this very burning theme we might add another likewise thorny problem for the Primo Minister. At the beginning of 1994, the Milan judges' inquests of political corruption incriminated Berlusconi's brother (who had confessed to corruption and accounting fraud), and investigations of Fininvest itself were building. In spite of that, on July 13, the Minister of Justice, Alfredo Biondi, advanced the Biondi decree, in which certain regulations regarding crimes of corruption were modified. In the face of the reaction of the Milanese magistrates, who resigned in protest, accusing the government of tying their hands and blocking the clean-up process, and in the face of the open dissent of the *Lega*, the government, notwithstanding its bombastic resolutions, dropped the decree. But the government did not stop promoting a harsh debate with the magistrates, accused by Berlusconi of "wanting to govern the country and decide its laws"—a debate that would continue throughout the year.

So, the first two political acts of the government, devoted to broadcasting and justice, touched very sensitive nerves of public opinion, and what is more, directly addressed the problem of conflict of interests, which until that moment had been almost academic. In other words, the economic activities of the Fininvest group, of which Berlusconi is the owner, are so diversified that virtually any government action could influence its accounts—positively or negatively. Moreover the ownership of three television channels, which have 90 percent of the commercial television audience, makes the problem of compatibility even more difficult. An anti-trust standard was insistently invoked, not only by the opposition parties but also within the majority itself, first by the League and, more diplomatically by Fini's so-called post-Fascists.

Berlusconi responded to these requests by naming a commission of three "wise men," one of whom was tied however to the Fininvest group, and by asking the President of the Republic to act as guarantor of their work. This unusual involvement of the president, who naturally responded that he could not be called upon to perform tasks outside if his constitutional mandate, was a final indicator (after the confrontation with the magistrature) of the Prime Minister's expansive conception of the relationships among the institutions. The conflict of interest and antitrust problems began to corrode the unity of the governing coalition. The close understanding between Berlusconi and Fini marginalized the League, which was the largest group in the parliamentary majority. In the face of this marginalization, which showed up in the way in which the *Carroccio's* major themes (federalism and privatization) were being treated as irrelevant, League leader Bossi reacted with a series of polemical broadsides against the Prime Minister. During Parliament's summer break, Bossi and Berlusconi met several times, usually in one of the Prime Minister's numerous Sardinian villas, and initialed a sort of understanding at Arcore, having themselves filmed smiling and happy before the television cameras. But neither federalism nor antitrust made any steps forward, and for that reason the debate soon re-ignited. In fact the government majority was split into two main camps: on the one side was the League, and on the other was *Forza Italia*, MSI-AN, and the other minor lists.

The Crisis

The opposition on the Left, still in shock after its electoral defeats in March and especially June, was not able until August to promote any political initiative. Only when the government began work on the budget proposal and brutally faced the question of retirement pensions, did the Left begin to give signs of life. The general strike against the government program to reform the pension system called by the CGIL, CISL, and UIL union federations for October 14, achieved a level of participation beyond all imagination. In the cities in which the demonstrations were organized, altogether three million people showed up—the largest demonstrations ever recorded in Italy. Galvanized by this success, the labor unions proclaimed another general strike for November and a national demonstration in Rome for November 5 (later postponed to the 12th because of the Piemonte flood). The Roman demonstration as well, launched with the slogan "a million workers in Rome," obtained full support. The government, pressed by labor union initiatives, was divided over how to react. Compared to the unyieldingness of Berlusconi, who responded to the demonstrations with a disconcerting "get to work" and that the budget would not be touched ("the numbers will not change for a strike"), was the understanding of the League and the embarrassment of the MSI-AN, which did not want to be more royalist than "King Silvio" and thought about its popular middle-class white collar electorate.

In the midst of all this, an *avviso di garanzia* for Berlusconi arrived, regarding an inquest by the Milanese prosecutor's office on the corruption of the Financial Police (*Guardia di Finanza*). Berlusconi reacted very harshly, accusing the magistrates of persecuting him, but above all asserting a sort of untouchability by ordinary justice. On a videocassette taped, sent, and played by all television news shows the day after his extremely long interrogation (seven hours), Berlusconi spoke of grave violations of his rights and of magistrates who are shattering justice. In this way the conflict —which had already stood out in July at the time of the Biondi decree, and was sharpened in September with the open denunciation of head Milan prosecutor Borrelli for some of his (innocent) declarations to the newspapers, and continued in November with the ministerial investigation of the Milanese prosecutor's office (to the point that this last event provoked the shocking resignation of the magistrate symbol of *Mani pulite*, Antonio Di Pietro)—reached its peak.

Caught between the dissatisfactions of its coalition, the investigations by the magistracy, the nervousness of the financial markets, the pressure from the *piazza* (to which a certain student effervescence, more a media than a university event, contributed as well), the government began to lose support. An SWG poll revealed that 71.9 percent of Italians were "little satisfied or not at all satisfied" with the work of the government.[19]

The agreement that was signed with labor unions on the budget and on pension reform on December 1, the day before a new general strike, was a surrender along the government's entire line. In this way the Left gave its assent to the rapid approval of a budget proposal in the Chambers before the end of the year, spurred as well by the pressure to which the lira, in free fall compared to the German Mark, was exposed in international markets. But at the same time it did not give up attacking the *Cavaliere* and presented a motion of no confidence in the government together with the PPI and the League. Once parliamentary debate was opened on the motion of no confidence, 343 signatures were collected. In reality, it was Bossi's League that decreed the government's the fall, accusing it of inefficiency and of having betrayed its initial agreements on federalist institutional reform, on privatization of the public sector, and on the liberalization of the economy (including the communications sector). Berlusconi, after having tried to defend his government by personally and violently attacking Bossi and calling him a "Judas," resigned on December 22 without waiting for a no-confidence vote.

What happens after Berlusconi lies outside the temporal sphere of this analysis, but in the space of the few days between the fall of the government and the end of the year, there emerged many portents of the shape of political conflict in 1995, at least for the first months.

The first regards the increasingly strong emergence of a vein of antiparliamentarianism on the part of the former Prime Minister. In the numerous interviews from that period and above all in the demonstration at the Manzoni Theater in Milan, shortly before his resignation, Berlusconi, appealing to an imaginary popular investiture obtained by means of the new plurality electoral system (such that he does not hesitate to call himself "anointed by God" in order to underline the sacredness of popular legitimation, with a significant logical and theoretical short circuit) contrasts the will of the people to that of Parliament: the March 27 vote was "ripped off," "betrayed," "sold" (according to circumstances) by Parliament. For one who professed commitment to liberalism at his entry in politics, this position, alluded to again and again, signaled a complete reversal in the direction of the most classic populism.

The second concerns relations with the other powers of State and above all with the President of the Republic. As is known, it is up to the president to nominate a prime minister who will form a government and present it to the Chambers for confirmation. The pressure on President Scalfaro to give the office back to Berlusconi in spite of the no-confidence motions reached the level of most grievous insults. Never in Italian political history, not even when President Leone was forced to resign in July 1978 under suspicion of connivance in episodes of corruption, were such violent expressions used. This attitude of "keeping the Quirinale under pressure," later theorized by the former Minister for Parliamentary Relations Ferrara, became an index of the total lack of comprehension of the necessity of checks and balances in a pluralist democracy. In fact, the political initiatives on the Right led, together with this populist line, to intolerance for other potentially non-cooperative organs of state. (The same attitude was shown towards the Constitutional Court as well in the first days of January, after its judgments on the admissibility of a series of referendums.)

The Revolution Is Still Running

The year 1994 closes beneath the Berlusconi meteor, which had entered the Italian political system with devastating force at the beginning of the year. But the fall of his government surely will not bring his exit from the scene, as many have predicted. The tenacity with which he has reacted to his parliamentary defeat shows how his presence in politics has not waned at all. Berlusconi's political course will be a determining factor for the future order of the party system. On the one hand, the *Cavaliere* can set out on his stated program of founding a genuine party in order to gather troops in addition to his employees. On the other hand, he can stipulate a unity pact of action with his faithful friend Fini (who, however, expects only to take his power away, in light of his own growing popularity) or with a reorganization of *popolari* and *leghisti* (or of fragments of these parties) who might abandon the "central" position and move toward the Right. In this last case, he could oppose Fini not only with television, but also with political experts and thus with rosier prospects for the future.

On the other side of the barricade, the year closed with a doubtless revitalization of the image of the labor unions, which obtained their greatest victory since the 1970s, but with a political Left still uncertain about what to do, caught between the hypothesis of a great "democratic" party which embraces all the elements between the increasingly social-Democratic PDS on one side and the other components, lay and Catholic, of the Center-Left in a federative pact. In the middle are still the League and the *popolari*. Bossi has paid a very high price in his battle against Berlusconi, losing more than a quarter of this parliamentary troops. But it is also true that the League's sudden expansion to be the leading parliamentary group, imposed a far-reaching recruitment on its leadership, and it is not certain that this hemorrhaging brings an effective weakening of the movement, since the organization—apart form the case in Milan—does not seem to have suffered from it. However, the League has few points of contact with the Left, and so the problem of a strategy of alliances remains. Rocco Buttiglione's *popolari* face the same dilemma, if in different terms. The young secretary-philosopher, elected after Martinazzoli's resignation following the March 27 defeat, aimed at the recovery of Christian Democratic votes that had ended up with *Forza Italia* and MSI-AN and so would have liked to approach these formations; he must however keep in mind the component of the Left that instead aims at a return to the alliances with the PDS which were so successful in the November-December 1994 local elections, and sees in the former president of IRI, Romano Prodi, a possible alternative (to Berlusconi) candidate for Prime Minister.

At the end of 1994, the party system was anything but solidified or simplified, with twenty lists having obtained parliamentary seats and having given life to eight parliamentary groups in the Chamber and ten in the Senate.[20]

The plurality system has not produced effects either on the format or on the style of competition, which instead of moderating, has returned to becoming inflamed and ideological, triggering repolarization after years of a contrary tendency. The Constitution has not been touched and so it is entirely improper to speak of a "Second Republic." The experiment of a government that is entirely new in its ideological presuppositions (liberalism, federalism, and latent nationalism), in its party composition and political personnel has been shipwrecked in quarrelsomeness, in inexperience, and in the absence of a precise identity. All this leads us to believe that the changes in the Italian political system have not yet come to an end, and that the phase of transition continues.

Translated by Sara L. Brann

Notes

1. Carol Mershon and Gianfranco Pasquino (eds.), *Italian Politics: Ending the First Republic* (Boulder CO: Westview Press, 1995), p. 52.

2. Ibid.

3. See chapter 3 in this volume.

4. The figures for the Chamber of Deputies are from Maurizio Cotta and Luca Verzichelli, "The Crisis of Partitocrazia: The Italian Earthquake from the Political Elites' Point of View," presented at the symposium "Political Parties: Changing Roles in Contemporary Democracies," Instituto Juan March de Estudios y Investigaciones, Madrid, December 15-17, 1994. Those for the Senate were compiled by the present author from biographies published in *Il Parlamento Italiano* (Rome: VAMA edizioni, June 15, 1994). Not all experience was consecutive, and it is possible that some former members did not mention that fact in their biographical sketches.

5. See the contribution by Gundle.

6. See the chapter by Patrick McCarthy.

7. For a discussion of antiparty sentiment in Italy, see L. Bardi, G. Sani, and P. Segatti, *Anti-Party Politics in Italy: Old or New?* Dipartimento di Studi Politici e Sociali, Pavia, 1993, and on a more general level, A. Schedler, "Antipolitical Opposition: A Framework for Comparative Analysis," presented at the VDD colloquium, Vienna, 1994.

8. The importance of the element of novelty is discussed by L. Ricolfi, "Il voto proporzionale: il nuovo spazio politico italiano," in S. Bartolini and E. D'Alimonte (eds.) *Maggioritario ma non troppo*, (Bologna: Il Mulino, 1995), pp. 273-316.

9. P. Segatti, "I programmi elettorali e il ruolo dei mass media," in S. Bartolini and R. D'Alimonte, cit., pp 147-173.

10. Ibid., pp. 165-166.

11. See the discussion by A. Manzella in this volume.

12. A. Di Virgilio, "Dai partiti ai poli: la politica delle alleanze," in S. Bartolini and R. D'Alimonte (eds.), pp. 177-231 at p. 195.

13. Cf. P. Ignazi, *Il polo escluso. Profilo del Movimento Sociale Italiano*, (Bologna: Il Mulino, 1989).

14. Cf. L. Verzichelli in this volume.

15. Cf. chapters by P. Neal and A. Carioti in this volume.

16. P. Ignazi, *Postfascisti? Dal Movimento Sociale ad Alleanza Nazionale,* (Bologna: Il Mulino, 1994).

17. Cf. P. Neal in this volume; S. Romano, "La politica estera italiana: un bilancio e qualche prospettiva," in *Il Mulino,* n. 357, 1995, pp. 63-70.

18. P. Segatti, *I programmi elettorali,* cit.

19. *L'Espresso,* November 25, 1994.

20. R. D'Alimonte and S. Bartolini, "Il sistema partitico italiano: una transizione difficile," in S. Bartolini and R. D'Alimonte (eds.), cit. pp. 429-466, at p. 432.

2

Forza Italia: The Overwhelming Success and the Consequent Problems of a Virtual Party

Patrick McCarthy

Forza Italia (FI) was the great victor of the March 1994 parliamentary elections. It obtained 21 percent of the vote, enough to become the largest party, while the coalition of which it was the core gained 42.2 percent and won an outright majority of seats in the Chamber of Deputies, although not in the Senate. In the European elections FI's vote jumped to 30.6 percent. Yet in the period from March to the summer the movement was racked by a dispute between the leadership and the rank and file, while in autumn FI apparently did not exist in large cities like Milan, Bologna and Venezia.[1] In partial local elections of November 20 this virtual party plummeted, losing 10.3 percent. Of the seven large towns that elected a mayor, the candidate of the governing coalition was victorious in only two.

Prime Minister Berlusconi's popularity had dropped as he failed to produce a convincing economic policy and instead concentrated on terminating the Clean Hands investigation with the botched July 13 decree, which aroused a wave of popular opposition. In the autumn came massive, union-led demonstrations against a budget which had to cut spending on pensions in order to reduce the government deficit and reassure the disappointed financial markets. As the government's problems increased, divisions grew sharper within the coalition, where Umberto Bossi was openly dissident and Gianfranco Fini embarrassingly loyal.

Moreover FI's fragility was exposed as a split appeared in its parliamentary group between the "hawks", who wanted to work with *Alleanza Nazionale* (AN), and the "doves", who looked towards the *Partito Popolare Italiano* (PPI). In the long run this may prove an advantage as the doves give FI a small measure of autonomy from Berlusconi, but there was no solace in the revelation of FI's weakness at the grassroots. When Berlusconi was summoned before the Milan magistrates to answer corruption charges, *Forza Italia* fought back with a series of demonstrations in Rome, Milan and Turin. However, while some ten thousand people joined the march in Turin, only a few hundred turned out in Milan.[2] AN, which cosponsored the demonstrations, proved that its base was stronger and better-organized than FI's.

We shall argue that FI owes its success to its "virtual" character, which also renders it vulnerable and may force it to change in order to survive. The strength and the weakness of FI stem from the historical moment, to which it has been a response but to which it has not as yet brought solutions.

This historical moment is complex. To simplify, one may say that in the spring of 1994 Italian voters, having lived through the destruction of the post-war political order, in the shape of the demise of the DC, the PSI and proportional representation, turned to a new but reassuring leader. The collapse of structures left a void which a charismatic leader could fill. Berlusconi's past as an entrepreneur and as a Craxi's supporter enabled him to respond to two particular traits of the moment.

The first was the growing preoccupation with the economy and the fear of unemployment. One survey showed that 77 percent of people interviewed considered that the first priority of the new government should be job creation, while only 17 percent felt it should be the elimination of corruption.[3] This may be misleading because it appears to indicate a willingness by the electorate to call a halt to the Clean Hands investigation, which was belied by the July protest. But the austerity programmes of the Amato and Ciampi governments and the world recession had created widespread fear of unemployment, even or especially in prosperous areas like Piedmont where FIAT was restructuring. Berlusconi's success in building a conglomerate and his promise to create a million jobs were powerful attractions. His allusions to a "new economic miracle" played on past memories, while his claim that he would cut taxes implied that in the future the achievements of the 1950s would be equalled without the hardships.

The second factor helping him was the left's victory in the local elections of June and of November-December 1993. These alarmed right-wing voters, the DC's orphans, and helped the MSI to gain over 40 percent of the vote in Rome and Naples. Anti-communism, fostered by the post-war regime as it had been by Fascism, its predecessor, had outlived Communism and fear of a government where the PDS would be the strongest force ran high. Berlusconi's visceral hatred for Communism, which to him meant any kind of statism, struck a popular chord.

He was able to piece together a right-wing coalition, which included his natural rival, the Northern League, and the MSI which he helped legitimize. After his victory he also received sympathetic interest from some members of the Church hierarchy.

The kind of movement he built stemmed from the regime crisis. The document *Alla ricerca del buon governo*, mainly written by the liberal political scientist Giuliano Urbani which was published in November 1993, argues that the De Gasperi-Togliatti vision of the mass parties creating a modern, democratic state has long since run its course.[4] The parties have become the problem because they have occupied and pillaged the state. Not only can the existing parties not be reformed but the phenomenon of the mass party is doomed. In this analysis Berlusconi's other advisors were reflecting on the crisis of politics which had been growing in Italy as in other Western European countries in the 1980s.

The weakening of class as a bond, the flagging ideologies, the end of Fordism and the increase in light, decentralized industry and in services were Europe-wide phenomena. In Italy they were reinforced by the bankruptcy of Communism, which drove the PCI to undertake its tormented transformation into the *Partito Democratico della Sinistra* (PDS), and by the revelations of systemic clientelism, which destroyed the DC. *Forza Italia* did not attempt to become a party with a base that had to be reassured or a bureaucracy that had its own goals.

Exactly what sort of a movement it would be was unclear in the *Alla ricerca* document. Two imprecise indications are given. The first is that Berlusconi's dislike of the state extended to the entire political realm so that the movement, *Forza Italia*, was to be limited to playing a cultural role in civil society. The manichaean view of a good civil society opposed to evil rulers is an old trait of populism which had been revived by the Clean Hands investigation. The second indication, implicit in the vagueness of the document, is that FI was to be no more than an electoral machine for the leader and his barons. The drawback of this is that, as we have already seen, the leader would be unprotected when problems arose.

In the strange entity of FI we may distinguish five elements. The first and most important is its leader, Silvio Berlusconi, while the second, which has no official status, is his company Fininvest. The third, the presidential council, was officially the organ which governed the party but in practice it has been little more than a projection of its leader. More important is the parliamentary group which has gained a measure of influence over Berlusconi's decisions, despite or because of its divisions. Finally the clubs, which have been kept powerless, may nonetheless hold the key to FI's long term success or failure.

The Seduction of the Electorate

Berlusconi was accustomed to selling. It is often forgotten that while Fininvest uses advanced technology in its television segment, its prime activity is selling: soccer, (AC Milan), consumer goods (Standa), insurance (Mediolanum), financial products (Programma Italia) and TV time (Publitalia). Berlusconi's role, as revealed by his speaking tours on behalf of Publitalia, was not to enter into details of advertising or marketing, but rather to project himself as the self-made millionaire.[5] Self-made so that the local businessmen, who were Publitalia's clients, might identify with him, and a millionaire so that they would see him as a model to emulate. Thus Berlusconi, aside from an embarrassing lapse when he claimed to have a kept a photo of Gianni Agnelli on his desk instead of a picture of the Madonna,[6] spoke coldly of FIAT as well as of the Employers Association. Instead he talked much of his early struggles to establish his commercial TV network.

In Italy, entrepreneurs of all kinds, ranging from the head of a family firm to the great *condottieri* like Carlo De Benedetti, are admired in a manner unthinkable in Britain, where a mere 32 percent of the population believes that entrepreneurs play a positive role in society. Berlusconi was a special example of the species because he was present in two popular and fashionable industries, soccer and TV.

Both played major roles in a campaign, which was organized like a Publitalia sales tour. Berlusconi used the language of soccer—"Let's go Italy" or "taking the field"—and surrounded himself with sporting figures like the runner, Alberto Cova, and the oarsman, Giuseppe Abbagnale. More important, he entwined AC Milan with the national side, calling his campaign staff the "blues", rather than the "red and blacks" after the Milan colours. Amidst the collapse of other élites, soccer stars like Franco Baresi and Paolo Maldini, became symbols of a populist patriotism. Association with them—especially when Milan won the European champions cup—allowed Berlusconi to present himself as the leader who would save Italy from Communism and recession. Conversely, as his political fortunes waned in autumn 1994, AC Milan slipped down the league table, which at least one soccer commentator attributed to Berlusconi's absence.[7]

Television was vital, although to attribute Berlusconi's entire success to it seems an exaggeration. A new movement could not have attracted widespread support without the battery of TV spots which FI deployed before the official start of the campaign, but the messages of the charismatic leader, popular patriotism and the family firm were just as important as the medium. However TV influenced and helped Berlusconi's campaign in other ways. He appeared surrounded by his familiar newscasters and he was endorsed by popular personalities who ranged from the quizmaster, Mike Bongiorno, to Ambra Angiolino, the queen of the pre-teens. The tone of optimism, required of commercial TV which must incite people to buy, was an antidote to Ciampi's call for austerity. Berlusconi, who once criticized a Fininvest serial because it depicted shabby streets and houses (and who also objected to the Mafia serial, *La Piovra*, because it gave too bleak a view of Italy,[8] radiated success in his well-tailored suits as in his casual but expensive sports clothes. Both reflected and reinforced the vision of TV as a realm of happy endings where the heroes become healthy, wise and above all wealthy. Voter-viewers were to be seduced.

TV is a cool medium and commercial TV must not shock or alienate. This suited Berlusconi's campaign to distinguish himself from his rival, Umberto Bossi. Where Bossi was virulent and made free use of invective and sexual allusions, Berlusconi reiterated the word "calm" and was exaggeratedly courteous. The *Lega Nord* and FI were akin in their neoliberalism but whereas Bossi's role had been to destroy the old regime, Berlusconi sought to unite the nation around a new set of values. Finally the example of the commercials helped guide Berlusconi to a direct, emotional but reassuring discourse, which made a stronger impact than the left's mixture of technocratic and residually marxist jargon.[9]

Berlusconi's language contrasted the pre-1992 politics, dismissed as "gossip" and "ideology", with the new politics, based on entrepreneurial efficiency and described with such words as "concrete", "real" and "organized". Similarly Berlusconi replaced the difficult, coded discourse of an Aldo Moro with deliberate clichés such as "call to arms" or "the trenches of work".

However the clarity of such a vocabulary is apparent rather than real and Berlusconi made lavish use of the magical elements, which Herbert Marcuse considered necessary in politics. The allusions to the "new economic miracle" had no rational basis because the present economic situation bears no resemblance to the post-war setting (nor did Berlusconi see fit to remind Italians that the explosive growth of the 1950s had its roots in Luigi Einaudi's austerity). Berlusconi was narrating a myth about the ingenuity of the Italian entrepreneur. Similarly Gianni Pilo's pseudo-scientific polls are best compared with the rounded figures of New Testament parables.[10]

At the centre of this magic realm stand the characters of the Man of Destiny and his people. Berlusconi does not hesitate to compare himself with Christ (or the Pope with AC Milan!). References to the "bitter chalice" which he must drink and to the "cross" which he must carry are amusing, albeit slightly alarming. However such narcissism was an integral part of the campaign to establish Berlusconi as a savior of the nation. At his first electoral meeting he declared he would relaunch the economy, adding "there is no one in Italy who can make this promise...with more credibility than the man who stands before you here".[11]

It is a traditional theme of populism that such a leader understands intuitively what his people feels. In the battles over the state television service Berlusconi invoked *la gente* against his parliamentary opponents. "The people agree with me" became a recurrent motif in his conversations. Once more pseudo-scientific polls prepared by Berlusconi opinion poll agency Diakron, formed the pretext rather than the reason for such claims.

Eugenio Scalfari wrote recently that *la gente* was a vast new sociological reality: the old bourgeoisie with its ethical values and its sense of the state has given way to a middle-class which possesses no cultural points of reference, perceives itself as a mass and is shaped by TV.[12] But this ignores the emergence of definable new social groups linked with economic innovation, such as computer technicians or health care workers. Although class distinctions are blurred by common consumption patterns, modern societies do not form an amorphous mass.

The notion of *la gente* belongs to political culture and represents a choice of strategy by Berlusconi (one might say that he tries to create *la gente*). He has two overlapping but separate goals: to break through the categories of the old regime—such as "interclass Catholicism" or "lay middle-classes"—and appeal directly to a more pragmatic, less ideological voter; and to use "the people" against his opponents in the parliamentary élite, especially those who could be castigated as theorizing, leftwing intellectuals.

When Berlusconi was shaken by the November crisis, his invocations of the leader and his people grew more extreme. If he was Christ, then Bossi must be Judas. Berlusconi complained of plots—by Communists, the press, the magistrates—and cast himself as the victim. His confident vision of himself faltered and he described himself as Jekyll and Hyde because of the difference between the way he saw himself and the way the media saw him. To escape this incipient schizophrenia he argued that he was "anointed by the Lord" because the people had voted for him.[13] The political implications of this view were that the people's leader could not be challenged by the magistrates, who did not represent an independent and legitimate branch of government, nor replaced by parliament, which represented the squabbling parties. Only the people could remove its leader in a new election.[14]

Our initial conclusion is that FI represents a brand of populism characterized by an ostentatious modernity, which does not, however, conflict with religious allusions or an invented economic tradition. Such modernity includes a cult of mass consumption and a myth of management. These reclothe the old structure of populism, which remains the charismatic leader and the reunited nation. However comparisons between Berlusconi and Mussolini are unseemly: Mussolini sought to coerce as well as to seduce.

The Company as Political Party

"Gentlemen our mission is accomplished. In a few months we have created a party, built an alliance and taken over the government. Now we must return to our company".[15] With these words Marcello dell'Utri summed up the achievements of the second component of FI—the Fininivest group. Once he realized, as early as the April 18, 1993 referendum, that the old regime had collapsed, Berlusconi planned to influence the course of the new order. The academics of the *Associazione per il Buon Governo* were to provide the themes of his political movement. The recruiting was entrusted to Fininvest companies, notably Publitalia, headed by Dell'Utri, Programma Italia and Diakron.

Much has been made of Fininvest's political activity, but the principal lesson is not the direct substitution of economic for political power. Nor is it merely the revelation of media power since Programma Italia has nothing to do with the media. The true significance of Fininvest's intervention is that in Italy the boundary between political and economic power, between state and market, had ceased to exist as the parties auctioned off public contracts, while industrialists competed for political influence. Now, after the defeat which the political class had suffered at the hands of the magistrates, an economic group could bid to replace it. But this change, while significant, did not mark the domination of economic over political power. At best it was the arrival of a new force, which would reform the clientelistic state. At worst it was a take-over by a new clan.

Through its contacts with the industrialists up and down Italy who bought TV time, Publitalia was able to uncover candidates and build networks of support in employers associations, Rotaries and the like. It also founded clubs, although much of this work was done by Programma Italia which had broader contacts, at a lower but still middle-class level, via its investment clients. Other segments of Berlusconi's conglomerate helped: some clubs were formed out of AC Milan supporters clubs, while enterprising Standa executives set up others.

Diakron (which is legally not a part of Fininvest but in practice is) conducted polls to discover which issues should be stressed and briefed the candidates. They were vetted, tested for TV performance, public speaking and ability to learn the issues quickly. Thus a dose of marketing was injected into politics and the methods and values of management came with it. To Berlusconi's lieutenants this was part of the change of regime: in place of the bankrupt political party, the company was the model. Efficiency, flexibility and pragmatic problem-solving were the new criteria.[16]

However these values amounted to little more than a myth of management. Certainly the campaign was well run, although some of the credit must go to Roberto Lasagna, a professional from Satchi and Satchi who was enlisted by Berlusconi. Once campaigning gave way to governing, the inadequacy of the managerial style became apparent. Berlusconi admitted that "it's not as easy as in the company where you listen to everyone but then make your decision. Here you have to mediate everything".[17] No serious attempt was made to run government departments using business techniques, as Robert McNamara had tried to run the US Defense Department.

Fininvest's entry into politics brought problems in its wake. As a company which had needed political friends—to make favourable zoning decisions for its property subsidiaries or grant licences to its TV networks—it was a natural target for the Clean Hands investigation. To mention only a few charges, Fininvest was alleged to have paid consulting fees, so high as to constitute a retrospective bribe, to an assistant of Oscar Mammì, the minister responsible for the 1991 law governing TV. Silvio Berlusconi's brother, Paolo, admitted paying bribes in return for zoning decisions, while in July 1994 he was arrested for bribing tax officials. AC Milan was investigated on the grounds that it had paid part of Gigi Lentini's transfer fee in Switzerland to avoid being taxed on the money. So it was unlikely that Prime Minister Berlusconi would escape investigation.

Another problem was the conflict of interest. A diversified holding like Fininvest was affected by a whole range of government decisions. For exemple, if tax on the coops was increased in the budget, that gave an advantage to Standa. The blind trust solution which was suggested made no sense since Berlusconi knew what his holdings were. Nor did he help his own cause after taking office by purging the state television, which was Fininvest's direct competitor. So far Fininvest has behaved more like a clan than like an agent of reform.

Without his company, Berlusconi could not have launched his electoral campaign. Until March 27, *Forza Italia* accepted Fininvest leadership, but then dissent broke out. Publitalia came under fire for reserving many of the proportional representation seats for its own members. Gianfranco Micchiché, Dell'Utri's lieutenant in Sicily, was one example, Roberto Cipriani in Lombardy was another and Enzo Ghigo in Piedmont was a third. When the FI parliamentarians met at Fiuggi in April for two days of study,Tiziana Parenti, the magistrate from the Milan pool who had gone over to FI, railed against the Fininvest contingent, whom she considered authoritarian and who had more access to Berlusconi.[18]

Dell'Utri, a former pupil of the Jesuits, emerged from the March and June victories with much power within FI. During the November crisis he called for a "military or company discipline" in the party.[19] However, in the myriad investigations of Fininvest by the magistrates, he was the object of the very serious charge of creating secret funds, on which no tax was paid and which could be used for bribery. This may be why, although he was considered for the post of national coordinator of FI in the autumn, he was passed over in favour of Cesare Previti, Minister of Defence and Fininvest's leading lawyer.

Despite the dissent, power in FI thus remained in company hands. It was paralleled by the strong Fininvest presence in the government. By one count this consisted of ten people, including, as well as Berlusconi and Previti, four undersecretaries, one of whom, Gianni Letta, occupied the sensitive post of undersecretary to the Prime Minister, and the Minister of Parliamentary Affairs, Giuliano Ferrara.[20] Publitalia alone had two undersecretaries: Domenico Lo Jucco at the Interior and Micchiché at Transport. Nor has Dell'Utri lost all power, for during the government crisis of December-January he acted as one of Berlusconi's emissaries: on January 6 he suggested to the PPI the solution of a government headed by Urbani or Dini which would hold early elections.[21] If there are fresh elections, Dell'Utri may well have a major role.

The Fininvest contingent is to be explained by the overlap of political and economic power mentioned earlier. From unification onward, Italian industrialists looked to the state for help more than their counterparts in other European countries. From the nationalization of the electrical industry in the 1960s onward, politicians have treated industry and finance as part of their territory. The boundary between state and market vanished, which is one reason for the post-1992 crisis. Hybrids arose: publicly-owned companies, like Egam, which conducted business in order to create slush funds for the parties; private entrepreneurs, among them Berlusconi, who could conduct business only with political support. Clans were formed to fight over the spoils: Andreotti's clan included Nino Rovelli, the head of a chemical company, the Caltagirone family, who had a construction firm and sectors of Catholic banking, as well as politicians like Vittorio Sbardella, who took care of Rome and Salvo Lima, who was responsible for Sicily.

Now Berlusconi, formerly a member of the Craxi clan, has taken over, using his company as his chief instrument. Fininvest is not a new kind of power, merely the nucleus of a new clan. Dell'Utri sums up the worldview of a clansman: "there is a general war, the magistrates have joined in, it's everybody against everybody".[22]

The Presidential Committee: Courtiers of the King

On January 18, 1994, some months after the work of setting up the clubs had begun, the political movement of *Forza Italia* was inaugurated at Rome.[23] Designed as a separate entity, it was to have far fewer members than the clubs: in June 1994 they numbered four thousand. This elite, which was supposed to exercize real influence, was an object of suspicion and jealousy to the club members. However they need not have worried because the average militant in the political movement had scant influence, while the organization itself was transformed in the Autumn reshuffle.

However its governing body, the presidential committee, had some power if only because of the close ties which some of its members had with Berlusconi. In short they were not so much members of a governing body as courtiers of the king.

In January there were, in addition to Berlusconi, four of them: Luigi Caligaris, a defence expert who proved too independent and had to be packed off to the European Parliament, Antonio Martino, the future Minister of Foreign Affairs, Mario Valducci of Diakron and Antonio Tajani, who had been a journalist with *Il Giornale* before becoming press secretary first to Berlusconi and then to FI. Once more the Fininvest contingent was strong.

An indication of how loose FI's structures were is that the movement had a coordinator who was not officially on the presidential committee. Domenico Mennitti had come over from the MSI where he had moved too quickly to please Fini. Already in the 1987 Congress Mennitti had proposed a break with the Fascist past. After the March elections he wanted to shake up FI, involving both the movement and the clubs in decisions. In June he was forced out as coordinator and FI was deliberately left to hibernate over the summer.

On May 28, partly as a first step towards reining in Mennitti, the presidential committee was expanded from five to eleven members.[24] Four of the newcomers were Fininvest managers with no independent power base: Paolo Del Debbio, a Catholic intellectual, Roberto Spingardi, who came from the personnel department, Alessis Gorla and Angelo Codignoni, the head of the clubs, who thus brought them under even more direct control by the leadership. However the heads of the FI groups in the Senate and the Chamber were designated as automatic members, which could introduce into the presidential committee the

clashes of the parliamentarians. In particular, Berlusconi imposed Previti as the new coordinator in September and blessed the appointment
of Vittorio Dotti as leader of the Chamber group in October.

The two choices strengthened diversity within FI, opening the way
to clashes and to a certain autonomy of the charismatic leader. However
the main theatre in which these clashes took place was not the presidential committee, which was left to languish in the Autumn re-organiza-
tion of the party. Previti, now second only to Berlusconi in the FI hierarchy,
was to be flanked as coordinator by Tajani, Del Debbio, and Nicolò
Querci, who had been Dell'Utri's assistant before becoming Berlusconi's
secretary. They were joined by three other members of the May presidential committee: Gorla, Valducci and Codignoni, who now brought
the clubs under Previti's control. Finally Menitti was allowed back, albeit
with the authoritarian Previti to keep him in line, while Gianni Pilo,
with his indispensable polls, completed the group.[25]

These repeated reshuffles reflect once more Berlusconi's preference
for working through tested loyalists rather than a party bureaucracy.
He was able to make decisions more quickly and there was less (or no)
opposition to his wishes. When he needed a committee, he invented it.
After he fell from power, he set up a Commission of Political Crises,[26]
made up of himself, Previti, Giuliano Urbani and Valducci, to decide FI
policy. The choice of Urbani reflects Berlusconi's willingness to listen to
collaborators of various political hues, provided that he could control
them. He understood that their presence widened FI's appeal. This explains
why he had blessed Dotti, although he was to discover that he could
not quite control the evolution of FI's fourth component, its parliamentary group.

Parliamentarians in Search of a Role

If we see *Forza Italia* as a new kind of populism and as the creation
of Fininvest, then the chief traits of its parliamentary group follow logically.
The group will be neoliberal in outlook, but it will have difficulty defining
its role because it will be caught between the charismatic leader and *la
gente*. However as it seeks to gain a role-looking for allies in other
segments of the movement like the clubs or the presidential committee-
so it may change FI. In particular it may help FI become a modern right-
wing party which, as the champion of free enterprise, seeks to create a
more modest but more efficient state and to establish a correct state-
market relationship. Along the way it will try to democratize the internal life of the movement.

The social composition of FI's 113 members of the Chamber reflects
its links with the private sector: 26 percent are entrepreneurs and 18

percent are managers; 12 percent are teachers (a term that includes university lecturers), 9 percent are lawyers and only 2 percent magistrates. The first two categories reveal the parallels and contrasts with the *Lega* which has 19 percent entrepreneurs but only 6 percent managers. FI is the party of large as well as small business. *Alleanza Nazionale* has weak ties to business—9 percent entrepreneurs and 1 percent managers—and it is the party of independent professionals and of the public sector, hence its 11 percent civil servants. Meanwhile the left is the party of teachers—31 percent—with 13 percent civil servants and 7 percent magistrates.[27]

The FI parliamentary group represented the social strata which was closest to Berlusconi. Populism is frequently a device which allows a leader to appeal to a particular social group in the guise of appealing to the nation. This group must be outside—or must be perceived as outside—the previous political categories; it may but it need not be the poorest group. Thatcher appealed to the upper-level of the working-class and the lower-level of the salariat. Berlusconi sought to create a "movement of concrete people, forged in the trenches of work and the professions".[28]

This was an appeal to the urban middle-class, which had grown steadily: in 1951 it was 26.5 percent of the population, by 1971 it had reached 38.5 percent and by 1983 it amounted to 46.4 percent. Within this class, the Northern small entrepreneur assumed special importance because he had helped pull the Italian economy out of the difficulties of the 1970s, but was politically under-represented. This is the class which, increasingly estranged from the old white and red cultures as well as from the mass parties which incarnated them, had looked in the early 1980s to Craxi's Socialists and to their slogan of modernization. Disappointed they had turned to the *Lega*, which attacked the old regime in the name of free enterprise and efficiency. In 1994 many of them were seduced by FI. Far from being *gente*, such people were the infantry of the capitalist party which Italy has never had. Could FI represent their interests?

Its programme drew on *Alla ricerca del buon governo* and called for the state to be pruned. It reflected the discontent with the old regime when it spoke of "bureaucratic muddles" and the "parasitic-bureaucratic class".[29] Such obstacles placed in the path of the wealth creators were to be removed. The welfare state was to be cut back and people would be given health coupons to spend how they chose. FI was proposing to resolve the crisis of the state by substituting for public dishonesty and ineptude individual effort and entreprenial ingenuity. The state was to be subjected to market discipline. Significantly, FI entrusted the economic recovery to tax cuts for individuals and business. There was scant mention of austerity, while the paragraphs on the need to defend the lira and reduce the deficit were generic. This may help explain why the Berlusconi government quickly earned the distrust of the international financial markets by its reluctance to raise taxes and its hesitation in cutting public expenditure. (One remembers too that Fininvest is a company dependent on consumer spending). When the government did turn to austerity in the budget, it revealed its class basis by making pensions the main object of its cuts and then it backed off when the unions organized massive protests.

This soft version of neoliberalism, which had nothing of Thatcher's blood-and-tears discourse, meshed with Berlusconi's messianic appeal. It was more reassuring to a right-wing electorate than the left's discourse of shared sacrifices. FI picked up 23 percent of people who voted DC in 1992, 31 percent of *Lega* voters and 25 percent of MSI voters. This was an interclass electorate which included a working-class component attracted by Berlusconi's promise to create jobs. Symbolically, FI carried the Lingotto-Mirafiori constituency in South Turin, the home of many FIAT workers. It was also the largest party in the North West, considered the most modern part of Italy.[30] It was, however, unlikely that the demands of many FI voters for a reformed state could be reconciled with the take-over of a new clan. This is one reason for the split which developed within the Chamber group in the autumn.

The problem of defining a role for the parliamentary party remained. People accustomed to making major decisions and earning high salaries did not take kindly to Montecitorio. The inexperienced FI parliamentarians were less skilled in the battle for spoils than AN and they also feared that AN, which did not hide its liking for the strong, central state, was pulling their party to the right. Moreover resentment of Fininvest's authoritarianism, personified in FI's new coordinator, Cesare Previti, ran high. The leader of the FI group in the House, Raffaele della Valle declared that Previti should not be both Minister of Defence and run the movement.[31] At last an FI spokesman was affirming the separation of the state and Berlusconi's clan.

These issues came to a head when Della Valle resigned his position to become deputy-leader of the House. The post belonged to FI but Previti tried to fill it with one of his supporters. He was unsuccessful but a much harder battle was fought over the choice of Della Valle's successor.

Although he too was a Fininvest lawyer, Vittorio Dotti wanted to free the Chamber group from the excessive influence of the company. He favoured a broader debate within the group and called for an opening to the PPI, which would counterbalance the influence of AN.[32] There was nothing of the populist in Dotti whose study in Milan became the haven for the doves. Significantly the group of parliamentarians which backed him was composed mostly of Northern Italian industrialists and free professionals.

Dotti was challenged by Previti's supporters. The Lingotto-Mirafiori member, Alessandro Meluzzi, who had moved from the far left to the far right, led the attack on Dotti. Next Umberto Cecchi wanted to run against him and, although he stood down when Berlusconi made it clear he preferred Dotti, 54 of FI's 114 deputies did not give Dotti their votes.[33]

The hawk-dove split came into the open again during the governmental crisis. Whereas Previti's hawks and AN supported Berlusconi's claim that only the people could remove him as Prime Minister, Dotti's doves were less extreme. Meluzzi organized the Turin demonstration but Raffaele della Valle criticized the violence of Berlusconi's language and warned against taking the struggle to the piazzas.[34] When Berlusconi's determination to force elections clashed with Scalfaro's refusal to grant them, the doves produced a document on December 26 suggesting that another exponent of FI be asked to form a government.

This notion, which had the backing of such FI ministers as Antonio Martino and Giorgio Bernini, was the germ of the eventual solution. In the days that followed, Scognamiglio stated that Parliament was not, as Berlusconi and Previti maintained, delegitimized, while Dotti declared his willingness to support a government headed by Urbani or Dini.[35] Although Berlusconi quashed such insidious subversion, he was gradually edged down the same path. When the Dini government was formed, the doves once more distanced themselves from Berlusconi's angry cries of betrayal. Della Valle suggested voting for Dini, which would also prepare the way for joint action with the PPI.[36]

Again Berlusconi dismissed such heresies and imposed the line of abstention. Yet the doves had established their identity within FI. At the moment they are still dependent on Berlusconi and, were he to disappear, the FI parliamentarians would probably split between AN and the PPI. If, however, they are allowed time, the doves might weaken the populist and company identities of FI and help turn it into that party of modern, reforming capitalism which Italy has always lacked. To do so they would need the support of FI's fifth component, the clubs.

What Future for the Clubs?

FI members explain lucidly what the clubs are not: they are not a militant base forcing its ideology on its leaders, nor are they seeking to monopolize power in their local communities. Indeed they are not political at all. They undertake "initiatives which are cultural, social and implicitly political, although not the kinds of things done by a party". At most the clubs may spread "the liberal-democratic view of life and of society".[37] One rediscovers here the notion, discussed earlier, that the clubs might, in representing the aspirations of civil society, be a response to the crisis of politics. Here again lies the basic ambiguity of Berlusconi's political venture: is this freedom from the occupation of civil society by the parties or is it freedom for one clan to plunder the state? So far it has been the latter.

The clubs are needed at election time to mobilize support. FI spokesmen compare this function with the role of electoral committees in American presidential campaigns, but in the US such committees, like public opinion in general, display far less deference towards their leaders. The quality of the participation in politics which the clubs have been allowed to offer is poor and they present in exacerbated form the contradictions of FI.

Their brief history falls into three periods: up to the March elections, from April until the autumn and a new departure, which is part of the restructuring of FI and whose outcome is as yet unclear. In the months before the parliamentary elections, clubs sprouted, sometimes nurtured by Fininvest and sometimes spontaneous. In February, Codignoni claimed that the clubs had more than 100,000 members. In reality, he had little idea how many clubs or members there were or what they were doing. Events had moved too quickly and Berlusconi's campaign team was both overwhelmed with work and reluctant to discourage supporters. Inevitably many clubs were formed by ex-Socialists and other adherents of the old regime, eager to recycle themselves.

After the March elections, the tensions exploded. Flushed with victory, the clubs sought a role in the choice of candidates for the European elections. The FI leadership envisaged no such role and no part in policy-making. When club members complained about Fininvest tyranny, they were dismissed as recycled intriguers and expelled from the movement. The protest by the presidents of a group of clubs in Treviso is not untypical: they "vigorously reaffirm their total refusal to allow the clubs to be transformed into mere electoral instruments to be used, when needed, by candidates imposed by the leadership without any regard for democratic procedures".[38] It is amusing that, like medieval peasants, the club presidents affect to believe that the good "King Silvio" does not know how badly his barons are behaving.

There were variants on this pattern. In Bologna, the struggle took place within Fininvest between Programma Italia, which had taken the lead in organizing the clubs, and Publitalia, whose executive, Massimo Palmizio, was an unsuccessful candidate in the European elections and also lost out within the movement. The boldest of the club revolts was led by Maurizio De Caro, who led a group of Milan clubs out of FI in May 1994 and formed them into an organization called *Libera Italia*.[39] The FI leadership dismissed him as a former supporter of Craxi. However it did not always spurn recycled politicians: the Bologna FI leader, Federico Bendinelli, had a long career in the DC and was its local secretary from 1989 to 1991.

Berlusconi responded to these rebellions by postponing all action until the autumn. However, the botched decree of July 13 revealed that he had lost touch with the country. A functioning movement, rooted in civil society but engaged in a dialogue with the political leadership, might have proved a more reliable guide than Pilo's polls.

In the autumn, hibernation ended. On the horizon were the local elections of 1995 for which thousands of candidates had to be found. Another spur to action came from AN, which had a good grass-roots organization and, whether for this or for other reasons, had reduced the 18 percent, which separated it from FI in the European elections, to 5.5 percent in the polls.[40] The electoral defeat of November 20 was a further warning.

Cesare Previti reorganized FI, retaining its centralized structure and its ambiguity. His principle was that the regional and local officials were to be, where possible, elected representatives of the national or European parliaments or of regional and local councils. This would prevent the growth of a party bureaucracy and make FI responsive to the voters. However these people were appointed rather than elected to their party posts. Moreover many of the regional delegates were graduates of Publitalia: Enzo Ghigo in Piedmont, Roberto Cipriani in Lombardy (except for Milan which was reserved for Pilo), Giancarlo Galan in the Veneto, Roberto Tortoli in Tuscany, Antonio Martusciello in Campania.

What then of the clubs? It is still impossible to assess how many there are, how many members they have and who these members are. In June 1994 Codignoni claimed there were 14 thousand clubs and a million members. Although the numbers jumped after the March 28 success, this figure seems exaggerated. Anyway there were many desertions over the summer. A census was supposed to have been finished in mid-October 1994, but in January 1995 its results are not available. Codignoni's deputy, Fabio Minoli, states that he has completed the analysis of 3,500 clubs with 6,000 still to be scrutinized. He suggests that the average membership of a club is around 50. As yet there are no figures on the geographical distribution of the clubs or on their sociological composition.[41] My impression, based on limited interviewing and on comments by club members, is that these are predominantly young, middle-class, professional people. If this is correct, then such people are not going to invest time and money without the reward of political power.

Previti has promised them a new role. The centralized structure is a quick way to rebuild the movement which will then be decentralized: "it is necessary to go ahead with the movement from the center to the periphery in order to arrive as quickly as possible at the reverse movement". The clubs, he added, are "our movement's reason for existence".[42] Perhaps, but Previti has never been considered an advocate of grassroots democracy.

In the future, as he describes it, the decision-making process is to begin with the clubs, which will elect the candidates-officials, who in turn will elect a national council, which will chose the presidential committee. A national convention is planned for the spring of 1995 (postponed from autumn 1994) and Previti's role as coordinator is considered temporary. Berlusconi's fall from power may well alter this plan. Certainly if there are quick elections the clubs will be pressed into rebecoming a machine to gather votes.

Conclusion

This is the challenge that FI is facing. It will not be easy to democratize a movement founded on one leader's charisma and created by a company accustomed to business discipline. Indeed internal democracy is incompatible with the clan, the company-party and the concept of la gente. The conflicting pressures from the center and the periphery are great and ambiguity is rampant. Berlusconi has stated that there will be "no more decisions made in Rome...with input only from the members".[43] This could mean either more power to the clubs or freedom for the leadership to reach outside the clubs to its local clients.

It is hard, however, to see how FI can become a useful force of government unless it changes. The historical crisis which brought it into being also contained a powerful drive towards citizenship. Certainly some of its voters see it merely as a barrier against the left, while others may be bought off with privatizations and more efficient public services. However, as the failures of Berlusconi's 1994 government demonstrate, efficiency requires citizen participation and control. Only by becoming a modern right-wing movement where the members have some say, can FI play a role in reforming the Italian state. An unreformed FI may regain power, but it will not govern better than in 1994. Berlusconi must decide whether to become less charismatic and more of a genuine leader or to rely on his TV networks and Ambra Angiolini's ability to seduce the next generation of voters.

Notes

I wish to thank Stephen Hellman for reading this essay and suggesting improvements.

1. *La Repubblica,*November 1, 1994 and November 16, 1994.
2. *La Stampa,*November 28, 1994.
3. Censis, *L'Italia in politica 1,* (Rome: Censis, 1994), p.8.
4. "Alla ricerca del buon governo" (text obtained from Press Office of FI in Rome).
5. Stefano E. D'Anna and Gigi Moncalvo, *Berlusconi in concert* (London: Otzium, 1994).
6. *La Repubblica,*October 26, 1994.
7. *La Stampa,*October 31, 1994.
8. *La Repubblica,*October 16, 1994.
9. For Berlusconi's use of TV see Roberto Grandi, Sandra Cavicchioli, Massimo Franceschetti, "Elezioni Politiche Nazionali 1994" (Paper published by Istituto di Discipline della Comunicazione - Università di Bologna).
10. For Berlusconi's use of language see our "Il linguaggio di Silvio Berlusconi". *Il Regno,* May 15, 1994, pp. 276-278.
11. "Il discorso di Silvio Berlusconi alla Convention di Forza Italia" February 26, 1994 (text obtained from Press Office of FI).
12. Eugenio Scalfari, "Meditazioni sul tramonto della borghesia", *Micromega,* 1994/4 pp. 23-31.
13. *La Stampa,* November 28, 1994.
14. *La Repubblica,* November 23, 1994.
15. *La Stampa,* September 9, 1994.
16. Roberto Spingardi, *La Repubblica,* May 28, 1994.
17. *La Repubblica,* October 16, 1994.
18. *LaVoce,* April 12, 1994
19. *La Repubblica,* November 26, 1994.
20. *L'Espresso,* May 27, 1994 p.42.
21. *La Voce,* January 7, 1995
22. *La Repubblica,* November 23, 1994.
23. Alessandrio Gilioli, *Forza Italia,* (Bergamo: Ferruccio Arnoldi Editori, 1994), p. 44. I have drawn heavily on this book for my analysis of the presidential committee.
24. Ibid. p. 216.
25. Ibid. p. 220.
26. *La Voce,* January 6, 1995.
27. *L'Espresso,* July 22, 1994, pp. 60-62.
28. *Forza Italia informa,* October 31, 1994 (from Press Office of FI).
29. Forza Italia, *Programma* p. 9.
30. Censis, *L'Italia in politica 3* p. 16. See also Ilvo Diamanti, "La politica come marketing" *Micromega* 1994/2 pp. 63-67.
31. *La Voce,* November 10, 1994.

32. *La Repubblica*, November 3, 1994.

33. *La Repubblica*, October 7, 1994.

34. *La Voce*, December 20, 1994.

35. *L'Epresso*, January 15, 1995 pp. 32-35.

36. *La Voce*, January 21, 1995.

37. Forza Italia, "Indicazioni utili" (text from Press Office of FI).

38. "Appello dei Club Forza Italia della provincia di Treviso al Cav. On. Silvio Berlusconi" April 1994 Author's archives.

39. Alessandro Gilioli, op. cit. p. 158 and p. 216.

40. *La Repubblica*, November 1, 1994.

41. Telephone interview with Fabio Minoli, January 31, 1995.

42. *Forza Italia informa*, October 31, 1994.

43. *La Repubblica*, November 5, 1994.

3

From the Ghetto to *Palazzo Chigi*: The Ascent of the National Alliance

Antonio Carioti

The year 1994 was an extraordinarily important year for the Italian Social Movement (MSI), not only for the fact that it was the last year for that traditional designation. The Movement arose as the heir to a regime and to an ideology both undone by war, and excluded until only recently from all meaningful political participation. For this reason it has been defined by the very few authorities on the subject as the "excluded pole" (*polo escluso*),[1] or as the party of the "exiles in their own country" (*esuli in patria*).[2] In 1994, however, the MSI became one of the pillars upon which the alliance governing the country was based. Nevertheless, it does not seem that the change in role has seen an equivalent transformation in the party's political philosophy. And the National Alliance, which formally took the place of the MSI after the January 1995 congress, cannot seriously be considered a new party, since it is the product of the absorption, into the old neo-fascist stump, of "loose cannon"-type parties which retain no autonomous political character. And so Italy continues to lack a liberal democratic Right comparable to those existing in other European countries.

The Flame Bursts

One of the most revealing peculiarities of the situation that came about in the last months of 1993, after the collapse of the parties which had governed Italy for decades, is the fact that the bipolar logic of the plurality electoral system, far from marginalizing the extreme Right, favored the destabilization of the Center, so that the MSI found itself as the only remaining credible point of reference for conservative public opinion in the South and Central regions.

The most prominent demonstration of this phenomenon was on November 21, 1993, when the first ballot for the municipal elections in some of the most important Italian cities saw the MSI-sponsored candidates advance to the second round in almost all of the major South and Central communities. In Rome, particularly, MSI secretary Gianfranco Fini received 35.8 percent of the vote, and in Naples, Alessandra Mussolini, the *duce*'s niece, reached 31.1 percent. Both were competing with opponents on the Left—Francesco Rutelli in Rome, and Antonio Bassolino in Naples—while the candidates supported by the Christian Democrats (DC), busy with its transformation into the Italian Popular Party (PPI), were literally swept away.

Two weeks later, in the run-off ballot, the hopes of both candidates of the MSI (known as "the Flame," for its tricolor symbol) were dashed in the major cities, which, just the same, showed respectable percentages (46.9 percent for Fini, 44.4 percent for Mussolini), never before imaginable for the neo-fascist party. And MSI candidates prevailed in four provincial capitals: Aimone Finestra in Latina, with 55.7 percent; Nicola Cucullo in Chieti, with 57.7 percent; Pasquale Viespoli in Benevento, with 71.5 percent; and Giuseppe Mancuso in Caltanissetta, with 51.7 percent. In centers of population with more than 15,000 eligible voters, the MSI was the strongest party, with 14.4 percent of voters. It was the voters who promoted the Flame to the role of protagonist in the Italian government.

For Fini the vote was his chance to harvest the fruits of a labor of renewal, launched with his return to the secretariat in July 1991, after having been replaced temporarily by Pino Rauti in January 1990. At that time the Flame seemed reduced to a flicker, having reached a historic low at the 1990 administrative elections (3.9 percent) and at the 1991 regional elections in Sicily (4.8 percent, compared to the 9.2 percent of five years before). Upon taking back the reins, Fini immediately tried to pull the party back to its strict rightist profile, more in keeping with its history, relegating to the attic Rauti's illusions of disrupting the Left. And he busied himself furiously with underlining a series of themes dear to the MSI electorate: capital punishment, tax revolt, abolition of RAI, severity toward non-European immigrants, and the annexation of Istria and Dalmatia. All completely in keeping with the "alternative to the system" program laid out by Fini's mentor Giorgio Almirante, and with a nostalgic appeal. "I conduct politics in the most appropriate way for my times," he affirmed for example in March 1992, "but I remain faithful to the roots of the MSI. And I am committed to preserving the era of Mussolini".[3]

The neo-fascist leader was provided with the most delicious opportunity, however, when President Francesco Cossiga made statements against the existing practices of cronyism (*consociativismo*) and partyism (*partitocrazia*). These remarks revealed Cossiga's apparent propensity for presidentialism, and perfectly matched the consolidated MSI position. Freer than most to completely adhere even to the harshest of stances, Fini ably established a sort of privileged rapport with the head of state, managing to exploit his popularity for the purpose of increasing public opinion in favor of his party. The MSI faced the 1992 political elections quoting Cossiga's slogan, "every vote a another blow of the pickax" (*ogni voto una picconata*), and the polls signaled an MSI revival (5.4 percent in the Chamber, 6.5 percent in the Senate), all the more significant in that it was achieved while the MSI confronted dangerous competition in the form of the Northern League.

The eruption of *Tangentopoli* subsequently favored the MSI party leadership, a force which had always remained completely separate from the system of corruption, and which could even boast of having within its own ranks members, such as Milanese communal councilor Riccardo De Corato, who had denounced that very system for some time. After Cossiga, the new idol of the *missini* became prosecutor Antonio Di Pietro.

The possibilities for expansion had already been glimpsed in the administrative elections of June 1993, with the capture of sixteen municipalities, including some rather important ones (Mola, Vasto Grottaferrata, Altamura), by Flame candidates. But it was doubtlessly the subsequent clamorous affirmation in Rome and in Naples that propelled the MSI to a new dimension.

In analyzing the reasons for this strong advance, we must first of all note that for the first time the old MSI aspiration to the entire conservative block no longer faced the insurmountable obstacle of the DC's centrality and its former role as dike against opposing extremes. The DC party leadership had in fact been decimated by scandals, while Martino Martinazzoli's new Popular Party (PPI) offered no confidence that it could close the Left down. The other centrist leader, Mario Segni, offered even less hope, and at one point had gone so far as to station himself among the progressives, with the illusory ambition of becoming their candidate for prime minister. Moreover, the claim that the *conventio ad excludendum* (agreement to exclude) towards the PCI had become in the 1980s a simple pretext for delimiting the area of the majority was loudly disputed. The anti-communist prejudice was just as deeply rooted in the opinion of the moderate electorate. Moreover, at the moment that the DC showed itself essentially disposed toward letting down that bar, a mass of support moved away from those who (everyone had assumed) would surely never open to the communists. The space on the right, which the MSI had always looked on with desire, no longer was as Marco Tarchi had defined it, that is, as a "forbidden fruit",[4] but rather, was ripe for the picking—at least where the League was not present.

Add to this the fact that Fini's party, immune from bribes because it had been almost completely excluded from power for decades, could present itself to the central and southern regions as a credible representative of renewal and could profit from the same climate of exasperation that had fostered the rise of the League in Val Padana. It is worth noting that in this phase, when the ballot for local government elections included a candidate on the Right and one from the Center, the voters for the Left usually wound up preferring the former, rather than risking a return to favor of the forces identified with the old, corrupt system.

It is also necessary to consider the fact that the MSI had characterized itself as the most intransigent champion for national unity in a period in which Bossi, with his secessionist aspirations, was sailing with the wind throughout the North. The League had entered into the collective imagination as a force which was very hostile to southerners and which intended to introduce discriminatory economic measures if nothing else. Fini, with a resounding argument against *Carroccio*'s "three Italies," billed himself instead as defender of the *Mezzogiorno*, for which he was abundantly repaid in terms of public approval. Besides, in the South, which had never seen the cruelest face of Fascism, either in 1920-22, or 1943-45, and which had lived the twenty years of Fascism in a phase of modernization, the anti-fascist prejudice had always been very weak. In vast sectors of the electorate it was practically nonexistent: already between 1970 and 1972, the MSI had garnered extraordinary successes in this area.

Finally, in an epoch dominated by television, the brilliant image that Fini managed to project whenever he appeared on the television screen was fundamental. Always clear, calm, self-assured, often sarcastic, but never excessive in his attacks, he was the perfect representative, at least in appearance, of the lower middle-class right: concrete and full of proposals, certainly conservative, but not a bigot. A far cry from the stereotype of the "thuggish" and intolerant Fascist. Besides which, the same Left which had first conducted a hard first round campaign against the MSI in the name of anti-fascism, in the following weeks showed itself to be quite lavish in its praise with regard to Fini.

An End to Isolation

Throughout its history, the MSI's principal problem has always been the unwillingness of other political forces to enter openly into agreements with it; the only possibility was under-the-table accords. Even when the shunning had lessened, on account of the weakening of the call to anti-fascism, the basic "hands-off" policy stood. And for almost all of 1993, the situation did not change. The evident strengthening of the MSI had in no way remedied its political isolation. So on April 18 of that year, Fini unexpectedly found himself again at the side of the Communist Refoundation in the disastrous campaign for the "No" vote in the referendum regarding the introduction of the single-member plurality system for election to the Senate. The MSI continued to rely on a logic of force wielded through anti-system protest. Incapable of coalescing with other groups, it was therefore committed to preserving the proportional vote. It had managed to enlarge the size of the ghetto, but it had not yet found anyone on the outside willing to open the gates.

All that changed with the entrance of Silvio Berlusconi on the scene, which makes sense since no one who proposed to create a winning moderate slate could ignore the MSI's supply of votes. On November 23, the day after the first round of voting for the local elections, the president of Fininvest declared without hesitation that, if he were a resident of Rome, he would vote for Fini in the run-off. Looking back on it, we can say that with that move, Berlusconi laid the first brick of the strategy that would carry him to the Palazzo Chigi. The signal immediately seemed clear: there was a new political actor at the ready, who did not care about the taboos of the First Republic, borne of the Resistance, and who was prepared to align himself even with Mussolini's heirs in order to overcome the power of the progressive line-up. For the MSI it was a long craved legitimization, since now Fini had the partner which his predecessors Michelini and Almirante had never managed to procure in their repeated attempts to form a conservative front under the banner of anti-communism.

The scheme the MSI leadership had worked for since the day after their crushing referendum defeat in the spring was taking shape. By April 24, 1993, Fini had sent spokesperson Francesco Storace as a scout, and Storace proposed that the party accept the challenge of the majority vote and promote a nationalist-conservative association that would be as broad as possible, capable of competing for control of the government.[5] And a few days later, the political scientist Domenico Fisichella, who had already been advancing that idea for several months, predicted in an interview the birth of a pivotal element on the right that would be like a "point of arrival of a meaningful process (already begun and not yet concluded) of the MSI's structural and cultural revision".[6]

On November 26 (not coincidentally immediately after Berlusconi's declaration of his candidacy), the National Alliance project was officially launched, in an attempt to gather vaster forces around the MSI, with the expressed goal of forming a coalition acceptable not only to the ordinary voters, but also to potential allies who might want to form a large conservative block. In reality it seems immediately evident that very few individuals were ready to come together under the banner of the Flame: a few renegade Christian Democrats from the right, like Publio Fiori and Gustavo Selva, and some intellectuals, including naturally Fisichella, the physicist Giuseppe Basini, and the economist Pietro Armani. But the Alliance's framework was entirely *missino*: charged with putting it together was Adolfo Urso, the ex-press secretary of the MSI.

After the municipal elections of December 11, the Central Committee clearly set the MSI strategy with an eye to the coming political elections. That very morning Fini went to pay his respects to the fallen men of the *Fosse Ardeatine*, who were murdered in retaliation by the Nazis in 1944. Then in a speech to the committee, he declared explicitly that Fascism now belonged to history. "No one," he added however, "can ask us to deny it again in the moment in which we declare clearly that we do not want it restored. Even we, like all Italians, are post-Fascists. Not neo-Fascists." But above all, the MSI leader proclaimed the necessity of "a clean and irreversible shift" (*una svolta netta e irreversibile*) in the party program. "A political alternative to the partitocratic system like that we have until now had," he went on to observe, "no longer makes sense for the simple reason that the partitocratic system no longer exists." It was now finally time to pose the question of access to government, and thus, of the alliances necessary to attain it. And the leader of the Flame, without ever excluding ties with any of the forces generically definable as moderate (the Segni Pact, the ex-DC, the League), explicitly showed his preference for Berlusconi, the only one, he underlined, "whose determination to stop the forces of the Left cannot be doubted".[7]

The Fini position passed without opposition, which is rather unusual for an ostensibly epochal turn-around. But without a doubt, some accepted him with a mental reserve that amounted essentially to a tactical move. On the other hand, the secretary's explicit allusion to the "don't deny, don't restore," (*non rinnegare e non restaurare*) formula which had been the motto of the MSI at its outset, let it be known that the break with the past was only apparent. The desired impression, however, was something else again. For this reason the party presented itself to the public with the new initials AN, forcing itself to absorb the largest possible number of independent personalities to show off as living proof that change had taken place.

The official launching of the new entity occurred with two distinct events, a week apart from each other: on January 22, 1994, the National Alliance was created; and from the 28th to the 30th, the MSI Congressional Assembly convened. From the first meeting it clearly emerged that the new movement which had been so hurriedly bound together was not at all a confederation of equally ranked entities, but a simple association of sympathetic interests, each more or less prestigious, revolving around the old neo-fascist party. The 800 delegates of the Alliance, meeting for only one day, limited themselves to nominating Fini coordinator by acclaim, conferring full powers on him.[8] As for the MSI Congressional Assembly, it too was a ritual celebrated above all for public consumption: it was not even a true congress in that no renewal of party executives took place. The program approved for the occasion (about which I will say more later) certainly was not novel with respect to the traditional positions of the MSI. And the symbol of the Alliance was the same unmistakable tricolor Flame, although reduced in size and dwarfed by the words *"Alleanza Nazionale"* written in large white letters on a blue background. It seemed more than just coincidence that on January 29, the *Secolo d'Italia* published a photo of the MSI leader pointing out the emblem with the following caption: "Gianfranco Fini shows the new symbol of the MSI." It was a truly Freudian lapse.

An Alliance Divided

Berlusconi's entry into the official field of candidates, on January 26, created a political polarization throughout Italy that was quite favorable to the National Alliance. Many years before, at another time of great electoral gain for the MSI (1969-1974), it had been Almirante's objective to arrive at a head-on confrontation between the Left and the Right. To all intents and purposes, Almirante's politics of a "national Right" must be considered the precedent which inspired the position now being staked out by Fini. At that time the Flame was aiming for the formation of an "explicitly anti-communist front" (*fronte articolato anticomunista*) which would benefit from the reaction of the "silent majority" against the youthful confrontation and the tumultuous hot autumn, with the aim of making all intermediary positions impracticable and arriving at a day of reckoning for the "Reds".[9] "The plan was," remembers Roberto Chiarini, "to eliminate the space which separates the anti-fascist front from the anti-communist front, until we could make them identical and consequently snatch out from under the feet of the Center the terrain which has furnished until now a profitable return and kept the Right in a perennial state of marginality".[10]

Now, in 1994, it was no longer so much the MSI-National Alliance, as much as Berlusconi in person who launched the challenge based on the front-to-front theory as regards the Left. Fini, however, easily inserted himself into this dialectic, for which his party was perfectly e-quipped. For this reason, Fini's continued appeal to overcome the fascism/anti-fascism opposition must be judged equivocal. Similarly, Fini's reference to Norberto Bobbio, which had already appeared in his speech to the National Alliance Constituent Assembly,[11] and was then repeated with much more resonance to the Chamber of Deputies the following May 20,[12] seems mistaken. Actually, Bobbio had predicted the end of the face-to-face contraposition between anti-fascism and anti-communism by means of a complete ideological depolarization.[13] Instead the Italian Right, just when it had declared anti-fascism obsolete, conducted an electoral campaign under the banner of the bitterest anti-communism, which was expressed, however, with much more vehemence by *Forza Italia* than by the National Alliance. Fini, therefore, whose voters' aversion to the PDS constituted such a settled motif that it did not need to be sparked again with any real vigor, could comfortably take hold of Berlusconi's coattails, while at the same time winning for himself more acknowledgments by the Left for his moderate tones.

This scenario, already clear even before *Forza Italia* officially came into being, met however with a notable stumbling block in the hostility between the Alliance and the League, an unavoidable component in forming a moderate front in the northern regions. Aggravated by the decline of the old power block, the contrast is solid and glaring, reaching beyond the ideological opposition between nationalism and federalism, to reflect the country's general split between North and South. *Carroccio*'s exclusively northern electorate demands less welfarism; the Flame's electorate, mostly southern, insists on the continuation of state economic intervention in depressed regions.

The polemic between the two parties reached a head right at the phase of preparing nominations. On one side, the League threatened to veto the presence of the MSI in the Freedom Alliance. On the other side, Fini, who attached great importance to the AN's national characterization, refused to give up the nomination of his men to the single-member plurality constituencies of the North. The editorial writer and future director of the *Secolo d'Italia*, Gennaro Malgieri, responded in kind to Bossi's coarse attacks against the MSI made from the podium of the League Congress in Bologna: "The League is not a contender like all the rest: it is an enemy to be beaten".[14] In reality these increasingly bitter tones seemed oriented toward the goal of diverting attention from the fact that the League and the Alliance, both on the point of allying themselves with *Forza Italia*, would be fighting the same battle separately. The question was finally resolved by creating two distinct coalitions based on the territorial realities: a sort of divided alliance that proved itself quite effective when it came to getting voter support. The Freedom Alliance, composed of Bossi, Berlusconi, Pannella and other moderate forces, was put forward in the North and in Tuscany (also for the Senate in the Marches). The Flame stayed back and proposed its own autonomous nominations in these regions. In the central and southern regions the *Polo del Buon Governo* (Good Government Alliance) was founded, fruit of an accord between the AN, *Forza Italia,* and the ex-Christian Democrats of the Christian Democratic Center (CCD): only a few constituencies (*circoscrizioni*) were left out (the Marches, Abruzzo, Molise and Campania 2 for the Chamber; Abruzzo and Umbria for the Senate) because of opposition between the interested parties.

Consolidated politically by a common desire to disrupt the Left, this strange coalition was however entirely non-homogenous with regard to platforms. Each party went to the elections with its own program. And the National Alliance's program (or, more precisely, that of the MSI) was situated in complete continuity with the neo-fascist tradition.[15] In fact, other than presidentialism, it proposed forms of corporative representation, and brutally attacked the federalist hypothesis. It gave in on the death penalty, but warmly supported stricter penalties for drug consumption, prostitution, and illegal immigration. Nor did it forego pleading against cosmopolitanism and consumerism, while the party's nationalist inclination peeked through in certain very critical passages regarding the privatization of public enterprises and the introduction of scholastic autonomy. In foreign affairs it contained a harsh attack on the Maastricht Treaty and explicit territorial claims (Istria, Fiume, and even Dalmatia) addressed to the Republics of the former Yugoslavia—this last point is one which sparked a huge debate between Alliance supporters and Foreign Minister Nino Andreatta in the electoral campaign.[16]

The verdict from the voting booths was however quite favorable for the Flame, which, with 13.5 percent of the vote, became the third strongest Italian party. Its success in the central and southern regions was resounding (20.3 percent), and good even where the AN was proposed in isolation: 6.7 percent in the Northwest, 9.1 in the Northeast, and above all 10.5 in the "red" regions, traditionally troublesome for the MSI. We must note that the supporters of National Alliance who were candidates of the *Polo del Buon Governo* in the single-member districts (*collegi uninominali*) obtained on average more votes than the *Forza Italia* supporters did, whether in the Chamber (37.8 percent, compared to 35.9) or in the Senate (33.8 percent, as opposed to 31.4), and they won much more often (77.5 percent of cases in the Chamber against *Forza Italia*'s 57.1). We can say then that the moderate voter no longer had any

Antonio Carioti

qualms about voting for the MSI.[17] Moreover, as Piero Ignazi has observed,[18] on the social, territorial, and personal levels, the vote for the AN was not much different from the votes which traditionally went to the MSI: the southernization of the party is even accentuated, as the tables show.[19]

Table 3.1   The territorial distribution of National Alliance votes and winners in the elections to the Chamber of Deputies

District	Proportion Votes	Seats	Single-Vote Seats	Total Seats
Piemonte 1	9.0	1	0	1
Piemonte 2	7.5	1	0	1
Lombardia 1	6.4	1	0	1
Lombardia 2	5.1	1	0	1
Lombardia 3	5.9	0	0	0
Trentino A. A.	9.0	0	1*	1
Veneto 1	8.3	1	0	1
Veneto 2	6.9	1	0	1
Friuli V. G.	14.2	1	0	1
Liguria	8.0	1	0	1
Emilia Romagna	9.0	1	0	1
Toscana	10.9	1	0	1
Umbria	16.3	1	0	1
Marche	15.7	1	0	1
Lazio 1	26.0	1	13	14
Lazio 2	23.2	0	5	5
Abruzzo	20.8	1	1*	2
Molise	19.1	0	2	2
Campania 1	19.1	2	8	10
Campania 2	21.6	2	6*	8
Basilicata	17.0	1	1	2
Puglia	26.5	1	21	22
Calabria	17.2	1	5	6
Sicilia 1	11.0	1	7	8
Sicilia 2	16.7	1	13	14
Sardegna	12.1	0	3	3
National average of votes and total of seats	13.5	23	86	109

* The single-vote seats indicated by the asterisk were earned by the National Alliance standing alone on the ballot, the others were included in the *Polo del Buon Governo*.

Table 3.2   Regional distribution of Senate seats won by the National Alliance

Region	Proportional Gain Seats	Single-Vote Count Seats	Total
Val d'Aosta	0	0	0
Piemonte	1*	0	1
Lombardia	1*	0	1
Trentino A. A.	0	0	0
Veneto	1*	0	1
Friuli V. G.	0	0	0
Liguria	0	0	0
Emilia Romagna	1*	0	1
Marche	1*	0	1
Toscana	1*	0	1
Umbria	1*	0	1
Lazio	0	11	11
Abruzzo	1*	0	1
Molise	0	0	0
Campania	2	4	6
Puglia	2	6	8
Basilicata	0	1	1
Calabria	1	1	2
Sicilia	0	10	10
Sardegna	0	2	2
Total	13	35	48

* Seats indicated by an asterisk were won in regions in which the National Alliance alone was nominated to the Senate.

Fini brought 109 members to Parliament (he had had 34) and 48 senators (formerly 16), political personnel almost entirely of MSI origin. In the Chamber, the MSI-AN was the party with the largest percentage of members with experience in the local elective assemblies (77.5 percent). As for reelected members, the MSI was outnumbered only by the League (59.4 percent against *Carroccio*'s 69 percent) and, for members with experience in the national branches of the party, only by the Refoundation (44.8 percent against the neo-Communists' 50 percent).[20]

The tendency was confirmed at the European election on June 12, signaling only a relative lull for the Flame (12.5 percent and 11 seats), keeping in mind the great growth in *Forza Italia* in the rush of Berlusconi's arrival to the premiership. From the European elections, too, one sees the virtual nonexistence of a non-MSI component. One need only consider that in the constituency of Central Italy, the independent candidate supported by Fini, Francesco Caroleo Grimaldi, was cleanly beaten in the preference voting not only by two candidates at the head of the list (*capilista*), Pino Rauti and Marco Cellai, but also by the young secretary of the Roman Youth Front, Roberta Angelilli. In fact the moment the National Alliance was essentially the new name for an old political party.

Fascists in the Government

Once successful at the voting booths, the MSI found itself struggling with the phantom of its past, as the composite slate in which it was participating prepared to translate itself into a government coalition. The presence of neo-Fascists in the Freedom Alliance aroused alarm—not just the somewhat cynical alarm of the Italian Left, which had been up until that moment quite generous with Fini,[21] but rather an alarm felt at the international level, where the unheard-of prospect of the return to power of those who had been defeated in 1945, just when the extreme xenophobic Right was flourishing all over Europe, seemed traumatic from more than just the symbolic standpoint. So, while the opposition was organizing a large demonstration in Milan on April 25, the anniversary of the Italian Liberation, the foreign press was getting excited over the threat of "Fascists in the government." Notable in this campaign were the large American newspapers like the *International Herald Tribune*, the *New York Times*, and even the conservative *Wall Street Journal*,[22] which, however, tended to waffle in its opinion.[23] The *Independent* and the *Daily Telegraph* of Great Britain attached much importance to the ascent of the AN[24] as did *Der Spiegel* in Germany,[25] and *Libération* and *Le Nouvel Observateur* in France.[26] Worried declarations arrived from various western government representatives and from prestigious personalities such as Nobel Prize winner Franco Modigliani[27] and the President of the Commission of the European Union, Jacques Delors.[28] On May 4, an indication of that alarm was recorded in the Parliament in Strasbourg, which wished for Italy, "a government faithful to the fundamental values that inspired the foundation of the Community."

During the formation of the government, the Alliance had to swallow the exclusion of those of its leaders who had taken part in the Italian Social Republic (RSI). The one who paid the price was Mirko Tremaglia, forced to give up the hoped-for Ministry for Italians Living Abroad and compensated with a position as President of the Foreign Affairs Commission of Montecitorio. In the end, however, the Flame obtained a sizable representation, and it tried to lessen the impact on public opinion by including a woman and two non-MSI members: for Giuseppe Tatarella, leader of the "Black Puglia," there were the deputy premiership of the cabinet and the Ministry of Posts and Telecommunications; for Adriana Poli Bortone, the Ministry of Agriculture; for Altero Matteoli, the Ministry of the Environment; for independents Fisichella and Fiori, Cultural Assets and Transportation, respectively. Twelve undersecretaries were named, the better to cover the key ministries.

Fini used the debate over investiture in the Chamber of Deputies on May 20, to confirm solemnly his opposition to totalitarianism and his full adherence to democratic values, recognizing as well that "anti-fascism was a historically essential moment in order for the values of democracy to return to Italy".[29] His words stoked bad feelings among those *missini* who were most attached to the philosophies of the past: Rauti, Tremaglia, Buontempo. Inopportunely the same day, the *Secolo d'Italia* published an article in which it exalted the RSI units that had fought at the side of the Nazis.[30]

All the same, it was Fini himself who fed the fires of debate over his party's past, with an interview immediately following the vote, in which he defined Mussolini as "the greatest statesman of the century".[31] He evidently wanted to reestablish the MSI's position with a call to its specific identity, after having appeared in an electoral campaign as an accessory to Berlusconi. Elsewhere the whole debate on the fascist threat, which was drawn out until the European elections, was dealt with by the National Alliance leadership on the tightrope of ambiguity, so as to avoid too rough a blow to the party. One day Fini asserted that, until the racial laws dating from 1938, Mussolini's regime had produced measures that were on the whole positive[32]—only a week after the *Secolo d'Italia* had honored the memory of Giacomo Matteotti, murdered by the Fascists in 1924.[33]

Naturally, the Flame leader's boldest interviews were released to the foreign press in order to remedy his party's image, which remained quite negative, so much so that at one moment Belgian minister Elio Di Rupo refused to shake the hand of his colleague, Tatarella, at a meeting in Brussels.[34] On June 18, Fini declared to *Le Monde* that he would even agree to call himself anti-fascist, if by this term "we mean the love of liberty, for democracy." And he managed eventually to win out over some hostilities. The *Times* of London defined him on November 17, as "democratic without a doubt." And a vague overture was conceded to him by Professor Norman Birnbaum's report to the American Senate, presented in October, in which it was still underlined that "the National Alliance's adherence to democracy is less passionate than its commitment to the promotion of other values".[35]

On the other hand, Fini's polite tones often coincided with rigid stances on concrete questions—for example, in the dispute over certain territories with Slovenia, whose membership in the European Union Italy vetoed above all because of National Alliance pressure tactics. On October 18, in Trieste, the MSI leader railed against the possibility of an "accord similar to the Osimo Treaty" and asked the Slovenians to apologize to Italy for the wrongs committed by Tito's followers. Three days later he reacted to the resulting difficulties in the negotiation by urging the government to declare its opposition to EU membership for Lubiana.

The Python's Strategy

In the highly conflicted coalition borne in March, the National Alliance at length took on the role of the calmer and reasonable member, even if the careless remarks of its exponents often partially blurred the judicious image which Fini constantly worked to promote. The ever-increasing reciprocal hostility between the MSI and the League was expressed for a while mostly in the strident contrast between Bossi's continuous attacks on Berlusconi and Fini's firm, guaranteed support of him.

In effect, the bridge between the AN and *Forza Italia*, the backbone of the majority, rests on foundations that are more solid than their simple aversion to the Left. They are both formations that suffer, albeit for different reasons, a certain lack of legitimization. And their understanding feeds precisely on the fact that each absolves the other of the "sin" for which it is characterized.

In taking for granted an evolution which has really only just occurred, Berlusconi has shut his eyes to the MSI's politico-cultural origins and to its past, even the very recent past. Just as he was painting the Democratic Party of the Left (PDS) as a Stalinist force of the old order, he accused of bad faith anyone who dared doubt the liberal-democratic conversion of the Alliance. Fini, for his part, closed his eyes to the anomalous situation created by the arrival in *Palazzo Chigi* of an entrepreneur with such strong interests in so many varied sectors—most of all in television, crucial for the control of information, where among other things one must work within the context of public concessions. On August 2, during the parliamentary debate over the conflicts of interest associated with the prime minister, the MSI leader gave a speech meant to minimize the impact of the problem, underlining that this was not the issue for which the government will be judged by its citizens.

Essentially the two allies sustained each other in the awareness of their mutual dependence, to the point at which a proposal to create a sort of federation, perhaps including the CCD and other minor forces, or even a fusion that would consecrate their association once and for all came to light. Moreover, it soon appeared evident that the AN could draw conspicuous advantages, in terms of party patronage, out of the iron pact with Berlusconi, whose personal leadership is undisputed.[36] From RAI, to the banks, to public corporations of every sort, Fini's party set out on a solid effort of penetration and affiliation, soon becoming, thanks also to Fini's diffidence with regard to privatization, the most solid reference point for functionaries and orphaned managers of the defunct five-party government.[37] The structural weakness of *Forza Italia* and the inexperience of the League provided vast openings to MSI initiatives, and to Tatarella's maneuvering talents in particular. The deputy prime minister worked a near miracle when he first gave the go-ahead to the summer offensive against the *Banca d'Italia*, presented as a "strong power" to be weakened,[38] and then donned the armor of defender of the institution's autonomy, and he is credited as the secret director of the operation which made Vincenzo Desario the general director in via Nazionale (Headquarters of the *Banca d'Italia*), against the objections of Treasury Minister Lamberto Dini.

For the most part, Fini's moderate stance has allowed him gradually to increase his personal popularity in a country that needs gravity, to the point of overtaking a Berlusconi impeded by the difficult job of governing. Meanwhile the MSI, by exploiting its roots in the political territory at its disposal, has managed much better than its allies to harvest the fruits of the shift to the right which had carried the Freedom Alliance to victory. Marcello Pera has proposed an image, which has acquired a certain plausibility, of the National Alliance as a python which wraps the *Forza Italia* antelope in its coils, suffocating and devouring it.[39] But in reality the Flame seems aware that it needs, at least for the moment, an ally more closely tied to the Center to lend it legitimacy.

The *Forza Italia*-MSI understanding meets some other obstacles, first of all with the underlying dissension between Berlusconi and the *missini* over the question of Berlusconi's stance toward the magistracy, especially the Milanese team directing the "Clean Hands" investigation. While the *Forza Italia* leadership displays an extreme coolness toward the prosecution directed by Francesco Saverio Borrelli, and considers the central role which the investigation has assumed in public life to be an anomaly which should be remedied, the MSI has been from the beginning one of the most ardent supporters of the magistrates, to whose actions it owes a significant part of its own fortune.

The dispute came to a head midway through July, with the decree on pretrial detention, which the Alliance first supported and then repudiated.[40] And it continued into September, when Di Pietro presented the investigating team's proposal to wind up the *Tangentopoli* episode, viewed with favor by the *missini* and with hostility by Forza Italia. But the contrast was carried even inside the AN, when Giulio Maceratini, Senate group leader, directed harsh criticism toward the magistrates at the October 22-23 Central Committee meeting, arousing the ire of the Lombard members of Parliament (La Russa, Tremaglia, De Corato). It is symptomatic that the new secretary of the Popular Party, Rocco Buttiglione, took his cue from this very theme in order to create divisions in the *Polo del Buon Governo*.[41]

More generally it is clear that the reappearance of a centrist, ex-Christian Democrat political initiative, a result of the new dynamism lent to the PPI by Buttiglione, creates a notable problem for the Flame. In fact the National Alliance, in order to consolidate its position, needs a political system arranged on a bipolar model: that way the line-up on the right will never be able to do without an AN contribution, and the risk of return to the ghetto will be avoided. But if instead there emerges an autonomous central force, ready to alternate its considerable package of votes between the Left and the Right, it will be able to dictate conditions for alliances with one wing or the other. It will also be able to demand, as Buttiglione does, that the Right push the AN out, or at least force out its most extreme components.

In the fall, there seemed to open between Fini and the PPI secretary a contest for which the prize was long-term hegemony over the moderate axis, which the too ephemeral and personalist Forza Italia does not appear to be able to handle. Each leader worked to divide his rival's party, moving toward the Center or toward the Right axis of the governing coalition. The MSI secretary wanted to oblige the majority of the *Popolari* to choose the conservative slate, breaking with the Left of Sergio Mattarella and Rosy Bindi.[42] Buttiglione worked at the contradictions in the Alliance, which was suspended between Gaullist ambitions and lictorian nostalgia.

The situation deteriorated when Bossi decided to break with Berlusconi, who was weakened by the negative outcome of the local elections (the Right was defeated by Center-Left coalitions almost everywhere), by the difficulty over the financial law, and by the investigation of Berlusconi initiated in Milan. The threat of a decisive change in majority, which Buttiglione could not help but support, obviously consolidated the relationship between the National Alliance and *Forza Italia*, because the MSI members were aware that only this prime minister's remaining in office protected them from the danger of renewed marginot as a victory of universal values, but, quite reductively, as "the political system that is most consistent with contemporary thought."

It would surely be excessive to read into these contorted writings Fini's permanent democratic unreliability. It is also plausible that he is planning, as Giorgio Galli believes,[48] a Gaullist type landing for the AN. His intention is to enact a smooth transition without losing a piece of the old anti-system party. Therefore a force within the party, which in the past located its *raison d'être* almost exclusively in the conservation of strong party identity, however obsolete, today refuses to question its own identity, because the question could get in the way of the new role that it has carved out for itself. In the place of the "fear of politics"[49] which had characterized the MSI in the 1980s, when it did not know how to accept Bettino Craxi's explicit overtures, there is now an attitude of *politique d'abord*, for which the party's entire vision seems to be consumed in the direct participation in the struggle for power.

From the organizational point of view, the change scheduled for the Congress in Fiuggi, January 25-29, 1995, consists in the fusion of the MSI apparatus with the nebula of the AN clubs , whose organization around the country was initiated only in July 1994. The National Alliance, outside of superficial speeches, had in fact never existed as a confederation between the MSI and other parties of equal status: the Alliance clubs in reality were merely local offices and were recognized through their direct relationship with the national coordinator (i.e., Fini) through his second in command Urso. And it should be emphasized that demands to support the circles can easily be deflected for reasons of incompatibility with the peripheral structures of the MSI.

Essentially, the transformation was a mechanism for admitting sympathizers without making them register with the old party, browsing through the various professional categories, in offices and workplaces, and in other places of social and cultural concern. The congress resolutions speak of approximately 2,000 circles already formed; Urso declared 1,700 of them ratified on November 30.[50] It is difficult, however, to trust these data because, for example, the official number of 8,337 MSI sections with 250,000 registered members is hardly credible, when in 1973, at the peak of Almirante's secretariat, there were only 4,335 sections, with 420,000 registered members.[51]

Evidently the AN circles do not possess their own political identities and will not be able to throw much weight around in the new organization: it is quite probable that they will split up and be distributed among the traditional MSI components, mostly in Fini's component. One might hypothesize just the same that they will have a certain role in the selection of candidates for the administrative elections of 1995, above all in the zones in which the MSI apparatus remains very weak.

nalization, while Berlusconi knew that Fini, for this very reason, only ally on whom he could count completely.

Politique d'Abord

The many unknowns of the political picture have led Fini ahead with the transformation of the MSI into the National All is a decision determined not by a critical appraisal of the nec experience, which to the contrary has been praised on every occ positive and winning, but rather by the need to render the actic party more effective in a new stage. The leader of the Flame e: it with extreme clarity in his September 30 press conference initiated the procedure:[43] the MSI had to become the AN in attract as much of the moderate vote as possible, to consoli agreement with *Forza Italia*, to lure votes away from Bossi, and off maneuvers that aimed to push it aside again. Arguments wh sayers Rauti and Buontempo, judging from their slim followir oppose only with ideological claims of little impact.

However, although the resolutions of the party Congress p by *Secolo d'Italia* on December 7 contain previously unpublished sions to federalism and privatization, they reveal no trace of a ɪ and deeply-felt theoretical revision. In fact, the call for a gen(tion on the right seems confused in its suggestion that people at absolute extremes, such as the Catholic democrat Luigi St the pagan traditionalist Julius Evola (together with classics like Gentile, Spirito, and D'Annunzio) are compatible. It seems si that the man who inspired all this, with his idea of an Ital "conservative revolution",[44] appears to be the same Marcello ᵌ whom Fini had cited in the 1990 Congress in order to attack vidualist and secularized West.[45] It is difficult, in this context, of an authentic reversal.

The same rejection of totalitarianism, already expressed mɛ before by Almirante,[46] sounds profoundly ambiguous, since easily disarm it by playing around with the words. In fact, if a rigorous and restrictive reading of the term in question, in the teachings of the social sciences, we are in a position tc Fisichella's statement that Mussolini's regime was not totalitariɪ the condemnation of totalitarianism does not necessarily imɪ demnation of fascism. If instead we broaden the concept out c tion, even the partitocratic First Republic—as Fini said in his the Chamber on May 20—can be considered totalitarian in its on the classic night in which all the cats are black. And iɪ emphasized that the resolutions of the MSI congress define d

It is this 1995 election, administrative, but perhaps also political, which provides a crucial deadline for the National Alliance plan, as the AN intends to succeed on the basis of an organized relationship with *Forza Italia* even in the North (in view of the Bossi's break with the Freedom Alliance), where the Flame appears to be in a phase of expansion. In effect, the administrative vote of November 20 - December 4 rewarded the Alliance in the northern cities (Brescia, Sondrio, Treviso), while it was disappointing in the South. The result in Puglia was disastrous, where the Right lost eight out of every nine votes cast.

More generally, Fini's objective is to make irreversible the process he began with the March vote, by consolidating a Center-Right front-line, of which the National Alliance is an essential component. Part of this strategy is the forceful renewed proposal of presidentialism in the congress resolutions, and likewise a change of position on the electoral law: while the plan adopted in January leaned toward the two-round majority system,[52] the resolutions opted for the simple majority (plurality) vote, which obliges pre-electoral alliances. It is not by chance that Fini has come down strictly in favor of the pertinent referendum promoted by Pannella, later ruled inadmissible by the Constitutional Court.

Seen in this light, obviously, the idea of an institutional government to be constructed on the ruins of the Freedom Alliance is being used as a smoke screen by the National Alliance, since remaining in executive office is the "corner stone" (*chiave di volta*)[53] on which Fini founded the transformation that he is bringing to bear. Significantly, a similar possibility was rejected with unusually harsh tones by a usually calm Fisichella.[54] And in effect, a lasting return to the opposition would nullify all efforts for legitimization made by the National Alliance, probably leading to the reemergence of extremist tendencies that are still deep-rooted in the party.

It is with a contradictory state of mind, then, that the MSI faces the year that should complete its metamorphosis, as it is buoyed by its pride for successes obtained and reined in by the disquieting fear of losing everything in a short time. It is one more reason to attend particularly to the problems of the immediate future, continuing to defer the fundamental problem of party physiognomy—a problem which cannot, however, be postponed indefinitely.

Translated by Sara L. Brann

Notes

1. Piero Ignazi, *Il polo escluso. Profilo del Movimento Sociale Italiano*, (Bologna: Il Mulino, 1989).

2. Marco Tarchi, "Esuli in patria". I fascisti nella Repubblica italiana, in *Lo straniero interno*, edited by Enrico Pozzi, (Florence: Ponte alle Grazie, 1993), pp. 185-209. An amply revised and updated version of this essay is in *Trasgressioni*, n. 18, January-April 1994, pp. 65-97.

3. *Il Messaggero*, March 2, 1992. For fairly exhaustive documentation of the political route followed by Fini since his return to the secretariat, up through the Roman municipal elections, see Francesco Storace (ed.), *La svolta. Luglio 1991 - dicembre 1993. Settanta interviste a Fini dal rilancio del Msi-Dn all'Alleanza nazionale*, Rome, Msi-Dn, 1993.

4. Marco Tarchi, "L'impossibile identità: Il neofascismo tra destra e sinistra", in *Trasgressioni*, n. 10, 1989, p. 16.

5. Cf. *Secolo d'Italia*, April 24, 1993.

6. *L'Unità*, April 27, 1993.

7. *Secolo d'Italia*, December 12, 1993. An even clearer and more prescient sizing up of Berlusconi's action came a few days later from the coordinator of the National Alliance organizing committee, Adolfo Urso: "Berlusconi is realizing, with the pragmatism that sets him apart, a fusion of the three realities which today cannot dialogue with each other but must do so if they do not want to hand the country over to the Left. Since the individual political parties are not able to do it, he will probably be the one to organize the winning candidates in the Padania with the League [...]; and he will do the same with the National Alliance in the rest of Italy... To be frank: if the "moderates" will have the courage to divide the DC, most of the job is done, and *Berlusca* will take care of the rest. In fact, he's already taking care of it." *L'Italia settimanale*, December 22, 1993.

8. See the agenda approved by the National Alliance constituent assembly in *Secolo d'Italia*, January 25, 1994.

9. For a reconstruction of the events, cf. Piero Ignazi, *Il polo escluso*, 133-165.

10. Roberto Chiarini, "La Destra italiana. Il paradosso di un'identità illegittima", in *Italia contemporanea*, n. 185, (1991), p. 595.

11. Cf. *Secolo d'Italia*, January 25, 1994.

12. Cf. *Secolo d'Italia*, May 21, 1994.

13. Cf. Norberto Bobbio, *La Stampa*, January 16, 1994. Bobbio's response to Fini is in *La Stampa*, May 21, 1994.

14. *Secolo d'Italia*, February 8, 1994.

15. Cf. *Secolo d'Italia*, February 27, 1994.

16. "No one has ever established that the borders settled on after the Second World War, and therefore fixed under a set of extraordinary circumstances, must remain untouched" writes Mirko Tremaglia in *Secolo d'Italia*, on February 17, 1994.

17. Cf. Stefano Bartoli and Roberto D'Alimonte, "La competizione maggioritaria" in *Rivista italiana di scienza politica*, XXIV (1994), pp. 631-686.

18. Cf. Piero Ignazi, "Alleanza nazionale," in *Milano a Roma. Guida all'Italia elettorale del 1994*, edited by Ilvo Diamanti and Renato Mannheimer, (Rome: Donzelli, 1994), pp. 43-52.

19. Cf. Piero Ignazi, *Postfascisti? Dal Movimento sociale italiano ad Alleanza nazionale*, (Bologna: Il Mulino, 1994), pp. 99-105.

20. Cf. Luca Verzichelli, "Gli eletti," in *Rivista italiana di scienza politica,* XXIV (1994), pp. 715-739.

21. With regard to this, Roberto Chiarini has observed: "After the victories in Rome and Naples, obtained also by agitating fascist fears, the Left hoped to be able to have the MSI as its only adversary in the central and southern regions, which would have guaranteed its success. It offered Fini advantageous terms because it considered him beatable... Only now, after their defeat, are they returning to a politics of anti-fascism, which I judge to be cynical and counterproductive." *Reset,* n. 6, May 1994.

22. For an analysis of the reaction in the American press, cf. Furio Colombo, *La Repubblica,* April 5, 1994.

23. Cf. *La Repubblica,* May 24, 1994.

24. Cf. *La Repubblica,* May 12, 1994.

25. *La Repubblica,* May 9, 1994.

26. Cf. director of the *Nouvel Observateur* Jean Daniel's comment in *La Repubblica,* May 8, 1994.

27. Cf. *La Repubblica,* May 3, 1994.

28. Cf. *La Repubblica,* June 6, 1994.

29. *Secolo d'Italia,* May 21, 1994.

30. Cf. Nino Arena, *Secolo d'Italia,* May 20, 1994.

31. *La Stampa,* April 1, 1994.

32. Cf. *La Stampa,* June 3, 1994.

33. Cf. Gennaro Malgieri, *Secolo d'Italia,* June 10, 1994.

34. Cf. the interview with Di Rupo in *La Repubblica,* May 31, 1994.

35. Quoted in Ennio Caretto, *Corriere della Sera,* October 11, 1994.

36. For example, Fini declared that "the National Alliance cannot ask for the premiership. And for the same reason, the League cannot ask for it either. The reason, for us and for them, lies in Silvio Berlusconi's role. He alone can bring about a fusion and remain in Palazzo Chigi with this majority." *Panorama,* December 9, 1994.

37. For a diagram of the AN presence in the abuse of party patronage, cf. Daniele Martini, *Panorama,* September 23, 1994. With regard to this topic, deputy coordinator Adolfo Urso asserts: "The AN is taking a few positions of responsibility for itself, but too many are already in the hands of people who are tied to the old system. Replacing them will be real challenge." *L'Espresso,* September 2, 1994.

38. Cf. *La Stampa,* August 10, 1994.

39. Cf. *Il Messaggero,* September 6, 1994. On the same idea, cf. Giuliano Amato, "Quel chiodo infisso nel Cavaliere," *Panorama,* October 7, 1994.

40. Cf. the interview with Fini in *Corriere della Sera,* July 18, 1994.

41. On October 2, Buttiglione declared: "There has been an attempt on the part of the Right to use Antonio Di Pietro as an alternative prime minister in case Berlusconi receives an *avviso di garanzia.*"

42. The MSI's congress resolutions offer a strong attack on the PPI, defined as "a political force which has turned *not choosing* into a source of pride," made up of "followers of the First Republic" who "miss the days of diminished democracy." Cf. *Secolo d'Italia,* December 7, 1994.

43. Cf. *Secolo d'Italia*, October 1, 1994.

44. Marcello Veneziani, *La rivoluzione conservatrice in Italia. Genesi e sviluppo della "ideologia italiana" fino ai nostri giorni* (new edition), (Carnago: Sugarco, 1994).

45. *Secolo d'Italia*, January 12, 1990.

46. "You find yourselves before a political party which rejects dictatorship, totalitarianism, racism, anti-semitism, and the behavior and the use of violence," declared Almirante in a televised tribunal over twenty years ago. *Secolo d'Italia*, April 20, 1972

47. Cf. *Corriere della Sera*, November 20, 1994.

48. Cf. *L'Unità*, November 8, 1994.

49. Cf. Piero Ignazi, *Il polo escluso*, op. cit., pp. 219-249.

50. Cf. *Secolo d'Italia*, December 13, 1994.

51. Cf. Piero Ignazi, *Il polo escluso*, op. cit., p. 165.

52. Cf. *Secolo d'Italia*, February 27, 1994.

53. Cf. Piero Ignazi, *Postfascisti?*, op. cit., p. 111.

54. The minister of Cultural Assets writes: "We see how many people have jobs in the public and institutional sectors in Italy. The Right is doing its duty when it agrees to renunciations, sacrifices, and even mortifications in this area. But now they've gone too far. For the good of all, let's hope that no one pulls the rope." Domenico Fisichella, *Il Tempo*, December 12, 1994.

4

The Failure
of the Progressive Alliance

Martin J. Bull

The year 1994 marked a new nadir in the history of the Democratic Party of the Left (PDS) and the Italian Left in general. The March national elections presented the left with its greatest opportunity since the war of gaining power. Yet the Progressive Alliance was roundly defeated by a conflict-ridden right-wing coalition containing neo-Fascists and led by a party—*Forza Italia*—only created three months before the elections. The defeat was followed in the June European elections by further poor results for all parties of the alliance. The combined effect of the two defeats was to cost Achille Occhetto his leadership of the PDS (he resigned in June) and the Progressive Alliance its unity (it began to disintegrate from May onwards). If in the first half of the year the Left was concerned with an attempt to crown its long history of opposition with expected political victories at the national and European levels, its attention in the second half of the year focused on trying to recover from two bitter defeats and rebuild the foundations for a victory in the future. At the same time, the left had to respond to a new question: what stance to adopt in its opposition to the government of Silvio Berlusconi.

This chapter documents the trajectory of the Left in this watershed year in five parts. The first part outlines the background to the emergence, in February, of the Progressive Alliance and the nature of its election campaign. The second part analyses the election defeat and explains its most likely causes. The third part assesses the impact of the defeat on the PDS (as the largest member of the alliance) and on the Progressive Alliance as a whole. The fourth part analyses the attempt to realign the Left in the second part of the year. The fifth part finally evaluates the role of the Left in opposition to the short-lived Berlusconi government.

The Progressive Alliance: Its Formation and Campaign

The formation of the Progressive Alliance was the product of a lengthy process of negotiation and conflict which began in earnest after the parliamentary electoral reform was approved in August 1993. This reform[1] meant that every party ideally needed to be part of an alliance. The problem was to agree on what type of alliance[2]. The forces of the progressive Centre effectively ruled out an alliance with the Left in the Autumn of 1993. From then on, the political forces of the Left and the Centre-Left sought to forge the Progressive Alliance.

The process was fraught with difficulties, mainly because many of the political forces involved in the negotiations wished to exclude Communist Refoundation (RC). The PDS, however, insisted on its inclusion, largely because Occhetto was worried that RC's presence outside the alliance would cost the PDS votes in its heartlands in central Italy. At the same time, he was aware that electoral victory would be difficult unless voters of the centre could be attracted, and this meant stretching the alliance as far as possible towards the centre. His aim, then, was to promote the bipolarisation of the party system into broad centre-left and centre-right camps, thus forcing the reformist centre to choose between the two.

The reformist centre refused to make (or even recognise) such a choice and the PPI and Segni's Pact stood as an independent centre grouping (the "Pact for Italy") in the elections, but the PDS had its way with regard to the inclusion of RC. The Progressive Alliance was launched in February 1994 as an alliance of eight political forces of the left and centre-left: the PDS; RC; the Democratic Alliance (AD, a centre-left umbrella movement launched in the spring of 1993); the relaunched Italian Socialist Party (PSI); Socialist Renewal (RS, an ex-PSI faction led by ex-leader of the PSI, Giorgio Benvenuto); the Network; the Greens; and the Social Christians (CS, a group of progressive ex-Christian Democrats led by Ermanno Gorrieri). The agreement was based on a common symbol (a tricoloured wave), stand-down arrangements for single-member constituencies, and a programmatic declaration of intent. The stand-down arrangements proved to be highly controversial, and had to be renegotiated more than once. The main fear of the smaller parties was that the PDS would take the lion's share of safe seats, and the PDS was subsequently forced to relinquish more than it felt it should. The drawn-out process around *tavolini* ("little tables") of different party leaderships proved to be disappointing for those who wanted to believe in Occhetto's description of the alliance as a "joyous war machine" ("*gioiosa macchina da guerra*"). The common programme provided the basis for the Progressives' election campaign, although the parties also campaigned on their own platforms for the Chamber of Deputies seats to be awarded by proportional representation. The programme was based on the following points: an extension of political democracy; a decentralisation of power; eco-nomic growth and an improvement in the state of the public finances; efforts to reduce unemployment; combatting abuses of the welfare state; a programme of moderate privatisation; protecting the poorest in society; an increase in the drive against corruption; improvements in education, health and social services; and protection of the nation's cultural and environmental heritage.

The striking characteristic of this programme was its moderation. If there was a common starting point for the parties of the alliance it was continuity with the outgoing Ciampi government and a recognition that in the existing economic circumstances there was only a limited amount of manoeuvre possible. Indeed, in the event of an electoral victory, the man who commanded most support amongst the Progressives to lead a government was Ciampi, even though not a Progressive himself. This moderation was championed by the PDS which—in the face of a fierce anti-communist electoral campaign by the right—arranged a series of high-level meetings with Italian and international elites to demonstrate that the left no longer posed a threat to the establishment.

That Berlusconi was able to mount a fierce, and ultimately successful, anti-communist campaign was symptomatic of the deep differences between RC (the second largest party in the alliance) and the rest of its partners. Indeed, the Progressives' campaign was, to a large extent, overshadowed by a growing gulf between RC's platform and that of the other members of the camp. RC's essential belief was that the electorate wanted a radical break with the past, the Ciampi government included. In domestic policy, the party proposed a tax on treasury bonds (the BOT); it voted against Ciampi's budget and opposed his proposals on reducing the public deficit; it was against the FIAT-trade union accord involving lay-offs and reductions, wanted to see the reintroduction of the wage-indexation system (scala mobile) and a shelving of plans to privatise key sectors of industry. In foreign policy, it proposed withdrawal from NATO, supported a non-intervention policy in Yugoslavia, and also expressed open support for Castro's regime in Cuba. In general, RC's policies were inspired by the orthodox objective of heightening class struggle while other members of the alliance were concerned with presenting themselves as the bearers of cautious renovation.

In short, the reconstitution of the Left into the Progressive Alliance was an intensely conflictual process which resulted in a broad alliance that included the far Left and the Centre-Left but excluded the political forces of the reformist Centre. The agreement which was reached papered over the inherent cracks in the alliance, particularly those between RC and the others, and the visibility of these cracks undermined the Progressives' election campaign right up to polling day.

The Election Defeat

Those on the left who were ruled by their heads rather than their hearts may not have expected a left-wing victory, but the scale of the defeat was a surprise even to them. The percentage of the vote obtained by the Progressive parties (34.4 percent in the "list vote") was the lowest the "Left" (a changing and unclear concept itself) had obtained since the historic defeat of 1948 (31 percent). The combined share of seven of the parties in the 1992 elections (the eighth, AD, did not exist in 1992) was 37.2 percent, so 1994 marked a 2.8 percent decline. The bulk of this loss was accounted for by the collapse of the PSI (down from 13.6 percent in 1992 to 2.2 percent in 1994) and the failure of the PDS to offset this collapse with what was otherwise an improved performance (up from 16.1 percent in 1992 to 20.4 percent in 1994).[3] The reason for this, as an analysis of electoral flows reveals, was that the bulk of those who had previously voted for the PSI defected to the forces of the right, a confirmation of the effective dissociation of the PSI from left-wing politics under Craxi. If, for this reason, the PSI's vote totals are excluded from the 1992 comparison, the Progressives actually advanced in most areas, and particularly in the central regions (from 35.1 percent to 43.4 percent) and southern regions[4] (from 21.3 percent to 31.6 percent).

These figures point to a first reason for the Left's defeat. When the PSI's rapid demise began in late 1992, Occhetto and his heir-apparent, Massimo D'Alema, mistakenly argued that this was a harbinger of victory for the left. The potential left-wing electorate in the post-war period was rarely above 40 percent (1976 being the exception) so victory in 1994 was always going to be difficult, but doubly so if one realizes that the PSI had increasingly harboured an electorate which was left-wing in name only. This suggests that the Progressives would have needed to attract at least some of the more progressive elements of the centre (Segni, Martinazzoli et al.) into an alliance. Yet, the tradition of "exclusion politics" and the suspicions and historic reservations on both sides weres too deep-rooted to be easily overcome in the two years between the 1992 and 1994 elections.

The divisions in the Progressive Alliance also played a significant role in the left's defeat. The failure of the Progressives to stand as a single party for the "list vote" cost the alliance dear because of the new 4 percent threshold rule: only the PDS and RC managed to cross the threshold and obtain a share of the proportional seats. Furthermore, the

Table 4.1   The Progressives and the 1994 National Elections (Chamber of Deputies)

| | List Vote | | | |
	Votes (m)	%	Seats	District Vote
Pds	7.9	20.4	38	Progressives 164
Rc	2.3	6.0	11	
Psi	0.8	2.2	-	
Greens	1.0	2.7	-	
Ad	0.5	1.2	-	
Network	0.7	1.9	-	

Source. Adapted from Bull and Newell (1995: 87)

Notes. Pds: Democratic Party of the Left; Rc: Communist Refoundation; Psi: Italian Socialist Party; Ad: Democratic Alliance. The "list vote" refers to the votes cast at the constituency level for the 155 proportionally-distributed seats. The figures for the list vote are given for those parties of the Progressive Alliance which stood. The "district vote" refers to the votes cast for the remaining 475 seats distributed according to the plurality formula. The figure for the district vote is given for the Progressives as a whole. Since, for this vote, the Progressives had stand-down arrangements, it is only possible to give the total number of seats obtained by the Progressives as a group.

absence of a formal organisational structure hindered the presentation of a united message to the electorate. Occhetto appeared to spend as much time explaining away the differences between RC and the rest of the alliance as he did publicising the policies of the Progressives.

The failure to achieve organisational unity also left the Progressives effectively leaderless, a cost imposed by the smaller parties' suspicion of the (hegemonic) intentions of the PDS. As leader of the largest party, Occhetto was the natural candidate to head a government, and it was he who met Berlusconi in a television duel. His name, however, was only put forward as a candidate for the premiership alongside two others, Napolitano and Ciampi, and, as already noted, it was the last of these who commanded most support within the alliance. This situation contrasted strongly with the right where Berlusconi appeared as the leader of the Freedom Alliance and the natural candidate for the premiership. In a campaign where alliances were campaigning as potential governments in waiting, the Progressives appeared to be rooted in the old politics with the leadership of the alliance dependent upon the negotiating power of the various party leaders (echoing the *tavolini*) after the elections. This, along with the inclusion of RC, left the Progressives barely credible as a governing (as opposed to electoral) alliance.

Greater unity, however, may not have overcome a more profound problem: that of the Progressives' image or identity. Occhetto's conviction that a bipolarisation of the party system would bring with it a stark contrast between a united, modern and reformist Left and a divided, extremist and old-style Right pre-dated Berlusconi's late entry onto the political scene. Berlusconi presented himself very effectively as someone who was new and who stood for real change. The core of his message was an emphasis on the value of the market against the state. Berlusconi chose the private sector as the primary terrain on which he launched a ferocious assault on the PDS and the Progressives as old-style *statalisti* ("statists"). The PDS and the Progressives responded inadequately to this challenge for three reasons.

Firstly, they found it difficult to present themselves as something new when: the PSI and PDS had become so closely associated with corruption in the previous year; RC had inherited the communist mantle and yet was in the alliance; the Progressives' behaviour (e.g. the different leaderships' endless bargaining to share out seats) reminded people of *partitocrazia* and the old politics.

Secondly, the relative success of the Ciampi government and the respectability it earned resulted in a subtle shift in PDS policy. The party increasingly began to argue that Italy's best prospects for renewal lay in a continuation of the policies of Ciampi under the guidance of a Progressive government. This position was guided not only by the need to find a consensus amongst the party's own allies, but later by Occhetto's quest for respectability with the establishment. By the eve of the election, the Progressives stood for "continuity with Ciampi", not (as Berlusconi did) for renewal through a break with the past.

Thirdly, the Progressives' opponents were able to link "continuity with Ciampi" to continuity with the Left's own political traditions, which meant state management of the economy and society generally.[5] The problem was not just that the ideology and practice of the new Right elsewhere had made state management of the economy look outmoded, but that in Italy the state had become inextricably identified with political corruption. Any programme, therefore, based on the state had to be based first and foremost on a reformed state, something which clearly eluded the Progressives' conceptual and presentational skills. Berlusconi's total commitment to the benefits of the free market could not have provided a greater contrast.

Two final factors which contributed to the Left's defeat should be mentioned, both of which focus on the PDS. Ruffolo and Tranfaglia[6] argue that the 1994 defeat was rooted in the failure of the PCI-PDS transformation to effect a genuine renewal of the Italian Left, leading to the abandonment of the PDS by many independent leftists. Secondly, the PDS leadership made a strategic mistake it was in assuming that the force of popular opinion which (through the referendums of 1991 and 1993) brought an end to the old politics, equated with a desire to build a Second Republic on the basis of left-wing power. In retrospect, it can be seen that the referendum results expressed a popular will to end the First Republic, but they said nothing about how a Second Republic should be constructed, particularly in a situation where, until January 1994, there were no real alternatives to the Left on offer.

The Impact of the Defeat: The PDS Changes Leader

The defeat of the Progressive Alliance fatally undermined Occhetto's leadership of the PDS. Although Occhetto at first refused to regard his position as in danger and some of his supporters even spoke of a "non-defeat" (because of the PDS's individual performance as against that of the Progressives as a whole), a whispering campaign against him eventually brought the leadership question into the open. In a survey carried out by *La Repubblica* (22 April 1994) 29 out of 40 PDS members of the Chamber of Deputies who were interviewed stated that there should be a change of leader. D'Alema's role in this was controversial. Although publicly supporting Occhetto[7] it is evident—from Occhetto's own account of things—not only that D'Alema wished to see his own leadership ambitions realised, but that he had even asked Occhetto to stand aside after the defeat, arguing that the leader had served his purpose for the Italian Left.

The European elections in June offered Occhetto his last chance of survival; the results left him little choice but to resign. The PDS vote dropped to 19.5 percent (from 27.6 percent in 1989 and 20.3 percent in the national elections), and the Progressive parties overall dropped to 31.3 percent (from 34.4 percent in the national elections). Meanwhile, *Forza Italia* saw its support consolidated (up to 30.6 percent from 21.0 percent in the national elections) as did the government parties as a whole (up to 51.8 percent from 46.2 percent).

Yet Occhetto did not go quietly and his subsequent action ensured that the leadership succession would be controversial. In a bitter resignation speech he criticised those whom he felt had hounded him from the leadership and distracted the party from reversing its electoral fortunes in the process. Furthermore, rather than convening a party Congress and announcing that he would stand down at it but lead the party until

Table 4.2   The Progressives and the 1994 European Elections

	Votes (in billion)	%
Pds	6.3	19.1
Rc	2.0	6.1
Greens	1.0	3.2
Psi-Ad	0.6	1.8
Network	0.4	1.1

Source. Adapted from Corriere della Sera, June 14, 1994

Note. For full party names see note to Table 4.1.

then (thus ensuring a smooth transition), he promptly resigned and left the party to agree on a method to find a new leader. This gave him complete freedom of action to try to stop D'Alema while still controlling the party apparatus (through his placemen).

The direzione did not wish to be without a leader for the lengthy period of time which convening a Congress would involve. It therefore organised a "popular consultation" of all the party sections and central leaders to see who were the most likely contenders for the leadership. This was followed by nominations and a vote in the National Council (Consiglio Nazionale), a large unwieldy body elected in 1991 (when the party was born) and which even contained some non-party members.

In reality, the "popular consultation" became a fierce competition for votes between Massimo D'Alema and Walter Veltroni, in which the occhettiani mobilised the party apparatus in favour of the latter.[8] Occhetto's tactics almost paid off. Although D'Alema obtained a majority amongst the central leaders (130 to 120)[9] Veltroni obtained a more significant small majority in the party sections (53 percent to 47 percent—see Table 3) and his supporters then argued that the National Council should respect the verdict of the party's grass-roots and elect him as leader. The d'alemiani were deeply critical of what they regarded as a form of manipulation of many party members by the occhettiani and of the latters' attempt to give an informal popular consultation the significance of a referendum. In the event, Veltroni's majority in the sections did not carry to the National Council and D'Alema emerged as the new leader of the PDS by 249 votes to 173.[10] Ironically, one of the main reasons for Veltroni's defeat was said to be the "Occhetto factor" ("fattore Occhetto"). The passionate support from the ex-leader and his troops suggested to many that Veltroni might not be his own man, and that not much would change under his leadership.

Table 4.3   The Pds's Consultation of the Party Sections on the Leadership Choice, June 1994 (by region and in numbers of members)

	Veltroni	*D'Alema*
Val D'Aosta (558)	194	251
Piemonte (23,697)	11,243	6,733
Liguria (22,802)	9,299	9,029
Toscana (104,552)	54,187	26,090
Umbria (19,392)	10,771	4,573
Sardegna (17,739)	4,306	7,256
Lazio (31,097)	11,203	13,037
Molise (2,248)	473	1,138
Lombardia (69,153)	23,904	27,258
Campania (27,945)	11,946	11,840
Trentino Alto Adige (1,267)	436	430
Friuli Venezia Giulia (6,410)	2,833	1,671
Veneto (27,432)	12,615	7,253
Emilia Romagna (219,245)	80,395	70,646
Marche (23,174)	10,099	8,230
Abruzzo (10,808)	4,384	4,641
Puglia (25,309)	5,055	15,976
Basilicata (46,678)	807	3,229
Calabria (22,733)	8,763	9,983
Sicilia (25,048)	9,467	11,602
Totals (685,287)	272,380 (53%)	240,866 (47%)

Source. Adapted from *La Repubblica*, June 29, 1994.

Note. Figures in parentheses after each region indicate the Pds's estimated maximum number of members consulted.

The other parties of the Progressive Alliance did not suffer as harrowing an experience as the PDS. Willer Bordon resigned as the coordinator of AD after the European elections, and Ottaviano Del Turco announced his intention to stand down as leader of the PSI (he would, in fact, end up dissolving the party, as noted below). These changes in the PSI and AD were less significant than the impact of the elections on the

Progressive Alliance as a whole. Although many argued that a failure to form a single-parliamentary group would amount to a betrayal of the electorate, no agreement could be found amongst all the parties on the exact structure and terms of action of a single Progressive grouping. Consequently, after RC, AD and the socialists refused to join a united group, the PDS, the Network, the Greens and the CS formed a four-party grouping called the Progressive Federation (*progressisti-federativi*). This was based on a single leader in each house and deputy leaders to represent each group. The effective disintegration of the Progressive Alliance after the national elections confirmed that it could not provide the basis for a united left in opposition, and that the Progressive-Federation was little more than a parliamentary expedient while the path to unity was rethought.

The Aftermath: Rethinking Left-Wing Unity

Despite the disintegration of the original alliance, the Progressive experience was not completely negative. Many on the left felt that a first stage towards unity had been achieved and that the experience should be built upon rather than liquidated. Terminologically, this was expressed by the replacement of the word "progressives" with "democrats" when the future composition of a united Left was being discussed. The problem, however, was the division of opinion over what exactly should be the next stage in the transition from progressives to democrats. This division stemmed from the paradoxical dilemma in which the Left now found itself, a dilemma which focused on the PDS.

If the elections showed anything with regard to the internal dynamics of the Left, it was that the PDS was more essential than ever to the Left's future. After the March elections the party accounted for something like 80 percent of the Left's support and was the only organisation to emerge relatively intact from Italy's crisis. Its 800,000 members were still a huge organisational resource which the Left could dispense with only at its peril. Yet, at the same time, the PDS was not strong enough by itself to be an alternative to the Right. It could construct an alternative only in an alliance with other parties of the left and, it would appear, of the reformist centre. And it is here that the paradox emerged, because if the presence of the PDS was a prerequisite for the future success of the Left, the party was also seen to be the chief obstacle to unity and even victory. Firstly, the very strength and historic tradition of the PDS cultivated suspicion and reluctance on the part of other parties (and particularly those in the centre) to enter into an alliance with it. Their fear was that any renovation of the Left based around the

PDS would be undermined by the party's hegemonic intentions, by its proximity to RC and by the continued dead-weight of its factions and organisational inertia. Even if unity were achieved, moreover, it would be these same factors which would ensure the Left's rejection at the polls.

The election defeat brought this paradox into sharp relief, and the first stage of the debate consequently focused on the future of the PDS.[11] Many outside the PDS argued that the party should finally recognise that its transformation from the old PCI was only half-complete and that it should now dissolve itself as a pre-condition to the formation of a new "Democratic Party". For this party to be genuinely different, moreover, it was necessary for the PDS dissolve first to prevent its organisation and factions monopolising and throttling the renewal process. Both Occhetto and, in his turn, D'Alema refused to court this possibility, and the latter laid out his own strategy for the Left in the course of the second half of the year. He argued that the PDS's new goal was a "coalition of democrats" based on the following principles: a strong PDS with a renovated identity which would not be conditioned in its behaviour by RC; a permanent alliance between the PDS and other parties and movements of the Left and Centre based on a federation with a single leader to be chosen through a primary election (and he conced-ed that it might be better for this leader to come from a party other than the PDS). He made it clear that an alliance with the political forces of the centre would be fundamental to victory over the Right. In his view, the left's basic error in March had been that it had asked centrist voters to change their identity and vote for the Left. The next time, the Left had to prove its commonality with the Centre in the form of a permanent federation or "coalition of democrats". Yet, he would not take the ultimate step of dissolving his party. He was prepared to place the party's resources at the Left's disposal and even to consider changing the PDS's name and symbol, but he was not willing to sacrifice its membership (another way of saying its organisation).

While there was agreement inside the PDS on the party remaining in existence, this was not the case with regard to D'Alema's coalitional strategy. The left of the party opposed the reconstitution of the political forces of the left and centre into one coalition which would destroy's the left's distinctiveness. They argued that a realignment of the genuine forces of the left should occur first followed, once unity is achieved, by an alliance with the Centre. Others, such as Occhetto and Veltroni, supported the idea of a "coalition of democrats" (indeed, Veltroni was probably the first to launch the idea), but feared that D'Alema's tactics were too much focused on achieving a political alliance with the PPI as a means of winning an election (something which D'Alema, in turn, denied). They expressed the fear that if the alliance did not correlate with social reality there could be a haemorrhage of support from both parties (the PDS and PPI). Any genuine coalition, therefore, had to go beyond party leaderships to include the participation of the trade unions and other social forces.

To the left of the PDS, RC rejected the idea of a coalition of democrats, and was fiercely critical of the PDS's new leader. RC's leader, Bertinotti, argued that all of D'Alema's ideas sprang from the conviction that the Right could not be beaten, and that the forces of the left had therefore to become "good liberals" in order to defeat "bad liberals". The firmness of this position raised the same tactical dilemma for the PDS as had existed before the election: whether to exclude RC from a potential coalition as a means of hastening the unity of the PDS with other non-communist forces of the left and centre-left. In 1994, D'Alema and Veltroni avoided the issue by stating that if the coalition were to be based strongly enough around a programme the choice as to whether RC entered the alliance would have to be made by RC itself. This position failed to satisfy those who argued that any alliance had to exclude RC on an a priori basis.

The political forces of the centre, although rejecting any notion of entering the government, refused to commit themselves to any alliance or coalition of the Centre and Left. The election of Rocco Buttiglione to the leadership of the PPI resulted in the party taking up a position "equidistant" (in the leader's words) between the left and the right. Buttiglione focussed more on the possibility of a reaggregation of the centre and right (through a possible breaking away of part of *Forza Italia*, a shift in the *Lega*'s position, the collapse of the government and the isolation of the National Alliance) than on possibilities to his left. Segni, meanwhile, in late October, "relaunched" his Pact, which, he said, aimed at bringing together "laical and reformist forces" into a "liberal, modern and democratic alternative" which would not fall under the dominance of any political party. The conviction of the two key players (the PPI and Segni) that the political centre could be refounded as the natural pivot around which a future government could be built was reinforced by the resignation of Berlusconi on December 22.

The refusal of the forces of the left (PDS) and centre (PPI and Segni) to change their basic tactical positions in the aftermath of electoral defeat left a myriad of non-PDS forces on the left in complete disarray. Many of them were not, in principle, against the idea of a "coalition of democrats", but they did not wish to enter such a coalition on the PDS's terms. Consequently, they all began pursuing independent initiatives which they hoped would generate sufficient momentum towards an alliance to force the PDS's hand, or at least to provide unity amongst the non-PDS left as a starting point. AD relaunched itself with the objective of achieving a "grand new alliance". The PSI formally dissolved (in recognition that the stain of corruption was too marked for the party ever to appear reformed) and reconstituted itself into the "Italian Socialists" (SI), with the goal of bringing together all centre-left reformers. Some socialists, under the leadership of Valdo Spini, broke with the PSI/SI and formed the embryo of a "Labourist Federation", inspired by the vision of the leader of the British Labour Party, Tony Blair. Its declared aim was to keep alive the socialist tradition, and it looked likely (late in 1994) to absorb the remnants of the Italian Social Democratic Party (PSDI). The ex-Prime Minister, Giuliano Amato, and others formed a political-cultural centre called "Italy Tomorrow" which was aimed at bringing together like-minded people to formulate ideas and policies for Italy into the millennium. Finally, the so-called "Progressive Mayors", who were swept to power in the December 1993 local elections and were alarmed at the lack of progress towards unity, started their own movement for a "Grand Democratic Coalition". Predicated on the idea of building a coalition from the grass-roots upwards the mayors ex-pressed the hope that a first victory would be achieved in the Spring 1995 local elections, from which the movement could be placed under the control of national political figures.

In short, 1994 witnessed a whole series of initiatives on the non-communist Left which were aimed at similar constituencies (reformists, laicists, progressive catholics) and at a similar type of project overall: a broad Left- of-Centre political movement. The manoeuvrings were not markedly different from those which had occurred before the 1994 elections. They reflected the continued failure of Italian politicians to fill a "liberal democratic" vacuum and provide a political movement distinct from, and independent of, catholicism, fascism and communism. By the end of the year, it was not clear that any of the initiatives had the potential to succeed. As Ernesto Galli Della Loggia commented, "Italy has passed from a land of political dinosaurs to one of political plankton struggling to hold together...They all say they are, or want to be liberal and democratic, but they plainly lack a liberal-democratic background or education".[12] This was perhaps most vividly demonstrated in the difficulties the left experienced in designing its opposition to the Berlusconi government.

The Nature of Opposition to Berlusconi

A prerequisite for alternation in government is not just a government which "governs", but an opposition which constitutes a potential government in waiting. The main criticism of the opposition after the elections was that it was failing to be this. There were two reasons. Firstly, the opposition failed to maintain (and expand) its unity. Not only were the divisions between the political forces of the centre and the left still present, but left-wing unity itself began to disintegrate. Significantly, one of D'Alema's first real actions on becoming leader of the PDS was to propose a "shadow government" consisting of all political forces in opposition and led by a member of the centre (i.e. a member of the PPI). The proposal was rejected almost universally as premature. Its rejection signified that no matter how divided the government of the day would become, the opposition could not pretend to offer an alternative, something confirmed when Berlusconi resigned in late December.

The second reason for the failure of the opposition was more profound and concerned the difficulties the Left experienced in responding to the changes in Italian politics ushered in by the 1994 elections. These changes brought with them demands for a reevaluation of the "culture of opposition" which had prevailed in Italian politics under the PCI. Traditionally, the nature of the PCI's opposition had been shaped by the party's delegitimisation and thus its likely permanence as a party of opposition. This embodied an ideological-style opposition which had questioned the government's right to govern and implied that transformative reform would follow the party's entry into government; it had been coupled with a form of "consociationalism" (consociativismo) by which, through obtaining a share in the spoils of government and administration, the PCI had maintained its influence and been compensated for its permanence in opposition.

The transformation of the PCI into the PDS, the demise of the Christian Democratic "party-regime", the partial bipolarisation of the party system and the victory of a centre-right coalition in March all suggested not only that the post-war style of government might be about to change but that there might be a concomitant need for a change in the post-war style of opposition. This was signalled in Occhetto's immediate response to the Left's electoral defeat which (paraphrasing) was that "the Right had won and now it should govern".[13] This suggested that the PDS recognised and accepted the centre-right's victory and that its opposition to the government would follow the Westminster model. Underlying this position was an assumption that a bipolarised system had emerged—or was emerging—and an expectation (or at least hope) that in such a system the centre-left's turn to govern would inevitably come.

Yet, that position quickly shifted as the style and controversial nature of Berlusconi's government became apparent. The government's conflicts with established institutions (such as the judiciary, RAI, and the Bank of Italy), its refusal to grant the non-governing parties the rights normally associated with an "English-style" opposition (best symbolised in the controversy over the government's nominee to the European Commission), its internal divisions (which provided an increasingly visible role for the leader of the neo-Fascists, Gianfranco Fini), and Berlusconi's own conflict of interests, led the PDS to adopt a more traditional stance which tended to deny Berlusconi's right to govern. When D'Alema became leader of the PDS he attempted to resurrect an "English-style" opposition (declaring himself ready to judge Berlusconi's policies on their merits and offering to meet the Prime Minister), but it lasted barely two months. In September, he publicly buried any such notions and the PDS henceforth placed more emphasis on the dangers of the new government than on advancing alternative policies.

The wavering in the PDS's position was not just a product of changes occurring under the government but of disagreements of a deeper nature inside the PDS about the nature of "Berlusconism". There were broadly speaking, two positions in this debate which had different implications for the type of strategy the Left should adopt in opposition.[14] On the one hand, there were those who believed that Berlusconi's election victory had been a product primarily of media manipulation rather than reflecting a genuine consensus in society. In this view, the government represented a danger to democracy not just because of the presence of neo-Fascists in its ranks, but because Berlusconi was interested in constructing a new "regime" based on the "enterprise-party" (*partito-impresa*), stringent control over mass communications and a marginalisation of the role of the opposition. In this situation, the priority for the opposition had to be to prevent the government doing too much, particularly in sensitive constitutional areas; Berlusconi had to be removed as quickly as possible. This "defensive" form of opposition implied seeking out political alliances designed to bring down the government, even if those alliances proved to be unrelated to a future governing alternative. Indeed, in the absence of an alternative alliance, an "institutional" (non-party-based) form of government had to be proposed to carry through important reforms to the electoral system and the regulation of the mass media. This was, by and large, the position adopted by people like by D'Alema and De Mita (of the PPI), the former of whom defined Berlusconism as the highest form of Craxism.

On the other hand, there were those who viewed Berlusconi's election victory as having been more than just a result of his control of the media. Berlusconi had proved able to interpret the Italian people's need for change better than the Left, and consequently, there was a genuine social consensus underlying his power. In this context, adopting a defensive posture would simply result in the Left closing itself into its fortress. The priority had to be to begin building an alternative to the government based on policies which were more coherent and competent, thus challenging the government on its own terrain. The logic of alternation should be accepted and the government allowed to govern. The alternative to Berlusconi, moreover, could not simply be the product of agreements between party leaderships, but had to be rooted in society and recognise that the traditional role of parties as mediators had, to some extent, been superseded. This position was emphasised by people like Occhetto (after his resignation), Veltroni and Adornato (of AD).

In the first four to five months of the new government the PDS wavered between the two stances (which were not necessarily mutually exclusive), unsure as to whether the Berlusconi phenomenon amounted to the beginnings of a new "regime" which would once again permanently exclude the Left unless it took immediate remedial action, or whether, in fact, the government constituted something genuinely different, reflecting a changed political system from which alternation eventually would occur. By the final two months of the year, however, the former stance quite clearly prevailed. This was a consequence of the November local election results (which suggested that Berlusconi's support was in decline), the judiciary's decision to place Berlusconi under official investigation for corruption, his subsequent interrogation by the magistrates, and the decision of Umberto Bossi to break with the government and pose a vote of no confidence.[15] From November onwards, the PDS began calling for the resignation of the Prime Minister and the establishment of a *Governo delle regole* (literally a "government of the rules"), a non-party based government which would have the task of carrying through the institutional reforms still required to complete Italy's transition to a more stable political order. The growing identification of the Prime Minister with Italy's crisis, as opposed to its resolution, left the PDS in no doubt that Berlusconism was a dangerous but ephemeral phenomenon produced by the continuing turmoil in Italian politics. It was deemed better, therefore, to adopt a non-cooperative stance to hasten Berlusconi's departure. That there were short-term benefits for the PDS in adopting this position was not in doubt, but, when Berlusconi's overthrow was achieved in late December, it prompted a new political crisis. The PDS had no alternative alliance to replace the outgoing government, but nor would it support Berlusconi's call for fresh elections while the latter still exercised a monopoly of control over the media. The party's proposal for an "institutional" form of government was a reflection of its (and other parties') failure, during the seven months of Berlusconi's controversial premiership, to galvanise the political forces of the left, centre-left and centre into an alliance which could have constituted the embryo of an alternative government.

Notes

1. Katz, Richard, "The 1993 Parliamentary Election Reform", in Carol Mershon and Gianfranco Pasquino (eds), *Italian Politics. A Review*. Vol. 9 (London: Pinter, 1994).

2. Bull, Martin J., "Another Revolution Manqué? The PDS in Italy's Transition", Paper presented to the "International Comparative Workshop on Scandal and Reform in Italy and Japan", Japanische-Deutsches Zentrum, Berlin, 19-20 August; Rhodes, Martin (1994), "Reinventing the Left: the Origins of the Progressive Alliance", in Carol Mershon and Gianfranco Pasquino (eds), *Italian Politics. A Review*. Vol. 9 (London: Pinter).

3. These figures are from the "list vote" (the proportional element of the electoral system) which, due to stand-down arrangements in the single-member constituencies, represents the most accurate comparison with 1992.

4. Bull, Martin J., and James Newell, "Italy Changes Course? The 1994 Elections and the Victory of the Right", Parliamentary Affairs, January 1995.

5. G. Pasquino, "Le ragioni di una sconfitta", in *La rivista dei Libri*, July-August 1994.

6. Ruffolo, Giorgio, "Coraggio sinistra, alzati e cammina", *La Repubblica*, April 6, 1994; N. Tranfaglia, "Il Pds rimasto in mezzo al guado", *La Repubblica*, April 13, 1994 and M. Riva, "Occhetto generale sconfitto", in *La Repubblica*, April 2, 1994.

7. Occhetto, Achille, *Il sentimento e la ragione. Un'intervista di Teresa Bartoli* (Milan: Rizzoli, 1994).

8. The key people involved in this operation were Piero Fassino, Claudio Petruccioli and Fabio Mussi.

9. 313 leading members were consulted, including members of the national direzione, regional leaders and presidents, federation leaders and trade union leaders. In total, 130 chose D'Alema, 120 Veltroni, 54 proposed other names and 55 did not indicate a preference (*La Repubblica*, July 2, 1994).

10. The National Council consisted of 461 members, although ten were absent for family or work-related reasons. To be elected the winning candidate needed an absolute majority of those voting (226 votes in this case). 428 valid votes were cast, plus five blank or spoilt ballot papers. With 249 votes (to Veltroni's 173), D'Alema surpassed the required majority by 23 votes (*L'Unità*, July 2, 1994).

11. For a flavour of this debate see, for example, Riva 1994, Adornato 1994, Ruffolo 1994 and Tranfaglia 1994.

12. Bompard, Paul (1994), "Pasta Joke", *The Times Higher Educational Supplement*, December 9.

13. *La Repubblica*, March 29, 1994.

14. Adornato, Ferdinando (1994b), "Resistenza o riforma?", *La Repubblica*, October 6.

15. There were three votes of no confidence, in fact. Besides Bossi's, both the PDS and RC tabled motions of their own. None were voted on because Berlusconi resigned before the debate was finished, aware that he would not survive

and fearful of Bossi's motion being passed because it included a clause which would have prevented him from becoming Prime Minister again until his conflict of interests was resolved.

5

The 1994 Elections

Jack Brand and Thomas Mackie

The New Party System and the Electoral Verdict

The first signs of change in the parties and party system appeared at least twenty years ago, with the emergence of a diffuse dissatisfaction with the political system and institutions. In his recent work Roberto Cartocci shows convincingly, for example, that since the pioneering The Civic Culture[1] Italians consistently have been more distrustful than other Europeans of their parties and other central political institutions.[2] The origins of the changes also include a more recent disappearance of the ideological bases of the party system.

One of the earliest steps on the road to a new party system was the transformation of the PCI into the PDS. The debate about how to change was started in the 1970s, long before the change of party name and form in 1991 which produced the PDS. For much of the run-up to the 1994 elections it appeared that the PDS would capture the largest individual vote and, for the first time since 1948, organize the government of Italy. But notwithstanding the PDS' promotion of the broad Progressive Alliance, which stretched from *Rifondazione Comunista* to elements of the *laici* such as *Alleanza Democratica* and the left of the PRI, the left won the votes of only about one elector in three.

Suspicion of extensive corruption was part of the general disenchantment to which Cartocci refers. There had been earlier cases, but no one of major importance was clearly implicated. With the *Mani Pulite* investigations, Italian electors were treated to a Niagara of revelations about the misdeeds of politicians. Since most of them were members of the governing parties, levels of disenchantment with the system increased even further.

The revelations of bribery are the backdrop against which one must see the rise of two new organizations, the *Lega* and *Forza Italia*, and the sanitizing of the Italian Social Movement (MSI). The work of the pros-ecutors confirmed the popular belief that the mainstream old parties of government were totally corrupt, and that only uncontaminated groups could safeguard public life in Italy. The centre ground of politics thus became vacant. It was contested by the newcomer, Silvio Berlusconi, and the left-wing Christian Democrat, Mario Segni, who had been the moving spirit behind reform of the electoral system. More important than either of these in 1993 was charismatic and raucous leader of the *Lega Nord*, Umberto Bossi, who had brought the *Lega Nord* to be the fourth party in terms of votes at the legislative elections in 1992, and in the municipal elections of 1993, the largest party in the North.

Some commentators on the rise of the *Lega* have suggested that it is a new party of the extreme right. It seems more realistic to accept Taggart's suggestion that it is best understood as a neopopulist party.[3] Bossi has gone out of his way to distance his organization from the fascists of the MSI. The *Lega* is certainly a populist party, with its constant references to the claims of and injustices towards the ordinary people of the hardworking North of Italy. It rejects the state and the parties which governed Italy as corrupt, and calls for a new system. On the other hand, the new system which it advocates would still have the character of a western liberal democracy. Bossi and his colleagues are certainly neo-liberals, placing the party firmly on the right of the spec-trum, and the state is to be reduced in power. There is no hint of glorification of the state and the sort of corporatism which is a hallmark of fascism.

The *Lega* was strikingly different from the MSI, which, until recently, was the inheritor of the fascist tradition. To complicate matters, the MSI and its successor, the *Alleanza Nazionale*, have followed their leader in describing themselves as "postfascist", denouncing the excesses of Mussolini's government. The MSI's support of strong central govern-ment and its nationalism, as well as its identification as a "Southern" party (in as much as the bulk of its vote comes from the South)[4] contrast sharply with the federalism and Northern orientation of the *Lega*.

Given this, it might be difficult to understand how these two parties could join in a government; it is not merely coincidence that the Berlu-sconi government lasted only nine months. The only thing they had in common was that neither had been involved in accusations of corrup-tion, because of their exclusion from the old political system. This now counted as a major advantage.

Silvio Berlusconi also enjoyed the advantage of being dissociated (overtly) from previous government parties. In setting up *Forza Italia* clubs over most of the country, he made it clear that they were bul-warks against any threat of a resurgent Left (the PDS) winning the next election. To do this, it was necessary to create a grand alliance. In making a pact with *Alleanza Nazionale*, Berlusconi acquired a loyal ally. And joining with *Forza Italia* provided a vehicle whereby the AN could break out of its Southern stronghold and become part of a national alliance. It could also be legitimated by close association with a group which no one could accuse of having fascist roots. Berlusconi and Fini needed each other.

But Berlusconi needed more. He could not ignore the growth of the *Lega* in the North, and, as the only other uncorrupted party of the centre, this also had to be brought into the coalition. Bossi made numerous statements before and after the election to the effect that he would never work with the fascists, but in the end the three were cobbled into an uneasy alliance, or rather two uneasy alliances. The differences between the *Lega* and AN were such that the election was fought by two alliances in alliante: the *Polo delle Libertà* in the North, consisting of FI and the *Lega*, and the *Polo del Buon Governo* in the South with FI and *Alleanza Nazionale*. Di Virgilio notes that these alliances looked much more insecure than the *Alleanza Progressista*, and were put together by Berlusconi only weeks before election day.[5]

Berlusconi was able to bring together his diverse and quarreling partners because of his own assets. He was a credible and even charismatic public figure who became the symbol for his alliance and subsequently for his government. A scan through any newspaper file from February to December 1994 will show his name in the headlines of most front pages, and many inside too. Moreover, as an extremely successful businessman, he had a huge fortune to spend on his political ambitions and contacts with other sources of funds. From his commercial base, he was able to advertise in newspapers and other media all over the country, recruiting members for his network of *Forza Italia* clubs. Their secretaries were members of his Fininvest company who were given a political sabbatical. Finally, his three commercial television channels gave him a spectacular vehicle to advertise himself. Their programmes were partisan and the message to electors was constant. For a foreign observer, there was surprisingly little of the street or door-to-door campaigning that is commonplace in Britain or the United States. Virtually the whole effort seemed to be put into the television campaign. For the owner of such a major part of this medium, the advantage was immense.

The picture of the electoral alliances, which represent the great novelty of the 1994 elections in comparision to previous campaigns and were the prime effect of the majoritarian electoral system, is completed by a fourth alliance called the *Patto per l'Italia* which consisted of the *Popolari*, the bulk of the old DC, and the associates of Mario Segni, who had broken off from the DC in March 1993. Segni's track is particularly striking. Segni and his followers started in an alliance with the PDS to link the centre left with the left, but moved out because the PDS refused to exclude broadening the alliance to include the *Rifondazione*. In November 1993 he founded the Pact for National Renewal with elements from the Republicans, Liberals, and Socialists, and later he moved back with the *Popolari*.

The general conclusion is that alliances were formed to fight elections and not to conduct the resulting governments. They did not rest upon real agreements about programmes of action which would be implemented if the association were to become the government. Events after the election illustrated this rather painfully.

Table 1 shows the transformation of the old parties and their new names and affiliations. For example, virtually all members of the old MSI went into the MSI-*Alleanza Nazionale*, while the DC and the PSI were much more split. In some cases, the bulk of the old party went to the same new home, with only a few going to smaller parties. Table 2 shows the ways in which the new parties co-operated to form the coalitions which fought the elections.

Before we look at the performance of these alliances in the election, we must say something about the electoral system which was introduced. It both encouraged the development of these alliances and moulded their chances of success.

The New Electoral System

For Chamber elections, Italy is divided into 26 multi-member constituencies (*circoscrizioni*) which return 155 deputies. They are in turn divided into 474 single-member constituencies (*collegi*). In addition, the region of Valle d'Aosta is a separate single-member constituency, bringing the total number of deputies to 630. Deputies in the single-member constituencies are elected by plurality. Deputies in the multi-member constituencies are chosen by proportional (PR). Electors have two ballot papers, one for a single candidate in his or her *collegio* and one for a party list in his or her *circoscrizione*. Candidates in the *collegi* must be formally affiliated to one of the *circoscrizione* party lists. In allocating the seats in the *circoscrizione*, the total number of list votes counted is reduced to allow for votes received by winning affiliated candidates in the *collegi*, more precisely by the number of votes received by the runner up candidate in each *collegio* plus one, i.e. the number of votes needed to win a seat (the socalled *scorporo*). The PR seats are first allocated nationally and then in individual *circoscrizioni* using the Hare quota. The introduction of the plurality rule for three-fourths of the seats was obviously the

TABLE 5.1   From the Old to the New Parties

OLD PARTIES (1980s)	NEW PARTIES (1990s)

Traditional Parties

Dc	Rete-Movimento Democratico (Orlando) (1991)
	Popolari per la Riforma (Segni) (1992)
	Patto Segni (1993)
	Cristiano Sociali (Gorrieri, Carniti) (1993)
	Partito Popolare Italiano (Martinazzoli, Buttiglione, Bindi) (January 1994)
	Centro Cristiano Democratico (Mastella, D'Onofrio) (January 1994)
	Alleanza Nazionale (Fiori, Selva) (January 1994)
Pci	PDS (1991)
	Rifondazione Comunista (1991)
	Rete-Movimento Democratico (Novelli) (1991)
Psi	Rinascita Socialista (Mattina, Benvenuto) (1993)
	Alleanza Democratica (Ruffolo, Benvenuto)
	Patto Segni (Amato) (1993)
	Partito Socialista (Del Turco) (1994)
	Federazione liberal-socialista Unione dei Democratici e dei Socialisti (Boniver, Intini) (1993)
Msi	Msi-Alleanza Nazionale (1994)
Partito Repubblicano	Pri (La Malfa)
	Alleanza Democratica (Bogi, Visentini)
Partito Liberale	Pli-Federazione dei Liberali (Zanone)
	Unione di Centro (Biondi, Costa) (1993)
	Alleanza Democratica (Battistuzzi)
Psdi	Unione dei Democratici e dei Socialisti (Ferri)
	Alleanza Democratica

New Parties

Partito Radicale	Lista Pannella (1992)
	Riformatori (1994)
Liga Veneta (1983)	Lega Nord (1991)
	Lega Lombarda (1987)
Verdi Sole che Ride (1985)	Verdi (1990)
	Verdi Arcobaleno (1987)
Forza Italia (1994)	

major change, but the remaining PR seats are allocated by less proportional rules than heretofore and with a 4 percent national threshold compared with the previous 300,000 votes and one constituency seat minimum.[6]

Although the electoral system for the Senate is based upon the same principle as that for the Chamber, namely that three quarters of the Senators were to be elected by plurality in single-member constituencies

TABLE 5.2 The Composition of the Electoral Coalitions

COALITION	PARTIES IN THE COALITION
Left	
Progressisti	Rifondazione Comunista
	Rete-Movimento Democratico
	Verdi
	Partito Democratico della Sinistra
	Rinascita Socialista
	Partito Socialista
	Alleanza Democratica
	Cristiano Sociali
Centre	
Patto per l'Italia	Partito Popolare Italiano
	Patto Segni containing:
	Popolari per la Riforma - Partito
	Repubblicano - Socialisti (Amato)
	Liberali
Right	
Polo della Libertà	Forza Italia
	Unione di Centro
	Centro Cristiano Democratico
	Polo liberaldemocratico
	Lega Nord
Polo del Buon Governo	Forza Italia
	Unione di Centro
	Centro Cristiano Democratico
	Polo Liberaldemocratico
	Msi-Alleanza Nazionale

and one quarter chosen by proportional representation, the electoral law differs in significant detail. As in previous Senate elections, the multi-member constituencies are the 19 regions (plus the single-member region of the Valle d'Aosta). Candidates can stand only in the single-member constituencies. There are no separate regional lists and the elector can cast only a single vote for an individual candidate. In previous elections candidates had needed to win 65 percent of the vote in their single-member district with any seats remaining unfilled allocated proportionately at the regional level. This happened so rarely that effectively the system was regional PR.[7] The new rules guaranteed that three quarters would now be elected from single-member constituencies. As in the Chamber elections there is a *scorporo*, but it is calculated differently, by summing the votes won by all the successful *collegio* candidates.

The d'Hondt formula and not the Hare quota is used to allocate PR seats.[8]

In an innovation designed to increase the proportion of women in Parliament, the new electoral laws provided that candidates on the party lists in the Chamber elections should alternate between the genders. With only 8 percent of Deputies and 11 percent of Senators elected in 1992 being female, Italy has one of the lowest proportions of female representation in Europe.

The Pre-electoral Alliances

The new local government electoral law for communes with more than 15,000 inhabitants introduced a two-ballot system for the election of mayors with a run-off between the two leading candidates if no one won an absolute majority. Parties standing for council seats were obliged to ally themselves with one of the mayoral candidates, with the winning mayoral candidate's list being guaranteed a majority on the council. The results of these elections demonstrated the importance of alliance strategies, and especially the effectiveness of those built by the PDS which included Green and "good government" groups as well as figures from the Democratic Alliance. The success of the Left contrasted with the dismal showing of the *pentapartito* parties, with the DC winning only 11 mayoral elections. Additionally, the strong showing of the MSI in Southern Italy, despite their failure to win control of Rome and Naples at the second ballot in December, pointed to another challenge to the established order. It also made clear that a vigorous challenge to the left would be difficult without the cooperation of the neo-fascists at least in the South. Consequently the building of electoral alliances was to be the principal drama of the months and even weeks immediately preceding the March poll.

As with the local election law, the intent of the new national electoral law was to encourage the formation of broad electoral blocs, and hopefully to enable the possibility of *alternanza* which Italian electors had been denied in the post-war period. But the continued existence of a PR element in the system still gave parties the chance to run independently. For this and other reasons, many commentators had urged the adoption of a two-ballot system on French lines instead. Moreover even as the electoral rules of the game were being modified in order to encourage alliance-building, the number of possible partners in these alliances was increasing as the governing parties of the *pentapartito* began to split and new parties, above all *Forza Italia* began to appear. (The decompositions and recomposition of the party system is illustrated in detail in Table 5.2).

Within the alliances of the right, the Northern League and *Forza Italia* had a quasi-monopoly of nominations in the single-member districts in Northern Italy (Piemonte, Lombardia, Trentino-Alto-Adige, the Veneto, Friuli-Venezia-Giulia, Liguria, Emilia-Romagna and Toscana) with 149 and 60 candidates respectively in 235 districts for the Chamber and a similar proportion for the Senate. Similarly in the rest of Italy the National Alliance and *Forza Italia* with 159 out of 185 candidates for the Chamber and 80 of the 99 Senate candidates dominated the scene. As in the North *Forza Italia* was obliged to cede an absolute majority of the single member districts to the established political party, in this case the National Alliance, which took 99 of the Chamber and 52 of the Senate constituencies.[9]

On the left, the PDS and Communist Refoundation, with 182 and 52 candidates respectively, stood in just over half the Chamber districts (with a similar proportion in the Senate). The Democratic Alliance provided 47 candidates, the Network 39 candidates, the reformed PSI 38, the Greens 32, the Social Christians 20, and independents and others 58.

The Results of the Election

The Electoral Participation

Turnout in the poll for the Chamber of Deputies was 86.1 percent and, at 85.6 percent, marginally lower for the Senate. Given this rather modest difference our discussion deals only with the Chamber vote. As usual, the national figures concealed considerable differences between Northern Italy and the *Mezzogiorno*, with turnout in the North averaging 91 percent and in the South only 78 percent. The slow decline in participation evident since the 1987 election continued with an overall decline of 1.2 percent compared with 1992. Again regional differences were clear with turnout in the South declining at four times the rate in the North. Not unexpectedly given the complexities of the new electoral system, the number of invalid votes cast increased, but again this increase was almost entirely accounted for by change in Southern Italy, where nearly 9 percent of the votes cast were invalid. Blank as opposed to invalidly completed ballot papers accounted for slightly less than half of the total. It is sometimes argued that, in a country where voting is regarded as a civic duty, a blank ballot could be regarded as a protest vote, whereas a spoiled one reflects simply voter incompetence, due, for example, to lack of education. The fact that the proportion of blank ballot papers increased sharply in the South, with virtually no change in Northern Italy, whilst the proportion of spoiled papers increased at much more similar rates throughout the country is suggestive. Overall the South saw both a much larger drop-off in turnout and an increase in blank ballots, which could be interpreted as signs of a much greater political malaise South of Rome.

Votes and Seats in the Chamber and Senate

The election offered the voters a clear choice between the Progressive Alliance and the centre right, even if the centre right was divided into three different alliances. With only 33 percent of the PR list votes going to the parties forming the Progressive Alliance, the result could be interpreted as a sharp reversal for the left compared with the 43 percent of the vote which the same parties had won two years previously. If one disaggregates the total left vote, however, the picture is a little different. Both the PDS and RC increased their share of the vote and the vote for the Network and the Greens was stable. It was the disappearance of the Social Democrats and the collapse of the PSI vote which explains the overall decline of the Left. It was that part of the so-called left which was part of the *pentapartito* which was sanctioned by the electors. Without panel or recall data it is not possible to identify with certainty the destination of previous PSI/PSDI voters, but given what we know of

TABLE 5.3   Electoral Participation - Chamber of Deputies

	Turnout	Invalid Votes	Blank Votes
1948-1987	92.1	3.4	1.7
1992	87.3	4.6	1.9
1994	86.1	5.9	3.0
North	86.1	5.9	3.0
Centre	91.1	4.1	2.1
South	79.1	8.8	4.7
Islands	76.7	8.8	4.3
Change 1992-1994			
Italy	-1.2	+1,3	+1.1
North	-0.3	+0.1	+0.2
Centre	-0.6	+0.2	+0.3
South	-2.3	+3.7	+2.8
Islands	-2.1	+2.8	+2.3

Source: calculated from figures provided by the Ministry of the Interior their social characteristics, the majority must have opted for the parties of the right. So for the core of the Italian Left the election marked a modest progression from a clear minority position. The Left remained clearly in a minority in the country as a whole.

TABLE 5.4 Election to the Chamber of Deputies, Votes and Seats

Alliance/Party	PR Vote Seats	PR Seats	Plurality	Total Seats
Freedom Alliance				
Polo della Libertà, Polo del Buon Governo, Forza Italia	21.0	30		
National Alliance	13.5	23		
Northern League	8.4	11		
Pannella Reformers	3.5	0		
Total	46.4	64	302[a]	366
Pact for Italy				
Popular Party	11.1	29	4	33
Segni Pact	4.6	13	0	13
Total	15.7	42	4	46
Progressive Alliance				
Democratic Left	20.4	38		
Communist Refoundation	6.0	11		
Greens	2.7	0		
Socialist Party	2.2	0		
Network	1.9	0		
Democratic Alliance	1.2	0		
Total	34.4	49		164[b]
Others	3.5	0	5[c]	5

[a] Comprising Northern League 107, National Alliance 87, Forza Italia 74, Centre Christian Democrats 22, Pannella Reformers 6, Union of the Centre 4, Liberal Democratic Pole 2.

[b] Comprising Democratic Left 72, Communist Refoundation 27, Democratic Alliance 18, Socialist Party 14, Greens 11, Network 6, Social Christians 3, Socialist Renewal 1 and Independent Left 10.

[c] South Tyrol people's party 3, Union Valdotain 1 and League of Southern Action 1.

Source: adapted from Bartolini and D'Alimonte, in *Rivista Italiana di Scienza Politica*, n. 3, 1994, p. 634.

The centre-right, however divided, was the clear winner both in terms of popular votes and in terms of seats. In this sense 1994 was comparable to 1948, except that the "party of order" won an even more substantial victory this time. At 15.8 percent, the Pact for Italy suffered a sharp reverse, winning barely more than half the vote of the DC in 1992. But it was the lay parties allied to the old DC which suffered most, with the Republicans, Liberals and Social Democrats effectively vanishing from the scene altogether. The big victors were clearly the MSI/AN whose vote nearly tripled and *Forza Italia*, winning one vote in five only three months after its formation. The *Lega* whose vote was stagnant was the big loser amongst the electorate. In terms of seats the *Lega* did very well, doubling its representation in parliament. But this advance reflected solely the working out the new electoral system, not an advance in the party's popularity with the electorate. Overall the most telling result of the election was the repudiation of the five traditional governing parties.

The new electoral system had the desired impact upon the distribution of seats in the Chamber. Candidates of the Progressive Alliance and the Freedom/Pole Alliance won all but nine of the 475 single-member seats. Tellingly, of these nine, five were won by well-entrenched local parties and only four by the Popular Party. If the single-member district seats produced a basically bipolar result, the PR seats provided, as intended, some compensation for the other parties. It was the successors to the DC which benefitted most. Standing independently, both the Popular Party and the Segni Pact gained PR seats, though with 4.7% of the vote Segni's party only just passed the four per cent threshold. The parties of the Progressive Alliance were less fortunate. Only the PDS and Communist Refoundation passed the threshold, so all the votes cast for the smaller partners in the Alliance were wasted.

Whilst the single-member district seats provided the solid majority for the centre right nationally, a regional breakdown provides a rather more complex picture. The *Polo della Libertà* won practically every seat in Northern Italy with the Progressive Alliance winning only 14 seats The *Lega* did much better in the distribution of seats than *Forza Italia*, reflecting, of course, the initial distribution of candidacies. Conversely in the four regions of the Red Belt the Progressive Alliance won all but three of the 80 seats. In the South, the *Polo del Buon Governo* with 129 seats was the clear winner, but the Progressive Alliance with 73 seats was far from marginalised. As in Northern Italy, *Forza Italia*'s popular support was not fully reflected in the distribution of seats, because the National Alliance's lion's share of single-member district nominations gave it a disproportionate share of Southern seats. Regional patterns of support for the different parties/alliances are best measured by inspecting the vote for PR lists, as electors' choices in the single-member districts were constrained by the particular patterns of local candidacies agreed by the various parties. The PR list vote is also more easily comparable with the vote in the 1992 election. In this section therefore we will focus on the PR vote, even though it was less important in terms of seat distribution.[10]

TABLE 5.5 Election to the Chamber of Deputies by Region (percent votes)

Alliance/Party	North	Centre	South	Islands	National
Freedom Alliance: Polo della Libertà, Polo del Buon Governo					
Forza Italia	24.8	16.8	15.5	30.4	21.1
National Alliance	7.4	11.3	22.9	13.5	13.5
Northern League	19.0	3.5	0.0	0.0	8.1
Pannella Reformers					
Total	51.2	31.6	38.4	43.9	42.7
Popular Party	12.3	9.7	11.1	8.6	11.1
Segni Pact	3.2	5.1	5.0	8.8	4.7
Total ex-DC	15.5	14.8	16.1	17.4	15.8
Progressive Alliance:					
Democratic Left	14.0	34.4	21.2	17.2	21.6
Communist Refoundation	5.3	8.4	7.1	1.6	6.1
Total ex PCI	19.3	42.8	23.3	18.8	27.7
Greens	2.7	2.7	3.1	1.1	2.7
Socialist Party	1.5	2.2	2.8	2.9	2.2
Democratic Alliance	1.0	1.4	1.4	0.9	1.2
Network	0.5	1.1	0.1	9.0	1.9
Total	25.5	50.2	30.7	32.7	34.9

The success of *Forza Italia* was nationwide, but with significant regional differences. In Northern Italy, the new party won almost a quarter of the vote. Predictably they performed less well in the Red Belt. Their strong showing in the South with 16 percent of the vote in peninsular Italy and 30 percent in the islands (rising to one third of the vote in

Sicily) was more of a surprise. *Alleanza Nazionale* became more of a nationwide force, doubling its vote in the North and the Red Belt. But it
was only in regionally peripheral areas in the North, where the MSI's
nationalist and irredentist rhetoric had already proved effective, that
the AN became a major player. Fini's presence at the head of the AN
list in Friuli-Venezia-Giulia, and the party's reparation claims against
Slovenia reflected the party's attention to this nationalist constituency.
The party won nearly 19 percent in central Trieste and nearly a third of
the vote in the city of Bozen/Bolzano compared with an average in
Northern Italy of only 7 percent. The Alliance's major breakthrough
was in its traditional area of strength, the South, as presaged in the 1993
local elections. Here the reborn MSI's vote almost tripled.

For the right-wing alliance, the only major partner which failed to
progress was the *Lega Nord*, whose national vote was stagnant. Moreover the overall picture of nil change concealed losses in all the Northern
regions except the Veneto where the *Lega* made modest gains, but only
at the expense of another regional league, the *Lega Autonoma Veneta*.

The principal heirs of the DC, allied in the *Patto per l'Italia*, suffered
losses throughout the country, losing 40 percent of the 1992 DC vote in
the North and a third in Central Italy. But the hemorrhage of DC support occurred in the South where the party lost over 20 percent of the
total vote.

Support for the PDS and RC increased throughout Italy (except for
RC in Sicily where they did not put up PR lists), but more in the Centre
and the South than in the rest of Italy. In the Red Belt, the two parties
retained a strong plurality position. The minor partners in the Progressive Alliance saw little change in their vote shares. The Network's ambition
to become a nation-wide movement was thwarted. It made hardly any
impact outside Sicily, where its vote increased from 8.8 to 11.5 percent.
But seen in the context of its successes in the 1993 local elections when
Leoluca Orlando had been elected mayor of Palermo with 75 percent of
the first round vote, this was a terrible disappointment.

The Right's overwhelming majority in the Chamber of Deputies was
not matched in the Senate, where they narrowly missed achieving a
majority with only 156 of 315 seats. Why was this? The distribution of
votes shows that both the Right and the Progressive Alliance won a
slightly smaller proportion of the PR vote, and the Pact for Italy and the
minor parties did slightly better. Minor parties, with six seats, won a
larger proportion of the total than in the Chamber, and the Pact for Italy
did better in the PR seats. But the main difference between the two
houses was the much more impressive performance of the Progressive
Alliance in the single-member district seats in the South. As in the
Chamber, the plurality seats in Northern and Central Italy were virtual-

ly monopolised by the Right and the Progressive Alliance respectively. But in the South the Progressive Alliance won a much higher proportion of this type of seat than it had in the Chamber elections.

The expectation that the electoral reforms might well reduce the representation of women proved to be mistaken. The proportion of women elected to the Chamber almost doubled to 15 percent, but only 44 were elected in the 475 single-member districts, whilst 51 were elected on PR lists. In the Senate only 27 women were elected. The Senate outcome reinforces the point that it was the obligation to alternate male and female candidates on Chamber party lists that was the key determinant, because in the upper house all candidates stood in single-member districts.

The New Party System

With the disappearance of major parties in these elections, one might think that a new party system emerged. It is evident at first glance that the new system has not clearly reduced the number of parties. That was supposed to be one of the major aims of the new electoral system with three quarters of the seats being elected by a first-past-the-post system.

One thing which has changed is that what Parisi and Pasquino called "the system of sub-cultural segmentation".[11] The erosion of the power of trade unions and of the Catholic church means that the major political formations of the left and right are not now associated with social communities. The importance of this is that the stability of the PCI and the DC votes, even given the high levels of dissatisfaction for the former system, are unlikely to be reached with the existing parties. Until some new consensus is reached, Italian electors are likely to shop around.

Earlier in this chapter, we suggested that the "alliances" and "poles" which contested the election appeared to be for this alone and not for co-operating to run a future government. This was confirmed for the government pole almost before the counting stopped. In the first place the *Polo della Libertà* and the *Polo del Buon Governo* had extremely vague platforms. Voters were asked to support them mainly as a way of keeping out the left. The apparent incompatibility of the *Lega*'s programme of federalization, or something near to it, and the Italian nationalism of the AN were constantly underlined by Bossi. For the *Lega*, Fini's party represented the area which, they believed, was milking the North of taxes.

Bossi had another problem. From its inception *Forza Italia* had targeted the *Lega* voters to join or associate themselves with Berlusconi's own organization. The degree to which *Lega* voters had actually been poached by Berlusconi is not known. However, there were several reasons why *Lega* support might have leaked in this way. Bossi's tone was extremely strident and rough. While this may have been appropriate for the leader of a grass-roots movement on the way up, it was easier to see Berlusconi, the immensely successful man of affairs, as the future leader of Italy. Secondly, although Bossi had good rapport with the bulk of his followers, Berlusconi could use his three television stations to speak to the nation.

There was evidence at the elections for the European Parliament in June that the vote of the *Lega* was falling from 8.3 percent in the March elections to 6.7 percent at those in June. Over the same period *Forza Italia* went up from 21 percent to 32.4. There was also evidence that a considerable proportion of the *Lega*'s deputies in the lower house preferred Berlusconi to Bossi, and this was confirmed in December 1994, when several of the group followed Roberto Maroni, their leader in that chamber, and rejected Bossi's call to vote for a vote of no confidence in Berlusconi's government. Maroni argued that the *Lega*'s position, as a partner in the governing coalition, had to be given more weight.

Despite his early success, Berlusconi also had problems. Keeping the coalition in place must count as one of the most important of these, and he was eventually unsuccessful. A second problem was his relations with President Scalfaro. To their personality differences was added Berlusconi's undervaluing the important residual powers which the president held, especially when the situation of the government required some external adjudication. The President was jealous of these prerogatives and insisted on safeguarding them. This side of the relationship was particularly important in Berlusconi's unwillingness satisfactorily to divest himself of his interest in Fininvest, and especially in the television stations. The President's was one of the most important voices which demanded that they should reach an agreement which would not allow the Prime Minister to dominate the mass media through his private resources.

Notwithstanding the fall of the government, there are two positive points to be made for Berlusconi and *Forza Italia*. The first is that the ex-Prime Minister still (February 1995) tops the poll ratings of individuals that electors would like to be the next Prime Minister. The second is that Fini and the AN have continued to evolve towards the centre-right and have been loyal partners for Berlusconi. The improvement in the positions of the AN and its leader might pose a future threat for Berlusconi, but at the moment he seems to have no hope without them. The leader of the *Popolari*, Buttiglione, has tried to build bridges towards *Forza Italia*, but even if he were successful, an alliance with the *Popolari* would not be nearly as attractive as one with AN.

TABLE 5.6 Change in Support for Parties by Region 1992-1994

Alliance/Party	North	Centre	South	Islands	National
Freedom Alliance: Polo della Libertà, Polo del Buon Governo					
Forza Italia	+24.8	+16.8	+15.5	+30.4	+21.1
MSI/National Alliance	+3.5	+5.9	+15.1	+8.0	+7.9
Northern League	+0.1	-0.9	-0.3	-0.2	-0.3
Pannella Reformers	+2.4	+1.8	+3.5	+2.5	+2.5
Total	+30.8	+22.6	+33.8	+33.5	+31.2
Dc/Pact for Italy	-9.5	-7.8	-20.8	-21.9	-13.9
Pli/Pri/Psdi	-8.7	-10.0	-11.1	-13.5	-10.0
Psi	-10.7	-9.8	-13.4	-11.5	-11.5
Progressive Alliance (excluding Psi):					
Democratic Left	+2.1	+4.4	+6.2	+6.0	+5.4
Communist Refoundation	+0.3	-	+0.3	-0.4	+0.5
Greens	-0.8	-0.1	+1.5	+0.5	-0.1
Network	-0.4	+0.2	-0.7	+2.5	-
Democratic Alliance	+1.0	+1.4	+1.4	+0.9	+1.2
Total	+2.2	+5.7	+11.4	+5.9	+7.0

Finally the old MSI had its flame extinguished by the party conference in February 1995, when Fini persuaded members to change its
name to *Alleanza Nazionale* with no incorporation of the old title. There
was surprising unanimity both on the change of name and on the confirmation of changes of policy and emphasis which would bring the
party into the mainstream of Italian democracy. It is tempting to think
that this was a complex bluff to smuggle the old fascists into power.
Obviously, this is only a suspicion. What seems certain is that the chance
to enter a government and take part in the future of Italy have proven
more attractive than clinging to nostalgia. There are old street fighters
left, but they seem likely to take themselves off to some other organization.

   In conclusion, the party system has certainly changed. The old system, based on rigid control over the course of events by the governing
parties (sometimes with the complicity of the opposition), has disinte-

grated, but without new forces having been able to take up the old positions of the DC or PSI and their allies. Berlusconi and Fini may be able to take over the old centers of power and reestablish the old style of politics. The only real guarantee that this would not occur is that Italy would develop a bureaucracy which was apart from politics. There is little evidence of moves in this direction.

Notes

1. G. Almond and S. Verba, *The Civic Culture. Political Attitudes and Democracy in Five Nations* (Princeton: Princeton University Press, 1966).

2. Roberto Cartocci, *Fra Lega e Chiesa* (Bologna: Il Mulino, 1994).

3. Paul Taggart, "Muted Radicals: The Emerging 'New Populism' in West European Party Systems" Paper prepared for delivery at the 1993 meeting of the American Political Science Association, Washington 1993.

4. Piero Ignazi, *Il Polo Escluso: Profilo del Movimento Sociale Italiano* (Bologna: Il Mulino, 1989).

5. Antonio Di Virgilio, "Dai partiti ai poli, la politica delle alleanze" *Rivista Italiana di Scienza Politica* XXIV, 1994, p. 505.

6. For further details see Richard S. Katz, "The 1993 Parliamentary Electoral Reform" in *Italian Politics: A Review* vol 9. (Boulder: Westview, 1994).

7. Aldo Di Virgilio, "Riforma elettorale e collegio uninominale" in *Quaderni dell'Osservatorio Elettorale*, n. 19, 1987, p. 93.

8. See Roberto D'Alimonte and Alessandra Chiaramonte, "Il nuovo sistema elettorale Italiano: quale opportunità?" in *Rivista Italiana di Scienza Politica*, n. 22, 1993, pp. 513-547.

9. These data are taken from Aldo Di Virgilio, "Dai partiti ai poli: la politica delle alleanze", in *Rivista Italiana di Scienza Politica*, n. 3, 1994, pp. 494-548, p. 505, pp. 515-23.

10. For this purpose, the North comprises Piemonte, Lombardia, Trentino-Alto-Adige, Veneto, Friuli-Venezia-Giulia, Liguria; the Centre the Red Belt provinces of Emilia Romagna, Toscana, Umbria and Marche and the South the rest of peninsular Italy.

11. A. Parisi and G. Pasquino, "Per un'analisi delle condizioni di governo in Italia" in A. Parisi and G. Pasquino (eds.) *Continuità e mutamento elettorale in Italia: le elezioni del 20 giugno 1976 e il sistema politico* (Bologna: Il Mulino, 1977).

6

The New Members of Parliament

Luca Verzichelli

The Extent of the Turnover

On March 27 and 28, 1994, Italy witnessed the almost complete disappearance of its political leadership.[1] A similar phenomenon was witnessed only in the 1946 elections, which occurred after an over twenty year interruption in democracy. During the life of the Republican Parliament, however, the turnover of members has always been kept below 30 percent. The 1992-1994 biennium represents, in this respect, a significant period of transformation (Fig. 6.1).

In analyzing this period we can distinguish two quite distinct phases, corresponding to the two electoral results. The initial phase, culminating in the 1992 elections, represents a partial renewal, which mostly affected the non-governing parties (the old opposition, in some ways self-renewed with the debut of the PDS, and the new opposition of the Northern League, and, to a lesser degree, the Network). It is also a matter of territorial renewal, since the South saw not only the strengthening of the governing parties,[2] but also the consolidation of a political class which was still able to attract ample public approval. The second phase, in the spring of 1994, saw the completion of the turnover in the northern part of the country (with the arrival of a second wave of League and *Forza Italia* representatives) and also the massive replacement of a parliamentary class that was waning in all the other regions. The new formation on the right took charge of filling the void left by the Christian Democrats, while the vertical collapse of the new Center had closed the doors of Parliament even to those many members of the old majority who were not directly involved in the *Tangentopoli* investigations and were standing again as candidates at the parliamentary elections.[3]

Figure 6.2 shows us just how the 1994 elections represent the central moment of the phase of substitution: the South also decided to bet on its new MPs (as well as new parties), while the area with the highest level of reelection is the Center, thanks above all to the success of the Progressive team in the two Red regions, Emilia and Tuscany.

Figure 6.1. Parliamentary turnover rates in Italy. The Chamber of Deputies (percentage values)

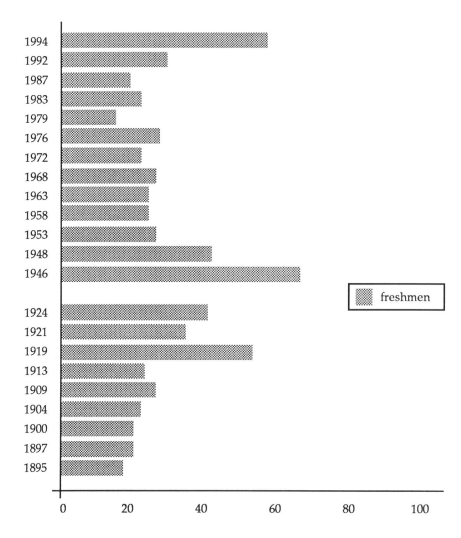

Figure 6.2. 1994 Parliamentary replacement by geographic region

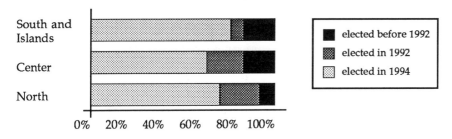

Note: The North includes Piemonte, Valle d'Aosta, Liguria, Lombardia e Triveneto. The Center includes Emilia-Romagna, Toscana, Umbria, Marche, Lazio e Abruzzo.

So the "physical" reorganization of politics in 1994 covers the spectrum of the party system. The disappearance of some traditional actors and the birth of new political formations accelerated the turnover, as seen in Table 6.1, which shows the proportions of freshman and "sophomore" MPs among the various parliamentary groups. It is evident that in addition to the *Forza Italia* MPs, all "new," both the Northern League and the National Alliance have managed, by virtue of their great success, to send a comparable number of freshmen to Montecitorio. Meanwhile, if we go on to observe the procedures of transformation of the political class through an analysis of the recent "shifts" between the legislatures (Table 6.2), we realize how the change has characterized the other parties as well—the PDS (especially with the 1992 elections, but also with the recent result) and the PPI in particular. On this occasion the turnover was directed, so to speak, by the parties themselves, which did not re-nominate many outgoing MPs. From this point of view, the most "permanent" parties with respect to past years are the Northern League and the National Alliance, which have managed to confirm wide sectors of their own re-nominated parliamentary class. The former sent the entire group that had "gone to Rome" on April 5, 1992, back to Montecitorio, while in the second party, there are lines of continuity with the traditional managing class of the MSI (the neo-fascist Italian Social Movement). In both of these cases the development of a new parliamentary class will depend to a large extent on the political postures taken and on organizational changes still to be defined.[4]

Although the raw data on the replacement of parliamentary personnel puts the historical significance of the elections into focus, it cannot tell us much about the real causes of such a pronounced change in the political class.[5] The turnover of MPs was widely expected as the result

TABLE 6.1   Parliamentary experience of 1994 deputies, by party (percentage values)

Party	Elected in 1994	Elected in 1992	Elected before 1992	Total	(Number)
Rc	62.5	27.5	10.0	100.0	(40)
Pds	59.5	24.0	16.5	100.0	(121)
Network	71.4	14.3	14.3	100.0	(7)
Greens	36.4	36.4	27.3	100.0	(11)
Psi	71.4	14.3	14.3	100.0	(14)
Cs	75.0	-	25.0	100.0	(4)
Ad	68.8	18.8	12.2	100.0	(16)
Ppi	51.5	18.2	30.3	100.0	(33)
Segni Pact	76.9	-	23.1	100.0	(13)
Pannella's List	33.3	50.0	16.7	100.0	(6)
Ccd	76.2	4.8	19.0	100.0	(21)
Forza Italia	94.0	3.4	2.6	100.0	(117)
Northern League	69.2	29.1	1.7	100.0	(117)
An	73.3	10.5	16.2	100.0	(105)
Chamber Total	70.8	17.5	11.7	100.0	(630)

of several unprecedented factors, such as the general sense of moral political crisis, the adoption of a new electoral system, and a de-alignment within the party system following the end of international bipolarity. The dimensions of such a turnover and the party redistribution in all sectors of the political class lead us to examine what has changed besides the identity of the new politicians themselves. In particular we must ask ourselves about the persistence and the eventual replacement of those models of recruitment of the political class that had been established in the first thirty years of the Republic and which even the innovative events of the 1980s could not erase.

Greatly simplifying the interpretations offered by the literature, we could say that the selection of the parliamentary class was historically based on the counter-position between two models corresponding to the two most significant parties in the first forty years of the Republic. On one hand there was the party-client model, toward which the Christian Democrats system of selection tended, hinging on internal competition within the list of candidates; once the party accepted (or confirmed) a nomination, thereby putting together a group of candidates representative of trends and social realities, every individual could play his own cards with a certain amount of freedom. In this scenario, obviously,

TABLE 6.2 Replacement and reelection of the parliamentary class. Chamber of Deputies 1983 - 1994[a] (percentage, total in parenthesis)

		VIII-IX (1983)	IX-X (1987)	X-XI (1992)	XI-XII (1994)
Dc	not re-nominated	14.1 (34)	7.8 (16)	16.2 (35)	62.4 (128)
	not reelected	20.4 (49)	13.7 (28)	18.9 (41)	25.8 (53)
	reelected	65.4 (157)	78.4 (160)	64.8 (140)	11.7 (24)[b]
Pci-Pds	not re-nominated	47.4 (83)	41.9 (68)	49.3 (76)	37.0 (37)
	not reelected	5.1 (9)	8.0 (13)	12.3 (19)	13.0 (13)
	reelected	47.4 (83)	50.0 (81)	38.3 (59)	50.0 (50)
Psi	not re-nominated	18.6 (11)	5.0 (4)	15.7 (15)	75.2 (70)
	not reelected	13.5 (8)	10.1 (8)	15.7 (15)	20.4 (19)
	reelected	67.7 (40)	84.8 (67)	68.5 (65)	3.2 (3)
Northern League	not re-nominated				25.4 (14)
	not reelected				5.4 (3)
	reelected				69.0 (38)
Msi-An	not re-nominated	15.6 (5)	11.3 (5)	34.2 (13)	24.,3 (9)
	not reelected	3.1 (1)	18.1 (8)	10.5 (4)	16.2 (6)
	reelected	81.2 (26)	70.4 (31)	55.2 (21)	59.4 (22)
Greens	not re-nominated			42.9 (6)	29.4 (5)
	not reelected			28.5 (4)	23.5 (4)
	reelected			28.5 (4)	47.1 (8)
Radicals	not re-nominated			50.0 (5)	33.3 (2)
	not reelected			20.0 (2)	16.6 (1)
	reelected			50.0 (5)	50.0 (3)
Rc	not re-nominated			33.3 (4)	40.0 (16)
	not reelected			8.3 (1)	15.0 (6)
	reelected			58.3 (7)	45.0 (18)
Network	not re-nominated				27.3 (3)
	not reelected				54.5 (6)
	reelected				18.2 (2)
Chamber Total	not re-nominated	23.9 (161)	20.3 (133)	34.1 (205)	50.2 (317)
	not reelected	12.2 (71)	12.7 (83)	15.0 (99)	20.6 (130)
	reelected	61.8 (391)	64.8 (423)	53.7 (356)	29.0 (182)

[a] The sum of the three values (those not re-nominated, not reelected, and reelected) is equal to the total of outgoing deputies. Among those not re-nominated we also find those who retired or died during the legislative term. Among those reelected we also find those who have transferred to the Senate.

[b] Of the 24 outgoing Christian Democrat deputies, 15 were elected by the Center coalition exactly 11 for the Ppi and 4 for the Segni Pact, 7 for the Ccd (2 of which were for the Senate) and 2 for An.

already to hold one of the coveted parliamentary seats (the obligatory point of departure for a government career), provided a great advantage over the challenging candidates.

In the mass party model, on the other hand, (communist) parliamentary personnel were chosen by the managing structures of the party (with rigid control from the center over local proposals). Internal competition was kept to a minimum, and the percentage of re-nominated members not re-elected was almost zero. In this way the length of service of Members of Parliament was held in check by the party, and the position of deputy or senator represented a necessary "moment of passage" in the career model of the communist politician, leading to other duties within the party organization chart.

All other parties used recruitment criteria inspired by these two models, or perhaps managed a compromise between the two, as in the case of the PSI. The one element common to all of them was always the centrality of the party in the consolidation of the political class and party professionalization, even if the mass party model showed a more evident dependence of parliamentary personnel on the (limited) party leadership.[6]

The use of this last model by the PCI began to undergo a transformation beginning in the second half of the 1980s. Weakened by electoral decline and stimulated by international events, the PCI showed signs of a renovation of its own political class—signs which did not, however, undermine the classic procedures of selection and control by the party apparatus.[7] Following the transformation at the Twentieth Congress and the birth of the PDS, this reorganization assumed a qualitative value as well, as the socio-political characteristics of the new party's personnel show. The PDS has tended then, albeit not without effort, to abandon the classic model of leadership recruitment that featured long labor union and party experience. The *Rifondazione Comunista*, however, itself renewed on the quantitative level, represents the continuity of that model.

In the case of the Christian Democrat's leadership, a significant change in the classic model of recruitment cannot be said to have taken place before the "earthquake" of 1994. In spite of the impact of significant factors like the evident party crisis (resulting in the loss of many seats, especially in the North) and the abolition of the multiple preference system, the confirmation of a high number of sitting MPs even in 1992, demonstrates just how such a model accompanies the whole life cycle of the party.

To consider the mystery of the decline or the transformation of these models at the time of the disappearance of the two parties to which they refer, it is useful to return to the data relative to the background of the MPs. To enhance the analytical capacity of such data, I have constructed two indexes relative to the political experience of the new parliamentary class: the first is the simple result of the intersection of the amount of parliamentary experience with the members' age (Table 3). The second instead is a (crude) index of political professionalization, obtained from the intersection of the data relative to party duties and local political experience (Table 4).[8] The results of these analyses will be discussed in the following pages by examining the three alliances borne of the March 1994 parliamentary elections.

The New Majority: A Fragmented Alliance

The political class represented by the alliances formed around *Forza Italia* is actually composed of two half-coalitions (the *Polo della Libertà* and the *Polo del Buon Governo*), made up of three distinct elements, corresponding to the three principle parties that supported the Berlusconi government. The data on the parliamentary experience of those elected show a substantial group of senior members on the one hand, almost all belonging to the National Alliance, and, on the other hand, an armada of *Forza Italia* freshmen. The Northern League delegation sits between the two, confirming almost all of its standing deputies and promoting, thanks to the fruitful electoral accord with *Forza Italia*, a comparable number of first-timers. The result is a substantially homogeneous group of representatives, composed of deputies with at most one (brief) term of parliamentary experience.

If we combine data on the MPs' seniority in office with their ages, obtaining a leadership replacement index for the various parties (Table 3), the gap between the personnel structure of the National Alliance, *Forza Italia* and the Northern League becomes even more apparent. In the first group, heir to a stable party of the First Republic, albeit a traditionally marginalized one, the continuity is identifiable not only in the highest level of reconfirmations, but also in the higher average age and by the other extra-political characteristics already typical to the staff of the old Social Movement.[9] In some sense it could be said that as a rule, an "old" political class prevails in the AN, implying with this adjective that we are referring essentially to the impact of a higher level of political or parliamentary experience among the elected members. The staff of the Northern League instead represent "new" political group, whether in terms of generation or in terms of moment of entry into politics (starting in the 1990s). With *Forza Italia*, finally, we are seeing the speedy recruitment of a rather young group of parliamentary beginners.

The same distribution can be detected by looking at the second index, constructed on the basis of political experience. The crushing superior-

122

TABLE 6.3 "Old", "new" and "brand new" deputies (percentages)

Party	Old	New	Brandnew	Total	(Number)
Rc	7.5	77.5	15.0	100.0	(40)
Pds	10.7	86.0	3.3	100.0	(121)
Network	28.6	57.1	14.3	100.0	(7)
Greens	9.4	90.9	1.7	100.0	(11)
Psi	7.4	97.5	7.1	100.0	(14)
Cs	-	75.0	25.0	100.0	(4)
Ad	6.0	87.5	2.5	100.0	(16)
Ppi	6.1	72.7	21.2	100.0	(33)
Segni Pact	-	92.3	7.7	100.0	(13)
Pannella's List	-	100	-	100.0	(6)
Ccd	28.6	66.6	4.8	100.0	(21)
Forza Italia	24.8	72.6	2.6	100.0	(117)
Northern League	29.9	70.1	-	100.0	(117)
An	12.4	77.1	10.1	100.0	(105)
Chamber Total	17.5	77.1	5.4	100.0	(630)

Note: The "brand new" deputies are those elected in 1994 and under 40 years old. "Old" refers to those MPs with least two legislative terms of experience, who are also over 55 years of age. "New" members are those who do not fall into the other two categories.

TABLE 6.4 Index of political professionalism among 1994 deputies

Party	Amateurs	Semi-professionals	Professionals	Total	(Number)
Rc	10.0	87.5	2.5	100.0	(40)
Pds	26.3	67.8	5.9	100.0	(121)
Network	28.6	57.1	14.3	100.0	(7)
Greens	27.3	72.7	-	100.0	(11)
Psi	21.4	57.1	21.5	100.0	(14)
Cs	25.0	75.0	-	100.0	(4)
Ad	50.0	43.8	6.2	100.0	(16)
Ppi	42.5	54.5	3.0	100.0	(33)
Segni Pact	84.6	15.4	-	100.0	(13)
Pannella's List	-	100	-	100.0	(6)
Ccd	23.8	71.4	4.8	100.0	(21)
Forza Italia	76.0	23.1	0.9	100.0	(117)
Northern League	28.2	70.9	0.9	100.0	(117)
An	11.4	77.7	10.9	100.0	(105)
Chamber Total	35.0	59.3	5.7	100.0	(630)

Note: "Amateurs" are those who have never held, before their election to Parliament, local elective office or party duties at least at the regional level. "Professionals" are those who have held either elective office at the reginal level or a party position at the national level.

TABLE 6.5 Professions of 1994 deputies, broken down by party (percentage values, number in parentheses)

	Rc	Pds	Other	Ppi	Patto Segni	Ccd	Forza Italia	N. League	An	Total[a]
Professional Politicians[b]	30.0	38.0	17.3	12.1	7.7	14.3	0.9	5.1	21.0	16.8
Professional Union Leaders[c]	7.5	4.9	5.8	6.1	-	-	-	0.9	3.8	3.0
Laborers	10.0	3.3	-		-	-	-	0.9	1.0	1.6
Craft Merchants	-	2.5	-	-	7.7	9.5	11.1	14.5	3.8	6.4
Entrepreneurs	-	-	1.9	-	7.7	-	15.4	3.4	2.9	4.3
Business Managers	-	-	1.9	-	-	-	14.5	2.6	1.0	3.5
Lawyers	-	4.9	11.5	3.0	23.1	19.0	7.7	9.4	22.9	10.3
Other Professions	5.0	9.1	13.5	6.1	7.7	14.3	18.8	30.8	19.0	16.8
Teachers	17.5	12.4	13.5	21.2	-	4.8	5.1	10.3	9.5	10.5
University Professors[d]	10.0	9.1	13.5	33.3	15.4	14.3	7.7	5.2	-	10.1
Public Administrators[e]	5.0	9.1	5.8	12.1	7.7	-	7.7	0.9	2.9	5.4
Civil Servants	10.0	3.3	5.8	3.0	-	19.0	1.7	5.1	7.6	5.1
Other	5.0	3.3	9.6	3.0	23.1	4.8	9.4	18.8	4.8	7.2
Chamber Total	(40)	(121)	(52)	(33)	(13)	(21)	(117)	(117)	(105)	(619)
	6.4	19.5	8.4	5.3	2.1	3.3	18.9	18.9	16.9	100.0

[a] The total number of deputies elected is not 630 because this table exludes the six deputies from the Freedom Alliance who belong to the Pannella-reformes movement and five other representatives of minor and local formations.

[b] "Professional politicians" as a category includes not only those with experience as "party functionaries" but all those who have carried out their political activities fulltime, without practicing any other profession.

[c] This category includes all those who have carried a labor union activity (at the managerial level) full time, or at least have declared that as their primary job.

[d] This category also includes university researchers.

[e] This category includes all public functionaires, judges, officers of the Armed Forces, and managers of para-state agencies.

ity of the element here defined as *amateurism* among the representatives of *Forza Italia* collides with the striking level of political professionalization in Fini's party. In absolute terms, this last group of deputies has the most solid party background, with the exception of the two PCI "heirs." Such professionalization did not weaken with the transformation of the MSI into the AN. We can suppose that the expansion of the party into intellectual sectors and both liberal and moderate sectors sympathetic to the Catholic Church has not stopped a conspicuous number of local exponents of the "old" MSI from successfully setting out on the road to national political consecration.[10]

Even within the Northern League one can speak of visible channels of institutionalization of a stable leadership class, but this process has come about with the briefest passage of time. Many of the *Carroccio's* parliamentary newcomers, however, received their first political experience through the acquisition of minor party posts or through election to various local political bodies. *Forza Italia*, on the other hand, relies on a staff that is completely foreign to the channels that have until now been typical of an MP's political socialization. The FI staff includes neither members with previous party experience (since FI came into being only a few weeks before the election and was consolidated, albeit in a limited way, only after the elections), nor those with an *administrative political background*, except for a small group made up largely of the group of ex-Liberals (UCD), here considered together with the FI. An analogous point can be made for another group that is inseparable from *Forza Italia* within the electoral arena (but considered apart here since it formed an autonomous parliamentary group): the ex-Christian Democrats of the CCD, who distinguish themselves from their colleagues on the lists by showing a considerable level of political professionalism.

A further distinction within the *Polo della Libertà* and the *Polo del Buon Governo* comes to light when we analyze the socio-professional characteristics of the elected members (Table 5). In short, we can break the larger groups of this line-up into three distinct segments within the larger set: the Northern League's staff remains a sort of *sociological mirror* of the low-middle class sectors, manual laborers and merchants, and of the professions. The National Alliance boasts a high level of political professionalism, sending dozens of functionaries and full-time party executives to Parliament. At the same time, Fini's party reflects some aspects of the traditional criterion of selection of its own cadres, continuing to recruit professional representatives and, in particular, members of the legal profession. Berlusconi's party instead represents an obvious departure, whether from the party-functionary recruitment scheme once belonging to the PCI, or from one based on the eminent figures of the local party élite. The social groups best represented by *Forza Italia* are in fact entrepreneurs and business managers. Thus, the three winning political formations have sent to Parliament rather different sets of representatives in terms of social profile. This fact tells us above all that a homogenization of political personnel does not follow from the logic of the associations. We can indirectly infer as well that the characteristics of the representatives still depend much more on the centralized choices of the various parties: the presence of the *Forza Italia* managers together with the former-MSI politicians looks in fact like evidence of negotiations over candidacies conducted at a level superior to the single-member constituency.[11]

The Center: Crisis and the Transformation of an Élite

As far as the socio-political characteristics of the centrist parliamentary groups are concerned, what grabs our attention is the level of continuity within the governing political class, as embodied in large part by the Christian Democrats, the party from which the current PPI is descended, and, in a different way, the movement formed around Mario Segni (*il Patto Segni*) in the months preceding the elections.

The low percentage of re-nominations in the PPI indicated, even on the eve of the elections, an effort toward renewal, which, however, has not convinced the electorate of the new party's determination to form a new political class. Mario Segni's own relatively good performance in the proportional competition, at least with respect to the PPI, might indicate a greater capacity for personal renewal in comparison with a party that only managed the symbolic act of changing its name a few weeks before the vote.

The comparison of the PPI and the deputies in Segni's Pact inevitably leads us to stress the greater continuity, and also the apparent rate of political professionalism, of those *Popolari* who survived the electoral earthquake. And yet on the level of parliamentary experience, Martinazzoli's work as mediator during the preparation of the lists of candidates, while belated and winning little public approval, determined the parliamentary debut of many new, young PPI members. Considering the breadth of the outgoing political class (and the resulting elevated competition, especially for nominations in the by-now-few "safe" single-member constituencies) and the greater traditional autonomy of the outgoing Christian Democrat members of Parliament with respect to party structure, we see a significant reorganization.[12]

Other interesting elements for understanding the transformation of the Center's parliamentary leadership can be gathered from the analysis of their professional qualifications. Among PPI deputies there is an apparent correlation with level of education and public employment. The percentage of university lecturers recruited during the party's reconstructive phase is high as well. We expect the new leadership of the political Center, still in the process of being defined, to emerge from this élite. The *Patto Segni* deputies instead show a professional origin less consistently characterized by political or trade union experience, and few Pact MPs hail from the world of academia or from the professions.[13]

As a rule, it can be maintained that the centrist parties have attempted a grand renewal, which however is not as evident as in the case of the other two alignments because of the reduced size of their parliamentary representation. It is more difficult to establish to what the change in organizational strategies proposed by the two groups active in this area corresponds. In fact, once the PPI overcame the party formula of factions and *clientele*, it seemed in search of an alternative system of leadership selection, and the result, in terms of parliamentary personnel, is the apparent rejection of political professionals in favor of intellectuals and members of the trade unions and associations. In the Segni Pact, however, the more typical personalities of a semi-profes-sional élite within a modern liberal-democratic party prevail. But the extremely low level of institutionalization and the high level of competition have weakened the party structure, as recent defections demonstrate, showing the limits of a coalition legitimated above all in the initial phase of the Italian transition: that is, the phase of destruction of the party system, just when Segni himself and his referendum movement were obtaining sudden and unforeseen success.

The Left: The Weight of the Traditional Logic and the Efforts for Renewal

The data on the elected members in the Progressive Alliance show the presence of new elements in the political class alongside other elements which reflect continuity with respect to the past. In this case, an interpretation is more difficult, since such elements intersect in every party group and in a special way within the PDS, the only major organization remaining after the collapse of all the Center-Left parties and, nowadays, the true torch-bearer of the leftist alliance. The strong quantitative renewal shown by the PDS starting in 1992 has introduced into Parliament a consistent segment of the political class which does not possess the party-labor union background typical of the traditional communist leadership. This sub-group of MPs, who are less tied to the mass party recruitment system, expands if we keep in mind the set of micro-parties belonging to the Progressive Alliance. In these cases we find not just new politicians (above all in the Greens and in the ranks of the AD), but it is also apparent that their career paths are much different from those of their colleagues in the PCI.

The maintenance of a Center-Left alliance and of a plurality electoral system might spark this transformation of the selection process of the political class, as the different proposals in the progressive camp, from the use of primary elections to the creation of a broad Democratic Party, show. On this point there might emerge profound differences with the *Rifondazione Comunista*, whose internal recruitment model remains much more closely tied to the traditional one.

By observing the current data we can say that the number of experienced members in the Chamber has gone down substantially, thanks above all to the change of 1992, when the PDS, making its national electoral debut, made a notable effort to replace its own parliamentary cadres. Many of the key players from that time remain in the Chamber and in the Senate today (the same might be said for the solid sectors of the parliamentary class of the RC, of the socialist-republican part of the AD, of the Greens, and of some elected members of the Network). The index constructed to include the members' ages as well shows us the preponderance of "new" but not "brand new" MPs. We can confirm this interpretation in qualitative terms, adding that with respect to the challengers on the Right (whether the newcomers of *Forza Italia* or the older, but traditionally "excluded" members of the AN) the rejuvenated and renewed team of Progressives presents itself as an élite with obvious features of continuity with the recent past: members who may have favored the perception of belonging to the "old" rather than the "new," thus contributing to their failure.

The social-professional profiles of the Progressive deputies also tells us that an apparent gap in the recruitment criteria exists between the two parties borne of the PCI and the other minor Center-Left forces: the PDS and the RC brought to Parliament a fortified group of professional politicians and union leaders, while the other forces have remade themselves by drawing mostly on the professions, on academia, and even on the business world. An internal recruitment model that is centrally controlled seems however less important than in the recent past, and the PDS especially is showing signs of change, coming for the most part from its candidates in the South, where the traditional apparatus offers less resistance.

In general, two characteristics of the new Progressive personnel stand out, as already highlighted: the PDS's clear organizational preponderance over every other group (or, if you prefer, the lesser weight of its allies, with the RC as the only exception) and the greater decentralization of the selection process, if not at the level of the constituencies, at least at the regional negotiating level. Regarding the first point, it must be said that the PDS "pays" the price of alliance by conceding to the other groups many parliamentary seats that would potentially be obtainable by its own votes (this lack of proportionality, which penalizes the PDS within the Progressive group, has been noted by all observers). This in turn brings about a reduction in the number of real PDS representatives and the entry into Parliament of a varied group of progressives who are surely far from the traditional organizational models of the parties on the left. At the 1994 elections, even within the limits of the Progressive parliamentary class, a series of phenomena could be observed which we might consider trends, like the effect of *Mani pulite* (or rather, the call for the candidacy of magistrates) or the presence of many personalities coming from the independent press and from the media. As has been said of the elected members from the *Patto Segni*, we will still have to wait for new elections to know how much of this "chance" parliamentary class plans to remain in the political arena in the future. The impression is that political forces and corresponding organizational structures do not now exist that are capable of reconciling the two models derived from the fracture of the old PCI: the more open model, centered upon less practical control over the parliamentary class (the PDS's current one), and that which is even today oriented toward the representation of class interests, reflected in MPs who have pursued party or labor union careers (*Rifondazione Comunista*).

Conclusions: Does a Political Class Exist in Italy?

It is much too easy to foresee, especially in the light of events following the elections, that the Italian political class is destined for further changes, due at least to the still considerable volatility of the electorate and to the surge of new alliance-forming strategies. It is less easy to say whether the characteristics of the politicians arising from the 1992-1994 period will form the basis of a consolidated model for the selection of party leaders or of the long awaited leaders of the Second Republic. This is not the place to offer conjectures regarding the future organization of the country's political class. But it seems plausible to affirm for now that the time for the consolidation of the new élite remains distant. The intra-alliance differences, in some respects even more evident than the inter-alliance differences, bring to mind a scenario of extreme fluidity in which certain organized actors try to attract scattered groups of elected representatives with a plurality electoral system that is still widely unknown to Italians and probably susceptible to further corrections. We see this mostly in the Center-Right alliance, where, even after the exit of the Northern League following the end of the Berlusconi government, two profoundly different organizations remain to contend over a very similar electorate. The same might be said, *mutatis mutandis*, of the alliance on the Left, which features two disparate interpretations of the inherited model of the old communist party, both in terms of organization and the resultant leadership class.

This last element is particularly important, whether we are thinking about the present—that is, about the existence of a parliamentary group that picks up representatives in the Chamber mostly from the combined lists of the Progressives[14]—or of the eventual development of a political élite. In effect, the current Progressive segment of the parliamentary class forms a very fragmented universe, no longer guided by a unique organizational machine like the PCI's, capable of renewing itself, but with centrally determined objectives and strategies. In this case we are not looking at two or more political actors allied in a cartel and antagonists within the coalition, but at an entire system that revolves around the PDS, a party which is still far from clarifying its final organizational model.[15] Unlike the other large parties, each of which foresees a model of personnel selection which, while surely temporary, will still be homogeneous, the PDS presents a parliamentary class which is substantially divided between the "professional politicians" of the generation of the Rimini "turning point" and all those Progressives who lack a visible political history and are not backed up by a party-union career.[16]

In fact, the transformation of the Italian political class, and of the whole party system of the Second Republic, does not seem complete. To return to a by now common refrain, one could say that the fate of the parliamentary class makes us consider the 1994 election to be the event that closed one phase of destruction of the "old," without yet clarifying how many and which actors were destined to promote stability and replace the ones who by now are forgotten.

Several motives lead us to this consideration: in the first place, the victories over the centrist and leftist alliances created more than just a compatibility problem among the various forces of Berlusconi's double coalition, which, moreover, is already on the decline. The redefinition of political equilibrium among the moderates entails problems and probable conflicts among the various actors present (today the two dominating parties on the center-right and the various smaller formations). Depending on the procedures chosen to resolve these conflicts there could be a different pattern of development for each of the various fragments of the current political élite.

The other element throwing a shadow of impermanence over the 1994 parliamentary class is connected to the very instability of the associative system: how many among the new local leaders of the various formations or among the professionals being "lent" to politics will still be available to accept the honor of hard and costly electoral campaigns, without being able to count on true parties and without at least some expectation of re-nomination? The abolition of the proportional quota could provide another blow to this unstable political class, obliging many forces to draw up new alliance-building strategies and to make new efforts of renewal in order to be more competitive politically.

Just the same, the political class of 1994 shows some characteristics which might persist even when, with the succession of elections and the consolidation of a new party system, parliamentary turnover will return to lower levels. In the first place, I would point out the requirement of local candidates, directly tied to the alliance-forming logic promoted by the single-member plurality system. This requirement was already revealed with the March 1994 elections, but it should lead to further and more visible developments, continuing to limit the presence of professional party members, and also eventually emphasizing a differentiation between the strategies of the various electoral alliances on the territorial level. Some of the strong parties, as for example the AN and the PDS show themselves to be today, could in fact place men and programs into the field that are very different according to the constituency or the region, alternating a series of centrally chosen candidates drawn from the party apparatus with local members recruited at the edge or even outside of the party itself.

The second novelty is that of greater competition than in the past in the attainment, on the part of the parties, of certain symbolic candidacies and of favorable public opinion tied to various cultural and associational sectors. Contributing to such a centripetal logic is surely the end of a monolithic party like the PCI and the diaspora of politically engaged Catholics throughout the entire spectrum of the new party system. Even in this case one may witness a consolidation of a much more elastic and less centralized recruitment than in the past, but, as above, this does not imply the cancellation of a typology of recruitment models in favor of a homogeneous system. Moreover, the presence of a well structured party in every alliance, and the eventual abolition of the proportional quota could lead to a re-conquest of the administration of recruitment on the part of better organized formations.

The third new element more specifically regards the characteristics of the new members of Parliament: the "enterprise-party" has been discussed at length as if it were a great novelty of this election. In this, we were referring to the way in which the cadres, which are formed by the many managers of *Forza Italia* and by all those new politicians, are already tied in some way to Berlusconi. If the appearance of the enterprise-party were only the manifestation of Silvio Berlusconi's personal success, we should probably think that the novelty would not form the basis of a real parliamentary class, but would be a phase of transition during which the new leaders would have time to form a consolidated group. In reality, we instead suggest that the development of the enterprise-party reflects a requirement felt over the entire political spectrum: the elevated number of managers, of professional politicians, and of various members of "civil society" in all three alliances provides the proof. On the other hand it would be worthwhile to remember how the over-representation of some categories already strongly rooted in Parliament (from university professors, to agriculturalists, to lawyers) does not correspond to the decline of the professional politician, but witnesses the parliamentary projection of a more complex society, which goes from the lower middle class of manual workers to small business (well represented by the Northern League) to the private managers (typical of *Forza Italia*), to the well-known faces of show business and the media.

Notes

1. I would like to thank Maurizio Cotta, who allowed the use of data from the "Centro di documentazione sulle élites politiche" of the University of Siena, which he directed. The disaggregation of these data was at the level of MP's party membership. I must, however, warn that these interpretations are open to correction because of the continuous movement of MPs from one formation to another. Obviously, taking into consideration the moment of entry into Parliament by those members elected in 1994, I did not consider the participation of many members in mixed groups and in progressive-federative groups (nor the recent formation around Mario Segni of the Democratic Group) and the exit of many members from the Northern League, together with a limited number of former Pact members, in order to favor the formation of a new parliamentary alliance (the Liberal Federative Group).

Other data for this analysis have appeared in the issue of the *Rivista Italiana di Scienza Politica* dedicated to the 1994 political elections (n. 3, 1994). That volume was subsequently published as a book, edited by R. D'Alimonte and S. Bartolini: *Maggioritario ma non troppo*, (Bologna: Il Mulino, 1995). I refer in particular to the article on the candidates (by Liborio Mattina) and the one on the winners (by Luca Verzichelli).

2. On the distribution of the April 5, 1992 vote, cf. G. Sani, "La destrutturazione del mercato elettorale" in *Rivista Italiana di Scienza Politica*, XXIII, 1992, pp. 433-474; and by the same author, "Le Italie del 5 aprile" in *Polis*, VII, 1993, pp. 207-228.

3. It is evident that the impact of *Mani pulite* had played a crucial role in the selection process, above all of the formerly governing parties, as some surpris-

ing exclusions (like De Mita's) show. Just the same, many were not re-elected (cf. Table 2) even with the attempt, above all in the South, of some departing MPs who were not re-nominated by their parties, to compete again with local lists.

4. The discussion is true especially for the AN, which could abandon the mediation taken thus far (also on the level of parliamentary recruitment) in order to give more tangible signals of a change of its own cultural horizon, as it has announced a number of times. On these fundamental problems, cf. P. Ignazi, *Postfascisti? dal Msi ad An*, (Bologna: Il Mulino, 1994). The same congress where the MSI was dissolved and the new party founded did not show any clear tendency of internal reorganization, at least at the level of the managing group. The exit of the Rauti and Pisanò group is not really that significant, since a large part of the old directing group has remained in the National Alliance, whose leadership now proportionally represents the various currents of opinion.

5. A provisional explanation of this phenomenon can be found in the paper by M. Cotta and L. Verzichelli, *Italy: The Breakdown of an Established Élite and the Rise of the New Politicians*, Berlin, IPSA World Congress, August 1994. In this study we used the classic Paretian argument of the challenge to the pre-existing political class, finding in the events of the past years the conditions for the substitution of the old élite (in particular, the governing élite, but also, with different tempos and procedures, that of the consolidated opposition on the Left).

6. This simplification refers naturally to some classic writings on recruitment of the political class in Italy, in particular that of M. Cotta, *Classe politica e Parlamento in Italia*, (Bologna: Il Mulino, 1979). The permanent elements and the corresponding elements of evolution of the following decade are evidenced in the work of A. Mastropaolo, *Il ceto politico*, (Roma: Nis, 1993).

7. Indicative of this partial replacement of the political class within the PCI during the 1980s are the progressively growing presence of independent candidates (which had already appeared in the Senate during the phase of national Solidarity) and the greater competition on the list, demonstrated by the slight rise in re-nominated candidates who were not elected (cf. Table 2).

8. The data relative to these variables, typically studied in the analysis of the political class, are available for the entire republican period. Regarding the first legislatures, cf. G. Sartori (ed.), *Il Parlamento Italiano*, (Napoli: Esi, 1993). For the following periods, cf. M. Cotta, *Classe politica*, op. cit., and A. Mastropaolo, *Il ceto politico*, op. cit. Regarding those elected in 1994, the data broken down for these variables are offered in L. Verzichelli, *Gli Eletti*, op. cit.

9. I refer in particular to the extremely low number of women: only six (equal to 5.6 percent of the deputies). It is the lowest percentage of female members among the new parliamentary groups. The other extreme belongs to the progressive groups, in particular, the PDS (34 women, equal to 26.2 percent) and RC (8, or 22.9 percent).

10. Among the deputies considered to enjoy a high level of political *professionalization* (cf. Table 4), I do not consider those who have held, beyond national party positions, local duties at the sub-regional level. In this way many AN

deputies remain in the central category (*semi-professionals*), although they display a long political career. This party has in fact today the most MPs with political experience at the local level. Cf. L. Verzichelli, *Gli eletti*, op. cit. p. 730.

11. About the problem of the conditions and of the procedures of the selection of candidates in 1994, cf. A. di Virgilio, "Dai partiti ai Poli," in S. Bartolini and R. D'Alimonte, *Maggioritario ma non troppo*, op. cit. pp. 195ff.

12. We should keep in mind the many problematic exclusions of some leaders of the old Christian Democratic *nomenklatura*-leaders who are capable of attracting a large amount of personal approval. In the first place is the already mentioned exclusion of Ciriaco De Mita at Avellino. In the PPI's case, reorganization assumes a very important value exactly because it was wanted by the group leaders and in particular by Martinazzoli's secretariat. The same thing cannot be said for the PSI, whose entry into the progressive slate had already excluded the possibility of re-nomination for many remaining leaders close to Craxi (who in fact left the party in 1993). Some of them have also returned to the "do-it-yourself" (*fai da te*) lists, to try to preserve their seats.

13. The low number of deputies belonging to Segni's Pact makes the descriptive capacity of these data weak.

14. Such as the Progressive-Federative Group, where the Greens, the Network, the Social Christians and some of the deputies of the AD are combined, along with the PDS. In the Senate, as noted, there exists a Green-Network Group (*Gruppo Verdi-Rete*) and a group called the Democratic Left.

15. One could say that after the success obtained by Occhetto's relatively repentant turnaround (measurable in electoral terms by the victories in the administrative returns of 1993), the PDS has returned to the dilemmas that were not resolved in its first two years of life, dilemmas to which are tied the possibilities of directing itself toward new organizational models and toward different social sectors. On these points, cf. the conclusions of P. Ignazi, *Dal Pci al Pds*, (Bologna: Il Mulino, 1992).

16. I am referring here not only to the parliamentary personnel under consideration, in the PDS column in the tables, but also to the other progressives. Many of them in fact do not identify themselves with any of the parties of the alliance, maintaining that they are representatives of the whole of the movements. In this sense the PDS embodies, by means of its electoral weight, a much higher proportion of MPs than those who actually registered with the party.

7

The First Majoritarian Parliament

Andrea Manzella

As most attentive observers warned, the first real test of the impact of the new electoral laws on the system of political institutions came about with the formation of the parliamentary groups. As is known, the existence of parliamentary groups was foreseen by the Italian Constitution as the organizing principle for the parliamentary committees and, thus, as an element characterizing the personal situation of each MP. The free and individual choice of party group, the relative numerical strength of the groups, their ensuing alliances, were all completely unforeseen elements in the transition from a proportional law to a quasi-majoritarian one. In order to understand the consequences on parliamentarian structures—and thus on the Parliamentary-Governmental regime—of the new electoral system, or to analyze the electoral data, it was necessary to await the organization of the new chambers of Parliament.

The law's split personality (plurality-proportional) was already shown in the electoral line-ups. The mechanism of the single-member constituency with a single ballot imposed electoral coalitions "of convenience" between emerging political entities (*Forza Italia*, the Segni's Pact, the Democratic Alliance, Christian Democratic Center) and existing political entities (DC-*Popolari*, PDS, Northern League, MSI, Communist Refoundation). The working of the *scorporo* (see Chapter 4), based rather on the proportional vote, had imposed the survival of party designations, symbols, and membership.

The Formation of Parliamentary Groups

The new electoral system's impact on Parliament has been entirely consonant with the law's split personality. On the one hand, the coalitions that were closed at the time of the elections "opened up" in Parliament and gave life to the proliferation of parliamentary groups that were already foreshadowed in the lists offered for the *scorporo* or even without reference to lists. On the other hand, those elected to Parliament in the single-vote constituencies (but, by contagion, also a certain number of those elected from the proportional lists) felt themselves invested with the "free mandate" of Article 67 of the Constitution, until now in some sense unfamiliar in the Republic of the parties.

First, this produced completely new parliamentary groups, different from those that would have been expected on the basis of the previous electoral coalitions. Second, MPs could join the major parliamentary group of their electoral coalition. Finally, they could join the *Gruppo Misto*.

The effects here described are the principal structural consequences deriving from the impact of an imperfect plurality law and from the related loosening of party bonds between originally distinct components. (We are beyond the casuistry of the historic crises of party discipline and alliance discipline in parliamentary democracies resulting from the dialectic between elected members of Parliament and party militants).

With the votes of confidence for the Berlusconi government and later for the Dini government, we had visible signs of political dissent within the parliamentary groups. Such dissent, although not unknown in our recent Republican history (consider the schism in the Socialist party at the time of the formation of the first Center-Left government) has now assumed features more characteristic of conflicting loyalties: loyalty to party as well as loyalty to the electoral constituency. The *turbatio sanguinis* (confusion of allegiances) among voters of various families of party opinion makes it so that, for many of those elected to Parliament, the "constituency mandated" creates a dependence that is entirely new in Republican parliamentary history.

Because of these intersecting motivations, upon the vote of confidence for the Dini government, the situation of the parliamentary formations was that shown by the following tables:

TABLE 7.1 Composition of Parliamentary Group (Senate)

XI Legislature		XII Legislature		
Group	April 14, 1994	Group	April 30, 1994	January 24, 1995
Dc	112	An-Msi	48	48
Pds	66	Ccd	12	14
Psi	50	Forza Italia	36	37
Lega Nord	25	Lega Nord	60	44
Rifondazione Comunista	20	Ppi	34	33
Msi-Dn	16	Progressisti-Federativo	76	74
Pri	12	Progressista-Psi[a]	10	10
Greens-Network	7	Progressista-Greens-Network	13	13
Pli	5	Rif. Comunista-Progressisti	18	18
Mixed	13	Democratic Left	*(born on May 31, 1994)*	10
		Lega Federalista Italiana	*(born on January 18, 1995)*	10
		Mixed	19	14
Total	326	Total	326	325[b]
Total groups	13	Total groups	10	12

[a] Starting from January 11 this group name is Laburista-Socialista-Progressista.
[b] Senator Giovanni Spadolini died during the Legislature.

TABLE 7.2 Composition of Parliamentary Group (Chamber of Deputies)

XI Legislature		XII Legislature		
Group	*April 14, 1994*	*Group*	*April 30, 1994*	*January 24, 1995*
Dc	203	An-Msi	109	109
Pds	106	Ccd	27	27
Psi	91	Forza Italia	113	108
Lega Nord	54	Lega Nord	117	95
Rifondazione Comunista	33	Ppi	33	33
Msi-Dn	34	Progressisti-Federativo[a]	143	167
Pri	26			
Greens	16			
Pli	17	Rif. Comunista-Progressisti	39	39
Psdi	15	Federalisti e		
		Liberaldemocratici	*(born on*	
			December 19,	
			1994)	24
Md-Network	12			
Mixed	17	Mixed[b]	49	28
Total	630	Total	630	630
Total groups	13	Total groups	8	9

[a] Greens, Network, Social Christians, Psi, Ad.
[b] Ad, Lega d'Azione Meridionale, Valle d'Aosta List, Segni's Pact, Svp.

So the prediction that the geography of parliamentary groups in the Chambers would be simplified appears to be unfounded: along side a contraction in the Chamber (from 13 groups to 9), we have an increase in the Senate (from 10 to 13). And the phenomenon of centrifugal forces is quite visible (we can add that the mixed group in the Chamber has 11 more members, compared to the last legislative term—28 instead of 17—and includes 5 distinct political components: AD, the *Lega d'Azione Meridionale*, Valle d'Aosta, the Segni's Pact, and SVP).

However the atomization of Parliament that was feared on the basis of single-member districts has not occurred. Group discipline (and, paradoxically, group secessionist indiscipline as well, such as most recently in the case of the Northern League) is nourished by the extension of the electoral campaign's strong ideologization, which preceded March 26, 1994, and also by the weight of the electoral machines put together by the Progressives (by traditional means) and by the Freedom Alliance in the North and the *Polo del Buon Governo* in the South (with the strong creative contribution of both personnel and funding by the Publitalia-Fininvest corporation).

We note again that the proliferation of coalitions has been based on the formal numerical requirement of 10 senators or 20 deputies. The rules that in the preceding proportional regime allowed the formation of groups beneath the prescribed minimum as long as they were representatives of parties or movements "organized within the Country" (article 14 in both Chamber and Senate rules), have fallen apart because of the impossibility of their application (but also because of the inconvenience of changing the rules that would be felt by the Rules Commissions of the two chambers).

It is evident, however, from this state of affairs, that the fundamental organizational rule for the Chambers—based on the translation of the proportional list system (or the grouping system, for the Senate) into the arrangement of parliamentary groups—has deteriorated at several junctures. It lives out its temporary existence awaiting a definitive electoral and institutional rearrangement—which indeed events in the parliamentary and electoral spheres make more urgent.

The Leadership of Parliamentary Commissions

Although the crude reality offered by the morphology of the parties has been a faithful and immediate mirror of the lack of a clear parliamentary majority, the majority formed in the first phase of the legislative term has superimposed onto this reality a behavior compatible only with an imaginary absolute majority. An inappropriate winner-take-all approach as far as the direction of parliamentary structures is concerned was initially imposed.

A *garantiste* parliamentary practice stemming from 1976 was gradually developed on the principle of allotting the presidency of one of the chambers of Parliament to a member of the opposition (Ingrao, Jotti, Napolitano). By convention, the presidents always have been elected on the first ballot and with greater majorities than those required. The exception was in the Eleventh Legislature when the first signals of turbulence appeared with Scalfaro's election as President of the Chamber of Deputies on the fourth ballot, and then Napolitano on the fifth ballot. The opposition's right to the chairmanship of the various oversight committees (the Commission on elections, on authorizations to proceed with prosecutions, on the supervision of the secret services, the Bicameral Commission for regional questions, the Bicameral Commissions of inquiry or of control) was also recognized.

The three party majority of the first phase of legislature (*Forza Italia* —National Alliance—the League) set its sights on the full occupation of all the chairmanships, in the name of a misunderstood struggle against "cronyism" (*consociativismo*). This denied Giovanni Spadolini the chance to remain President of the Senate after a grueling and dramatic head-to-head contest with majority candidate Carlo Scognamiglio. The Chamber presidency was easily won by Irene Pivetti. And the coalition expected to win for itself the leadership of every other committee, both supervisory and substantive.

The reaction to this approach hit the majority with a sort of boomerang effect. The Senate opposition parties exploited a loophole in the rules to change the precarious numerical balance with respect to the majority supporting the Berlusconi government to their own advantage. Turning to the rule (article 21) that authorizes the representation of groups that have at least a minimum number of members, the evening before the constitution of the permanent Commissions of the Senate (May 31), ten senators (led by Libero Gualtieri and with prestigious members like Senators-for-Life Norberto Bobbio and Leo Valiani and Senator Bruno Visentini) left the progressive-federative group to form the Democratic Left. The appearance of this new group, immediately before the meeting of the Commissions to select their chairmen, allowed Berlusconi's Senate opposition to win the chairmanships of nine permanent Commissions out of 13 (five to opposition parties on the left; three to opposition parties in the center; one to the Northern League, but with considerable support from opposition parties with respect to the other candidate of the then majority). In the Chamber, the majority instead took advantage of its large margin to assure itself the chairmanship of all 14 permanent Commissions.

But the majority was forced to reject *sine die* the setting up of units in which it felt itself to be "in the minority." (For example, and paradoxically given "its" federalist banner, the Bicameral commission for regional questions had not been established ten months after the beginning of the legislature, and neither had the Senate Commission for European Community Affairs, the commission that is the interface with analogous organs of other national parliaments of the European Union). And it must list another failure in the chairmanship of the Bicameral Committee for the Secret Services, (which went, for reasons of seniority, to the progressive Brutti).

These unforeseen (but predictable) difficulties are perhaps not unrelated to the return to the traditional practice of proportionality in parliamentary votes for lay members of the Superior Council of the Judiciary (after which the President of the Republic, without listening to the voices that were asking for a postponement in anticipation of an electoral law, held elections for the members). In fact, 6 members indicated by the majority, one by the opposition parties in the center, and three by the opposition on the left were elected.

The Chairmanship of the Assembly

But the most surprising proof of the failure of the two Chamber presidents to conform to a majoritarian logic lies in the visible recomposition of a *super partes* role that the two Presidents "from the majority" have assumed.

Both Carlo Scognamiglio and Irene Pivetti also immediately adapted themselves to an institutional role that is highly constrained by customs and regulations and too highly vulnerable to assembly control to be party-oriented. The President of the Republic has helped in this "recovery" of independence by offering himself and the two new Chamber Presidents as a fertile triad of guarantee for the Italian transition, an arrangement already tried with Giovanni Spadolini and Giorgio Napolitano in the Eleventh Legislature.

However, the initial affirmation of a conception of the presidencies as expressions of the majority caused a general crisis over the "power to nominate" of the Chamber Presidents (which in the last legislative terms had grown with the increase in the placement of neutral guarantors in the most varied sectors: Guarantor for broadcasting and publishing; Commission of guarantee for the implementation of the law on the exercise of the right to strike; guarantee authority for free market competition; authority for public works). Above all the nominations to the new board of directors of the RAI (after the previous board, still validly in place on the basis of their nominations by the previous presidents, was "overturned") signal the peak of opposition criticism of the two Presidents (July 12, 1994). But for Chamber President Pivetti, the criticisms came above all from her own party, the Northern League. This criticism was weakened, however, when one of the directors nominated by Pivetti, Alfio Marchini, resigned (November 10, 1994), signaling the dissent of both the League and of the opposition parties regarding the politics of occupation of the RAI pursued by other members of the majority, *Forza Italia* and the AN.

The nomination of Giuliano Amato to chair the Antitrust board might seem then to return the power of nominations by the presidents of the two chambers to its previous status of "incontestability."

It is curious to observe that the first phase of the legislative term closes, as far as the "regime of the presidents" is concerned, with a virtual return to the old ways. After the vote of confidence for the Dini government, the Senate president, elected in the coalition on behalf of *Forza Italia*, became in some ways a president representing the "*quasi*-opposition." One branch each, just as from 1976 to 1994.

A significant testimonial of this recovered independence might be seen in the acknowledgment even by majority of the Senate president's power to declare amendments that conflict with the Constitution (see the Rules Commission meeting of December 16, 1994) out of order.

The rebuilding of the chamber presidents' *super partes* position has formed, as can be seen, the basis for the stabilization of a correct relationship between majority and opposition in Parliament, in the face of the new semi-majoritarian law (a significant worry raised in Scognamiglio's speech at his investiture: "I consider myself president of all the senators," and Pivetti's: "president absolutely *super partes*").

And, in reality, as the exemplary experience of the majoritarian British House of Commons shows, the best guarantee for minorities in the unpredictable development of events in Parliament lies with the Speaker as interpreter of parliamentary law—"flexible" between legalism and politics, between written norms and unwritten customary practices. An example of such discretionary power in *bonam partem* vis-a-vis the opposition is offered by President of the Chamber Pivetti in the December 14, 1994, meeting. Having to establish a forum for the examination of the burning topic of television broadcasting, she decided—with some procedural strain and in one of her most hotly contested decisions—to form a special commission, apart from the permanent Commission for Culture, under the debated chairmanship of the On. Vittorio Sgarbi.

Procedural Guarantees for Minorities

Nevertheless, there are automatic procedures that protect the opposition, both in their individual initiatives and investigative actions, from obstructionism by the majority. The crucial field of radio-television news was also the spur to the demand of one third of the members of the Chamber of Deputies which resulted in the automatic convening of the Chamber on October 26, 1994, in conformity with article 62, paragraph two, of the Constitution. In the Senate, the series of automatic procedural mechanisms introduced in 1988, which had already established a formal status for the opposition parties in that branch of parliament, continued to develop with a good deal of functional success.

Consider the debate and the vote—within the brief period required by the rules (30 days)—on the motions introduced by the opposition parties on the RAI situation (debated at the November 10, 1994, session). Consider above all the formation of two monocameral Commissions of inquiry—the Commission on the health system and the Commission on the exploitation of seasonal workers (*caporalato*)—: developments made possible by the particular procedure named in Senate rules article 162, paragraph 2, with the prescription of particular times for the consideration of a call for an inquiry proposed by at least one tenth of the Senate.

According to certain observers, these opportunities for minorities afforded by Senate rules might elevate the function of this chamber as a chamber of control (as proposed by the Bozzi Commission), but likewise, it could cause a greater "distraction" of the Senate from its legislative function, a distraction motivated by the propensity of the government, in the first phase of the legislative term, to introduced its bills for the conversion of its most prominent decrees in the Chamber of Deputies—because of its ample majority—rather than in the Senate.

However, in the phase initiated by the formation of the Dini government, the propensity of the government to initiate legislation in the Chamber could reverse itself because of the lessened force in the Senate of the "*quasi*-opposition" of *Forza Italia* and the National Alliance.

In any case, both the numerical relationship between the coalitions (because of a different result of the electoral law for the Senate with respect to the one for the Chamber, variously explained by the specialists on the subject) and this difference in the status of minorities have produced, for the first time in republican experience, a sort of imperfect bicameralism.

Legislative Initiative

It cannot however be said that this situation in Parliament has either particularly disadvantaged or favored the government. In reality, this first phase of the legislature has been characterized by very meager legislative initiative of the Berlusconi government (if we exclude bills to convert decrees and bills to ratify international accords, there are only 26 bills proposed by the government). The sustained use of the decree laws has continued (192: following the trend of the preceding government; but the Prime Minister was called upon to justify the actions of his government in the unusual venue of the Senate Commission for Constitutional Affairs on August 3, 1994, while in the Chamber—after the October 6, 1994, examination of the Minister for Parliamentary Relations by the Commission for Constitutional Affairs—a special meeting was devoted to the problem of making urgent decrees the following October 11).

There has been a counter-tendency in the use of the power of delegation and of repeal of legislation with respect to the authentic "revolutions" effected with those powers or set out by the Amato and Ciampi governments.

This parliamentary inactivity of the Berlusconi government has been imitated by its majority. In the Chamber, where the government should have rested on a solid majority, in the first 114 sessions there was no quorum present 28 times (in 21 sessions). What's more, in order to pass the 1995 finance law, the government was forced to ask for a vote of confidence three times (November 14-16).

This situation of substantial continuity, on a more modest level, of the practice of the period in which the Parliament was elected by proportional representation, united however with the paralyzing effect of the announcement of a dishonest majoritarian logic (as usual, the accumulation of the worst of the two systems) has also characterized the work of the parliamentary Commissions. Here the sectoral logic has prevailed, as has dialogue with the opposition in addition to that within the majority, despite the negative ghost of "*consociativismo*." They are characteristics revived with exemplary synthesis in the work of a key commission, the Chamber's Commission for Constitutional Affairs, characterized by three fundamental elements:

— the government's the substantial refusal to defend a policy of its own on institutional matters and to muster its majority on these themes.

— the consequent absolute prevalence of parliamentary initiative in the identification of solutions and in the drafting of texts. In this area, the experience of the Twelfth legislature continues that of the last legislature, with the difference, however, that in the 1992-1994 period, the

Commission, above all in electoral matters, arrived at effective compromises on a series of bills. In the current legislature, the elaborations of proposed texts have not managed so far to build consensus, but rather, if anything, to exhaust opposition.

— the notable fragmentation of political forces, including within the major blocs (the "galaxy" of the Progressives, the various components of the Alliance) making quite easy the formation of transverse majorities, which are, however, volatile and thus incapable of "controlling" debate for the entire journey of a proposal.

The Head of State "in" Parliament

Given this lack of comprehensive "control" of the working of the Chambers, it is no wonder that the first vote of no-confidence in the constitutional history of the Republic struck the Berlusconi government. And it struck it, paradoxically, where its margin of majority was strongest (and not in the Senate, where the opening of the crisis would have also been much less "costly" for the Northern League). Even if it was not voted upon, the motion of no confidence, once it was signed by more than 316 deputies was, so to speak, self-enforcing of the sanction of removal.

It is clear that an emblematic image of a segment (perhaps the most ambiguous one) of the Italian transition emerges from this summary of the first phase of the Twelfth Republican Legislature. One in which, on the one hand, an irreversible institutional evolution is taken for granted ("we are at the passage from the First to the Second Republic," Irene Pivetti had proclaimed in her investiture speech to the Chamber). But also one in which, on the other hand, while reflecting the elimination of a large fraction of political personnel (except for those who had taken refuge, in order to survive, in the great coalitions on the Right and on the Left), there is nothing, either on the parliamentary level or at the level of governmental practice or regarding relations between the government and Parliament, which substantiates that "transition" in institutionally meaningful words and deeds.

These contradictions between an imaginary Constitution and the intact institutions of constitutional arrangement in force—contradictions marked by the terminological recovery of concepts that are otherwise quite glorious in the history of law (the "material" or "substantial" or "real" constitution)—end up exhausting themselves in debates over the position and the functions of the President of the Republic.

So Oscar Luigi Scalfaro continues to live out his extraordinary constitutional destiny. Elected as *defensor Parliamenti*, after the iconoclastic fury of his predecessor, he soon had to reconcile his original mission with the political and constitutional course marked by the electoral referendums of 1991 and 1992, that is, with the fact of extra-parliamentary direct democracy. Therefore, he devised and carried out the 1994 loosening as a duty required after the approval of the majoritarian electoral law in August 1993. But now that the inadequacy of an electoral law by itself to change the institutional picture of which it is part is clear, Scalfaro strives to defend the parliamentary establishment against a new attempt to weaken it in a situation of disparity of substantial electoral guarantees (verified in the March 26 elections and now recognized by all political forces, none of which in fact opposed that point in the Dini government's program that called for *par condicio*—that everyone should be on an equal footing in political debate).

But there is more. In order to guide the transition toward a balanced system, but in the new majoritarian parliamentary form, the President of the Republic has been forced to assume a role that is comparable to that in a semi-presidential regime.

Three "Prime Ministerial Governments" within the space of two years (Amato, Ciampi, Dini) and the last two not presided over, for the first time in Italian history, by Members of Parliament (and the last also composed entirely of non-MPs); penetrating powers of protection in the most arduous passages of "their" governments (a protection often shared with the presidents of the two houses of Parliament); public conditioning of the government issuing from the precarious political majority resulting from the elections: these are the stages of a constitutional tendency that must reach the extreme limits of its institutional role in order to assure, for all political forces, an evolution toward a definitive order under conditions of democratic balance.

Here is revealed the full truth of the intuition of great constitutionalists who saw in the Head of State, even for parliamentary regimes, the institution capable of extending its role in political emergencies to that of "Commissioner for crises"—endowed with *reserve power*.

This decisive influence is extended to Parliament. It happened indirectly, in the parliamentary debate on investiture of the Berlusconi government, when the unprecedented exchange of letters between the Head of State and the Prime Minister came into evidence on the eve of the division of "reserve power." In the first letter, the President addressed himself to the responsibility of the Prime Minister regarding the choices that he was about to make. The new foreign minister should have "assured full fidelity to the alliances, to the politics of European unity, to the politics of peace." The new Interior Minister, in his turn, should not have "taken political positions in contrast with the principles of liberty and legality, not to mention the principle of a single and indivisible Italy, which are the foundation and the soul of our Constitution." The entire government should have "been respectful of the principle of social solidarity, which gives substance, first of all, to the protection of employment, with particular regard for the possibility of assuring work to the young." The President concluded by confiding that the Prime Minister put into office should "give every personal guarantee regarding these matters." Prime Minister Berlusconi replied by assuring the President that he "intended to exercise without reserve his power and his responsibility to coordinate and to guide the executive office," confirming as well that "none" of the people considered for the ministerial posts "shows orientations contrary to the principles to which you have chosen to call my attention."

The Head of State's influence over Parliament was instead direct when on September 30 and November 11, 1994, two letters from the President were received by the two chamber Presidents (genuine "messages," according to Constitution article 87, if it were not for the lack of a counter signature). In the first "message," Scalfaro lamented in the first place, that the government submitted to him a 1995 financial proposal with such delay as to have "denied him the exercise of the power of control over legality," according to Constitutional article 87. In the second place, he once again called the attention of the chambers to "the delicate theme of the conformity of the content of measures related" to the resolution that adopted (August 4, 1994) the Document of economic and financial planning. In the third place, the Head of State himself argued against the "suggestion," already approved by the government, that "the reform of the pension system forms an object of an autonomous and distinct legislative proposal."

In the second "message," the President called the chambers' attention back to a theme that is vital for democracy: that of the *par condicio*, which must be recognized for all political entities (parties, movements, coalitions) as regards [...] the equal opportunity of expression and of being heard, above all through the means of mass communication. "He was signaling—therefore—the insistence that the Parliament be able to confront and resolve the situations in question, in ways that might be considered opportune, but with the urgency that they require also in relation to the next electoral deadlines."

The Italian transition, as we see, shows an extreme flexibility of institutional behaviors and even suggests a model of "presidential *garantismo*", a "semi-parliamentary" model, a form of "divided government", in order to allow a return to institutional normalcy.

This return is rendered problematic by the eruption, with vast public approval, on the Italian parliamentary scene of phenomena themselves incompatible with the system of political guarantees of the Constitution,

a system based on the fundamental norm of equality in political participation (Constitution article 3) and on the related division and balance
of powers. Such phenomena are the political profit assured by the
domination of a vast system of information; the confusion of political,
economic, and media powers in the same hands; the corporatization of
politics.

The first phase of the legislative term closes, then, with an exceptional turn in republican practices. Paradoxically, the "guardian of the
Constitution" reaches the extreme limits of his role in order to be able
to carry out informally his neutral function of guarantee. Parliament,
which has recovered, with the opening of the crisis, an essential function of stopping a government that presumes its own self-sufficiency
from direct electoral investiture, now operates within the confines of a
situation in which the powers of the Head of State stand out (powers
that are contested and defended in unprecedented ways).

But already the prominence of the elections, dominated for the first
time by the counter-position of two line-ups unified behind particular
candidates for the premiership, calls, in the changing Italian transition,
for new roles both for the Head of State and for Parliament.

Translated by Sara L. Brann

8

Mani Pulite, Year III

Valerio Onida

The set of investigations and criminal proceedings that go by the name *Mani pulite* (Clean Hands) without a doubt represents an event of utmost importance in Italian judicial, governmental, and political life. It is not that these investigations revealed and combated the diffuse phenomena of political and administrative corruption for the first time. There have been investigations, trials, and convictions in the past, as well. It is the first time, however, that the prosecutor's office of Milan has not stopped with a single incident of corruption, but has widely extended the investigation to the point of getting its hands on the system of corruption, with the disclosure of accords, often of a potentially permanent nature, which allowed the constant flow of funds to political parties from business concerns, and which have provided jobs and supplies to the public sector by means of kickbacks (*tangenti*).

The investigations have spread link by link, involving more and more people. Although the number and length of the hearings have been greatly reduced by plea-bargaining, the trials and convictions are still numerous. We are no longer faced with fairly shocking inquiries, but with a chapter in judicial history, already largely written in terms of the "truth of the trial" (*verità processuale*), whose meaning and overall effects it is now possible to explore.

These effects can be understood and described from several different angles. First of all, we can view the investigations as a genuine judicial event, that is, at the level of judicial procedure and the ability of the magistrates to restrain corruption working within their traditional, established role, in which successes previously had been much more limited. In this light, *Mani pulite* represents the struggle against political-administrative corruption. There is also the standpoint of Operation Clean Hands' impact on judicial and investigative practices; or more generally, its impact on the distribution of judicial power in our government structure, on the relationship of the judiciary with other governmental institutions, and its effects on the *modus operandi* of the other institutions, especially the public administration.

Finally, another aspect to be examined is the repercussions that the judiciary's inquiries and the subsequent greater "visibility" of the judicial apparatus have produced and are still producing on the political system and on its collective actors—the political forces—that form that system, and on the tide of public opinion. Here we enter the sphere of temporary, indirect, and even in some ways improper effects that the situation has produced because of extraordinary circumstances and the political context surrounding it.

The Attack on Corruption

Let us begin by considering the investigations as a judicial event. The systemization of investigations and inquiries was the counterpart for the first time to the diffusion and the "systemization" of the phenomenon of corruption. The veil of resigned silence and *omertà* that covered the phenomenon has fallen, and the solidarity between the corrupters and the corrupted and the various "links" of the chain of corruption have ruptured. Many facts have been confirmed—definitively in several cases.

The balance then is fundamentally positive. Corruption in public structures—understood here in the widest sense, that is, as the mixture and interlacing of private accords and flows of money for private ends (and "private" includes the parties, from this point of view) to influence the procedures and decisions of the public administration—sullies and de-legitimates the institutions, both those founded on the elective principle (representative) and those based on technical expertise (professional), and radically jeopardizes the circle of trust between institutions and citizens.

There are still supporters of a cynical doctrine, according to which corruption would be tolerable if the efficiency of the system were nevertheless assured. And of course history offers evidence of the frequency with which illicit "payoffs" are intertwined with the exercise of public power at all levels (from the highest ranks to the lowest level of petty bureaucrat, who has inherited the customs of the ordinary citizen)—all for private purposes. And yet it is necessary to re-affirm that a system of public functions and public functionaries—that is, an organizational system of collective life like the one in which we have lived for centuries, founded on the State and on public law—radically loses its claim to legitimacy if the faith and the presumption that the one who carries out of such functions receives no private favors for himself or for others in connection with his actions is undermined. This is the essential difference between the modern system of public functions and the older one of public offices awarded as private "favors" to their holders. It is this which renders public power "impersonal" and allows us to distinguish the authority of the one carrying out a public function from a pure position of force, and to distinguish the right of the citizens to avail themselves of the "product" of public administration from a mere private "benevolence" proffered by the one who administers.

However much Italian mistrust of all that is public, and the long established experience of so many private "histories" have spread skepticism in this matter, it is not true that the citizens expect nothing other than a pervasive system of corruption when dealing with public agencies. Just consider how the suggestion that a teacher received money to pass a pupil, or that a magistrate received money to rule in a certain way, is still considered a "scandal" (notwithstanding the emergence of just such cases). Even with respect to officials who are assigned strictly administrative duties, although the phenomenon of petty corruption is taken for granted, it is not internalized as "normal" and acceptable. It might be viewed with greater "resignation," or, more frequently, "utilized" by someone who himself wants to get away with his own illegal deed, whether great or small (corruption by "closing one eye"). In this case, complicity between the corrupter and the corrupted is tighter, and the corrupter comes to exploit, so to speak, a double advantage over the citizen, who asks only that which is his due: he disguises his own illegality and uses a sort of privileged access with the administration. This is perhaps also the reason why, in a country of tax evaders like ours, the revelation of corruption in the Financial Police during tax audits seems to evoke less public reaction than the discovery of corruption involving bribery in the letting of public contracts.

The Future of *Mani pulite*

The success of the *Mani pulite* investigation signals, then, a fundamental point in favor of the establishment of the Constitutional State. It seems that corruption does not necessarily enjoy immunity, that it is not a "necessary evil," that it can be discovered and pursued. From now on one can say that Italy has one of the most corrupt governments among the developed nations. But one would also have to say that it is one country in which the magistrature has been employed with greater success in combating corruption. This is no small matter, as evidenced by the wide interest of judicial and political sectors in other solidly democratic countries in the experiences of our investigations. There now are two key problems. One is how eventually to draw investigations of the past to a close. The other is the response of governmental and political organizations to the problem of administrative corruption in the future.

The first problem is temporary. We have long spoken of a political or legislative solution, but so far no fully convincing proposal seems to have come to light. It is still too early for a genuine amnesty. Indeed, amnesty is appropriate when a great quantity of crimes of a particular kind have been committed, discovered, and prosecuted. Then, in evaluating the extraordinariness of the surrounding circumstances in which the crimes were committed, one might judge that the benefits of "reconciliation" are greater than the risks of weakening the deterrent function of punishment—risks deriving from the refusal to apply such punishment because the surrounding circumstances have changed. In the case of corruption, one would at least need to be reasonably certain that the surrounding circumstances in which the offenses were produced really were changed, that is, that the "system" of corruption was fundamentally defeated.

That brings our attention to the second, more permanent, problem—that of the response for the future. Here legislative solutions actually have been proposed and attempted: from the new law on public bribery (which, however, is now suspended), to the proposal to introduce a new action of immunity from punishment for a participant in corruption who denounces the fact within a certain time period. It is obviously a matter for different responses, on one hand in the area of administrative procedure, and on the other, that of criminal law.

The last proposal must surely be evaluated with attention, and closely examined in all its implications—something that I do not intend to do here. What seems certain to me is that what we need (or one of the things we need) is a response at the administrative level. But that response cannot simply be, much less be limited to, new legislative regulations on administrative procedures. Regulations of this type already exist, and are for the most part detailed and rigorous. What is missing, fundamentally, is a response in terms of the organization of the administrative apparatus.

As for the elected officials, one can hope that a radical turnover of that class as a result of the upheaval of the political system, the inauguration of a practice of alternation, and the public's greater sensitivity to what at one time was called (and now?) the "moral question," can also help control the phenomenon of corruption (although the problem of the costs of politics, and of related temptations, appears anything but resolved). But better distinguishing the functions of elected and professional administrators (which, moreover, are never clearly separated) remains a problem for professional administrators, a problem sharpened by the tendency to reinforce the role of these professionals, to the detriment of elected officials.

It is necessary that this question be confronted in all administrations, especially at the organizational level. It is surprising that in all these months since the criminal investigations of corruption have spread, no one within the administrative apparatus has gone beyond an expectation that is defensive and more or less fearful of the magistrates, much less opened general administrative investigations, anticipating and actively assisting the magistrates, encouraging citizens' statements, giving life to genuine internal "task forces" in order to search in the folds of administrative structures, to see clearly, to modify structures which might be susceptible to favoring or tolerating corruption, installing effective mechanisms of internal control. If it were true, as is whispered, that where the magistrates's offices have not yet arrived everything continues more or less as before, then perhaps only with an increase in the "price" will the struggle against corruption really be lost. That would be an "amnesty" of a different sort altogether!

The Relationships
Between the Bench and the Public Administration

The investigations of administrative corruption have also affected—not always in a positive way—those aspects of judicial practice that are not directly or exclusively connected to this inquiry. Public opinion has managed above all to grasp the excitement of the "action" on the use of preventive detention. Without minimizing the real risks of a weakening of the spirit of rigorous guarantee of the rights of the accused, which can follow from the "easy" use of this instrument, I believe that many polemics are largely self-serving, reflecting the underlying hostility of a political class that has felt and feels itself under accusation by the magistrates, more than any genuine preoccupation with the protection of the rights of (all) citizens and their relations with the justice system. In any case, the excesses of judicial practice in this area can and must be combated beyond the legislative level, through the use of remedies which the trial system itself offers, in particular through the control of the Court of Appeals over restrictions on personal liberty.

An entirely different matter to consider is the risk of distortions in judicial practice, that is, the criteria of judicial in control over administrative activity. We are just now beginning to see symptoms of the criminal magistracy's disposition to expand its own control over the discretion and responsibilities of the administrators, which has brought conflicts to the attention of the Constitutional Court at times. The extension of the investigations to crimes within the public administration and the discovery of vast zones of illegality could naturally lead, and sometimes probably have led, to a sort of generalized presumption that every administrative action is illegitimate, or to a more frequent "conversion" of dysfunctions and of inefficiencies into criminal offenses.

In other words, the magistrates, spurred by the trust of public opinion and stimulated to intervene by our widespread habit of turning to the criminal justice system as the principal, or almost only, instrument of justice, intervene more and more often in administrative activity. When intervention aims to ascertain and repress corruption, regarding events in which illicit payoffs are interlaced with administrative choices, there is no question: the criminal judge's intervention in these cases is sacrosanct and irreplaceable.

It is something else when the supervision of administrative activity translates itself into charges of "abuse of office," potentially equating abuse with illegal action, and any alteration of the balance of interests that is achieved through administrative activity with the illicit advantage or prejudice of third parties. In such a way more questionable hypotheses are introduced: it is no longer a matter of ascertaining objectives and intentions of corruption of administrative activity, like the kickbacks paid (in this case the "deed," if proven, is incontrovertible), but to investigate every possible departure of administrative activity from the normative "model" constructed by the judge. And so we risk turning the criminal court and its investigative arm into a tool for the general inspection of the legitimacy of the administration and radically displacing attention from general administrative procedure, and from the search for ways to make it more efficient and more appropriate, focussing instead on the behavior of individuals, seen as the basis for possible criminal prosecution.

The more probable effect, and sometimes the more visible one, is flight from responsibility because of imminent fear of the prosecutor and the criminal judges. In an administrative system characterized by ever more intricate laws and increasing reliance on administrative action to resolve conflicts of interest, where every choice might be subject to review in court as possible proof of criminal culpability, according to criteria whose application is somewhat subjective because they pertain to more internal aspects of discretionary administrative power, anyone working within that system might be inclined to take every precaution by not choosing—or by choosing poorly, but in a formalistically unassailable way. From this point of view there is the real risk that heightened "pressure" from the magistracy on the administration effectively will be a cause of confusion or paralysis rather than an incentive to improve levels of regularity and efficiency. The criminal investigations which have been initiated in other cities following the Milanese example are not, from this point of view, all the same or all worthy of equal appreciation. In general we can say that the Milanese investigations have had a high level of credibility because they were based on specific facts regarding illicit payoffs, not on debatable legal reconstructions of the criteria of legitimacy in administrative activity. We cannot say the same, it seems to me, of all the other investigations.

The Power of the Bench

The indubitable success of the *Mani pulite* operation has certainly reinforced the overall position of the magistrature in the government organizational structure. We should remember that the operation got started and developed in a climate in which wide political sectors had been arguing for some time with the magistracy and with its governing body, the Supreme Council; and that the investigations' destructive effect on established positions and political reputations of people and parties has led to the intensification of debates and the exploitation of every occasion to attack the magistrates, especially those of Milan (one thinks for example of the storm raised, at the end of the last legislative term, after the famous visit of the Financial Police to Montecitorio, in search of party balance sheets).

The victories of the magistracy in the clash with that part of the political establishment that most opposed its action have been enough, in recent months, to lead to a position of power that hardly seems assailable today (if the political climate does not change): from the constitutional reform of parliamentary immunity, on the wave of a constitutional conflict in which the Milan prosecutor's office challenged the Parliament's use of its own privileges, to the failed issuing of the "Conso" decree that envisioned the de-criminalization of the illegal financing of the parties, to the most recent fall of the "Biondi" decree that tried to prevent the implementation of preventive detention for many of the crimes subject to investigation. Consider, in other words, the climate of much greater calm and respect in which the Supreme Council of the magistracy can now operate, compared to the not distant times in which Cossiga sent the police to monitor its sessions or tried to deprive the vice-president of authority.

The effort to establish political control over the action of the prosecutors, by lifting the constitutional principle of compulsory prosecution in criminal cases, has not been given up completely. But it is a great deal less likely that it can succeed if current conditions persist. So one could say that the independence of the Bench and of the prosecutor, which in our system enjoys of a level of legal assurance superior to that found in most other developed nations, appears today more firmly fixed. That does not mean that there are no institutional problems tormenting the Bench: just consider the permanent failure to provide the new judicial positions promised by the Constitution, or the unresolved dilemma of finding a fairer process of training and selecting magistrates. But it is certain that today we can pose these problems knowing that we do not have to go back to fighting a rear-guard battle in defense of basic guarantees of freedom.

Magistrates or Heroes?

The growth of the role of the courts and the strengthening of their general position have intertwined with the genuine "revolution" which has laid siege to the political system in the last three years, contributing in no small part to the definition of that "revolution". It has been said by many that in its turn the action of the Milanese prosecutor has been made possible by the weakening and subsequent collapse of the political system dominated by those parties which the investigations showed to be involved in rife lawlessness. It is idle to discuss whether the chicken or the egg came first, or whether the investigation or the weakening of the old parties came first. It was certainly a combination that included other important factors, from the growing annoyance of the voters with party procedures, to the 1993 referendum and to the subsequent electoral reform. The fact remains that the Milanese investigations have dictated for quite a while the "agenda" for debate and political action. As long as it has been intended to force the parties to change or to disappear, to pose the question of administrative corruption as central, to compel us to revisit the problem of political financing (which is, nevertheless, still a largely unresolved problem), this has been a stimulus for good, even if not always leading to a healthier political system (an objective, moreover, which is still far from being attained).

But, just as the lack of legitimate response from government has also led to the risk of changing the essential role of the judiciary, so the political system's inability, in many ways, to furnish, at least in the short term, a cogent and comprehensive response to the crisis which had assailed it has created effects of occasional overexposure and of inappropriate "mythologizing" the magistrates. The Milanese team, and in particular its embodiment, Antonio Di Pietro, have been especially prone to this phenomenon, and this led not coincidentally to the point of breakdown with his unexpected resignation.

It is probable that with time these effects, too, will recede, and perhaps they are already receding. But whoever wants to portray the signs of fragility of the new political system which is being delineated, and also the risks of movement in a plebiscitary direction demonstrated by that system, certainly cannot ignore the recurring suggestions for Di Pietro's accession to government office, including potentially to the highest office (a suggestion offered even by a usually reflective leader like Segni). Nor can one ignore the calls for a "Di Pietro party"; the conviction stated by many that anyone could win an election if he managed to bring the former prosecutor of Milan into his own camp. All of these are mani-festations—real or fanciful—of a sort of short circuit of public opinion, in which the job of building a new political system is symbolically entrusted to the magistrates, who, in nicely carrying out their own assignment, have demonstrated that we can do better in maintaining the constitu-tional state than a political system undermined by corruption.

The realism of the key-players has until now prevented the attempt to activate this short circuit. But if that were to happen, it would not be another success for the investigative team or for its symbol: it would only be the demonstration that in Italy the myth of the "hero" is still stronger than the message of solid and productive "normalcy," which is the most precious contribution offered us by the work of the Milanese prosecutor's office. Let us hope that is not the case.

Translated by Sara L. Brann

9

The New Foreign Policy

Pernilla M. Neal

When the Berlusconi government came to power in the spring of 1994, there was reason to believe that there would be something new about Italy's foreign policy. Italy had new political leadership. Berlusconi was a businessman with no prior experience as an elected governmental official. His foreign minister, Antonio Martino, was a university professor, an economist by training, not a diplomat. Although they differed in style and emphasis, both were members of *Forza Italia*.

Another factor promising change in Italy's foreign policy stance was the inclusion of the *Alleanza Nazionale* (which incorporated the *Movimento Sociale Italiano*) in the government; for the first time since the end of World War II, fascists (or "neo-fascists" or "post-fascists", depending upon whose label was being used) were members of an Italian government. Given the pronouncement of some AN leaders regarding Slovenia and Croatia, it was plausible that Italy was poised to add to the havoc being wreaked in Europe related to nationalist claims.

Finally, changes in the setting in which foreign policy decisions were to be made reinforced the expectation that Italy's foreign policy profile would change. Many realities of the Cold War period had ended. The Soviet Union had ceased to exist. Germany had reunited. The United States was reducing its military presence in Europe. Yugoslavia had broken apart. Italy had experienced a political housecleaning, breaking the domination of its political order by the Christian Democrats. It almost seemed that by the spring of 1994 Berlusconi and Martino had a clean slate on which to draw their own grand designs for an Italy entering a new political era. Berlusconi's clearly stated intention was to elevate Italy's foreign policy profile. Both he and Martino felt that Italy should assume a larger, more consequential role on the international scene. Over the course of the year, they worked to enhance Italy's diplomatic standing.

They faced myriad policy issues. Among the most important were the maintenance of peace on the European continent, given the destructive forces of nationalist sentiments, and the speed of the movement to further integration within the EU. The situation in Europe was paradoxical. In the west, there was movement toward greater unity and the maintenance of peace. In the center/east, there was disintegration (or threats to the unity of countries) and violent conflict. Political strife in places such as Albania and Bosnia (as well as portions of Northern Africa) made Italy a destination point for people fleeing those areas. Therefore policymakers in Italy, along with their counterparts in countries such as France and Germany, came under pressure to cope with increasing numbers of immigrants. High rates of unemployment within these countries made them reluctant to expose themselves to new waves of immigration. Maintaining the standards of living for their own citizens during an economic downturn proved difficult to do.

Finding solutions to problems in these issue areas called for keen problem-solving skills and capabilities. Policymakers were increasingly compelled to pay more attention to "quality of life" concerns of their citizens. This meant identifying and solving problems related more to economics, the physical environment and the provision of social services. There has been growing recognition by policymakers of the necessity to work together at the international level to resolve these types of problems, highlighting the continuing blurring of the distinction between "domestic" and "foreign" policy. Decisions taken within the setting of the G-7 annual economic summit or the EU constrain Italy (as well as other members of those groupings) in developing its policy options. Berlusconi encountered strong opposition to financial reform measures he attempted to institute in order to bring Italy into compliance with EU-mandated economic performance levels. Economic considerations have assumed more importance in the formulation of foreign policy.

The appointment of Antonio Martino as Minister of Foreign Affairs was particularly noteworthy in light of the emphasis on economics in foreign policy. He had a command of the theoretical aspects of economics not typically possessed by a foreign minister. He was an economic liberal who had studied at the University of Chicago and who strongly favored free markets. He was well-placed to develop and implement successful foreign policy initiatives related to "low politics" issues.

Against this backdrop, what then was "new" about Italian foreign policy in 1994?

The Global Perspective

Throughout the years of the Cold War, Italy lined up neatly behind the United States in its face-off with the Soviet Union, and the Cold War was perceived by many to be a key underpinning of the Italian political system during those years. The United States was determined to see that the PCI (largest Communist party in Western Europe) never came to power in an Italian government, and thus, the United States supported the Christian Democratic party as a bulwark against possible Communist accession to power. Now that the Christian Democrats have lost their chokehold on political power domestic politics has been freed to find its own level of equilibrium. Concomitantly, Italian foreign policy has been set free as well.

Despite this freedom to chart new courses, the Berlusconi government refrained from doing so at the global level. In Martino's initial forays into the field to meet with other foreign ministers, as well as in press conferences and interviews he gave immediately following his appointment, he repeatedly emphasized that there would be "continuity" in Italy's foreign policy goals and objectives. An examination of the broad outlines of foreign policy under the Berlusconi government leads to the conclusion that they did not differ in substance from those which Italy had followed in the past.

In his May 1994 visit to Washington, D.C., Martino made a concerted effort to reassure U.S. government officials that Italy remained a loyal ally and that there would be no fundamental changes in its foreign policy choices. Throughout the visit he insisted that "continuity" would prevail in Italian foreign policy and there was no cause for alarm, neither on the part of the U.S. government nor the U.S. public at large. He further affirmed his conviction that an appreciable portion of the political opposition in Italy would support the foreign policy stance of his government.

"Continuity" of broad foreign policy guidelines signaled a willingness on the part of the Italian government effectively to continue to take its cues from the United States. This reflected a longstanding practice in Italy's global foreign policy; on more than one occasion, Italy found it convenient to put itself on "automatic pilot" where foreign policy was concerned. Domestic political considerations dominated political debate, almost to the exclusion of foreign policy issues. During the life of the Berlusconi government, that trend continued.

Threats to the stability and survival of the Berlusconi government appeared continually, distracting the government attention's from foreign policy and undermining its attempt to strengthen Italy's diplomatic standing. As in the past, it proved convenient for Italy to take a "follow the [U.S.] leader" foreign policy stance at the global level as it turned inward to grapple with pressing domestic issues.

The Regional Perspective

While the Berlusconi government chose to pursue "continuity" on the global level, it took a different approach on the regional level. There it sought to carve out a new identity for Italy as a "major player." As Martino noted more than once, Italy's message to other members of the EU was that it wanted to count more. In his opinion, there needed to be a larger and more incisive Italian presence in various international organizations, especially the EU.

Within the setting of the EU, this push for a higher profile was marked by two strikingly different tendencies—one where Italy was a strong advocate of further integration of the members of the European Union and another where Italy favored restraint and a lessening of the concentration of control of the EU bureaucracy in Brussels. These two positions were supported by the two members of the government having the most voice in the determination of Italy's foreign policy—Berlusconi and Martino. Berlusconi made a point of indicating support for the movement toward integration. Martino on the other hand tilted in favor of a slowing down of the integration movement and a reduction in the powers which the EU's headquarters could exercise over member countries.

The Berlusconi position was consistent with Italy's historical pattern of allying with the dominant power on the continent. Germany, now ranks as the most powerful country on the European continent. Despite the murmurs of others concerning the composition of the Berlusconi government, Germany's Chancellor Kohl extended a warm and cordial welcome to Berlusconi as he joined the ranks of European heads of government. In Berlusconi, Kohl found not only a supporter of his (Kohl's) enthusiastic and full-speed ahead push for greater integration in the European Union, but also someone who agreed that the European Union should expand even further, admitting the Eastern European countries into the organization.

In contrast, Martino effectively allied himself with the British position of slowing down the integration process. This can be traced in part to his economic training at the University of Chicago where he came to appreciate the teachings of those who argued against extensive governmental regulations to govern market activity. He left Chicago an economic hawk, firmly in favor of privatization, deregulation and free markets. As a result, some perceived the creation within the EU of an Anglo-Italian axis in opposition to the dominant German-French one. It is readily apparent that Berlusconi and Martino worked toward the same goal—greater recognition for Italy—but they took different paths to realizing it.

During the life of his government, Berlusconi actively participated in the business of the EU and fully supported the implementation of the terms of the Maastricht agreement. In particular, he expressed strong support for bringing Italy into compliance with the stipulations of Maastricht concerning economic performance, while readily acknowledging how difficult it would be to achieve them in Italy. For example, he noted that Italy's public debt was 124 percent of GDP compared to the 60 percent set by the Maastricht agreement and that its budget deficit was triple the maximum allowed under the agreement. Given the growing political instability of his coalition by year's end and the public's unwillingness to see the imposition of stringent financial reforms, there was little Berlusconi could do other than pay lip service to Maastricht.

In voicing his strong support for the creation of a single currency, he steadfastly rejected the notion of a "Europe at two speeds." The Germans advanced that idea during September 1994 in an effort to speed the movement toward monetary union. They reasoned that those countries which were well on the way to satisfying the requirements of the Maastricht agreement should not be delayed by those (such as Italy) which were lagging behind. In the year-end prime minister's press conference, Berlusconi drew an analogy between Italy and the EU to justify his negative response to the "two speed" proposal. Briefly, he argued that despite the differences in the economic strength of northern Italy and southern Italy, both used the same currency and were none the worse off for doing so. Thus, he reasoned, all members of the EU could travel together down the road toward currency union, despite striking differences in their economic condition.

Berlusconi and Martino succeeded in achieving greater prominence for Italy in European diplomacy, but that did not necessarily result in the presentation of a united front on policy issues—either in substance or style. Further, the resignation of the Berlusconi government at year's end effectively marginalized Italy in European diplomacy. While once there had been the perception on the part of Italy's European partners that the advent of the new Italian government might signal the dawn of a new political age in Italy, by the end of that government's term it appeared that once again no one was in charge in Italy and no one could be held accountable to fulfill promises made by the departing Berlusconi government. Ironically, a response by Martino to a question during an interview in Peking in November 1994 provides insight into this situation. When asked why certain promises made (by Italy to China) had not been kept, Martino noted that (1) an Italian government lasted on average 10 months and (2) it fell the lot of succeeding governmental ministers to accept the blame when promises which had been made with great fanfare by their predecessors could not be kept. Thus, he felt that Italy had to change and focus its attention on longer time frames. As it turned out, the Berlusconi government did not even last the 10-month average.

Coping with the Fascist Legacy

The presence of the *Alleanza Nazionale* in the governing coalition had a direct bearing both on the development of Italian foreign policy during 1994, and on its perception by people inside and outside of Italy. It is no exaggeration to say that concerns about fascism (be it the "neo-fascist" or the "post-fascist" variation) and its irredentist cries touched virtually every facet of Italian foreign policy during the year.

The inclusion of the *Alleanza Nazionale* in the Berlusconi government raised the question of how the new government would be regarded by other countries given Italy's fascist experience. Throughout the post-World War II period, the United States in particular had been concerned about how deeply democracy had become embedded in the political systems of (West) Germany and Italy. With strong U.S. support, democracy and a market economy were established in each. However, there has also been a residual fear of the reappearance of fascism. A number of countries, not just the United States, warily eyed the composition of the Berlusconi government.

Throughout the life of that government, the leader of the *Alleanza Nazionale*, Gianfranco Fini, steadfastly maintained that his political group was post-fascist and committed to democratic values and practices. On the one hand he sought to reduce fears about the effect on Italy of having post-fascists in the government. On the other hand, however, he engaged in some activities which served to increase anxieties on that score. More specifically, he openly called for a renegotiation of the Treaty of Osimo and for the return of property to Italians compelled to flee Yugoslavia at the end of World War II. The *Alleanza Nazionale* sought to influence Italy's foreign policy, especially with respect to Slovenia and Croatia. Its actions contributed to growing concern about the negative effects of nationalist sentiments and ties on European populations.

Italy's allies were not at all comfortable with the idea of the *Alleanza Nazionale* being a primary member of the governing coalition. Consequently, one of the first tasks undertaken by Martino was to make visits abroad in an effort to reassure allies about the soundness, stability and democratic leanings of his government. Martino's trip to the United States in May ranks as one of the most important of those meetings. In talks with U.S. Secretary of State Warren Christopher, Martino sought to calm any fears the State Department had concerning Italy's new governing coalition. In response, Christopher stated that the United States was looking at the "new political process" in Italy with a great deal of interest. Further, he expressed a belief that the Italian government would respect the democratic process which had brought it to power. Thus, officially, Martino succeeded in obtaining a favorable response (if not enthusiastic and active support) from the United States for his government.

Before meeting with Christopher, Martino had another critical meeting in Washington, D.C. It was a session with representatives from some of the largest Jewish organizations in the United States. That group of Jewish leaders represented one key section of the U.S. public which had been particularly disturbed by the composition of the Berlusconi government. The meeting with Martino succeeded in calming their fears. In fact, one of them declared that the governing coalition was "the most pro-Israel Italian government of the last twenty years." (*La Repubblica*, May 25, 1994, p. 19).

The Israeli government itself made no secret of its dislike for the inclusion of members of the *Alleanza Nazionale* in the Italian cabinet. The number two man in Israel's foreign affairs ministry—Yossi Bellin—called for Israel to have no direct dealings with any Italian minister who was a member of the *Alleanza Nazionale*. Shimon Peres, as head of Israel's foreign ministry, met with Martino in Luxembourg in June. At that meeting, he acknowledged the friendly intentions of Berlusconi and Martino toward Israel. However, he stated Israel was definitely concerned by statements made by Italian ministers who were members of the *Alleanza Nazionale*. Further, he indicated that Israel would make decisions based on what those ministers actually did and said and not simply on the basis of what others had to say about their statements, actions and intentions.

After having calmed the fears of policymakers in the United States and in Israel, Martino faced biting criticism on the issue of the composition of his government closer to home. That criticism came most pointedly from the president of France, Francois Mitterrand. In responding to it, Martino effectively turned the tables on Mitterrand, stating that the best response to Mitterrand's criticism of the inclusion of the *Alleanza Nazionale* in the Italian coalition could be found in Mitterrand's own response to criticism of his inclusion of several Communists as ministers in the first socialist government of the Fifth Republic. Mitterrand declared all such criticism to be "unacceptable." In Martino's eyes, Mitterrand's criticism of the composition of the Berlusconi government was likewise "unacceptable."

While fending off criticism from abroad and keeping diplomatic relations more or less on an even keel with Western allies, Martino faced growing discord with Italy's immediate neighbors to the East, especially Slovenia. This situation stemmed from the ethnic cleansing program implemented by Tito in Yugoslavia in the 1940s. That action resulted in the loss of Italian lives, homes and property in what is today Slovenia and Croatia. Even before the installation of a new government following the elections of March 1994, the *Alleanza Nazionale* had begun to call for (1) renegotiation of the Treaty of Osimo (signed by Yugoslavia and Italy in 1975 to normalize relations between them), (2) the return of property to

Italians forced to flee Yugoslavia at the end of World War II and (3) greater protection of the rights of Italian minorities residing in Slovenia and Croatia. (Today there are approximately 3,000 Italians living in Capodistria, Slovenia, 2,000 in Fiume, Croatia and 15,000 in Istria, Croatia.)

Throughout the life of the Berlusconi government, members of the *Alleanza Nazionale* remained in the forefront of efforts to bring about those changes and, if possible, a re-drawing of the boundaries between Italy and the former Yugoslavia. Initially, Berlusconi attempted to ignore these issues. However, the *Alleanza Nazionale* kept putting pressure on him to take a hard line with Slovenia and Croatia. This situation increased tension within the governing coalition and generated considerable criticism of the government from opposition parties.

When Slovenia refused in July to agree to Italian requests to renegotiate the Treaty of Osimo and other matters of concern between the two countries, Italy proceeded to strike back in dramatic—and hard—fashion. At a meeting of the EU at the end of October to vote on associate status for certain Eastern European countries, Italy cast a veto against the granting of such status to Slovenia. The Slovenians had argued all along that the dispute with Italy was a bilateral question and should not be factored into the multilateral issue of Slovenia's accession to the European Union. The Italians turned a deaf ear to their pleas and (for the time being) blocked their entry into the EU.

The entire episode with Slovenia (and Croatia since the two effectively have established a joint front vis-a-vis Italy regarding the Treaty of Osimo and the treatment of Italian refugees and minorities) added something of a new twist to Italian foreign policy by engaging the attention of domestic constituencies (e.g. refugee associations), and causing them to lobby the government to take action on their behalf. Given the sympathetic ear they found in the *Alleanza Nazionale,* along with the critical role of that political grouping in the survival of the governing coalition, they succeeded in having the national government adopt foreign policy positions favorable to their interests. The Treaty of Osimo and the return of property to refugees became a part of the mainstream political discourse in Italy, and transformed foreign policy into a tangible concern of ordinary citizens.

The Spillover Effect

The participation of the *Alleanza Nazionale* in the government had wide-ranging effects in many policy areas. During the year, Italy was under pressure to provide troops for UN peacekeeping forces in Bosnia. One argument in favor of providing the troops was that it was Italy's duty to do so, especially given its desire to achieve a higher profile internationally.

Additionally, it would have been a sound move to strengthen its bid for a Security Council seat. However, offsetting that argument was the inadvisability of a government which included the *Alleanza Nazionale* sending troops into the former Yugoslavia. After all, the *Alleanza Nazionale* went beyond the mere expression of hostility towards the former Yugoslavia. As far as the *Alleanza Nazionale* was concerned, the harder the policy line taken by Italy vis-a-vis Slovenia and Croatia, the better. Additionally, it was pointed out that the UN Secretary General opposed using troops from neighboring states in peacekeeping operations. Consequently, Italy remained on the sidelines in the efforts to end the fighting in Bosnia.

In December, NATO inquired about the availability of Italian troops to assist in the withdrawal of UN peacekeeping forces from Bosnia. The feeling was that Italian troops would not actually be sent to Bosnia, but would staff a communications center in Puglia in connection with the proposed UN withdrawal.

Nonetheless, many of the reasons advanced for non-Italian participation in the UN peacekeeping force in Bosnia were used to oppose direct Italian participation in the NATO effort to facilitate a UN withdrawal from Bosnia.

Aside from constraining Italy's options in terms of troop deployment, the presence of the *Alleanza Nazionale* in the government contributed to a weakening of the lira on financial markets. By the end of the year, as tensions between the members of the governing coalition peaked, the lira was reaching new lows against the German mark. Investors' confidence in Italy's ability to cease interminable political wrangling, implement needed financial reforms and put its economy on a sounder foundation fell.

Conclusion

The Berlusconi government did not last very long. Its short life adversely affected its efforts to bring about a lasting "new" foreign policy for Italy. At the outset, it held much promise of change. In the end, it failed to meet those expectations.

The major foreign policy goals of the government were reasonable and within reach. At the global level, it avoided jeopardizing Italy's international standing by adopting a policy of "continuity." By declaring that it was not going to make any dramatic changes in broad policy guidelines, Italy provided welcome reassurance to allies and others who had grave concerns about the inclusion of the *Alleanza Nazionale* in the governing coalition. It remains to be seen how much the attempt of the fascist component of the *Alleanza Nazionale* to transform itself into a less-threatening political entity helped the government's efforts.

At the regional level, the time seemed right for Italy to identify itself as a major member of the EU. The Germans and the French still had the loudest voices in policymaking, but with the expansion of the EU there would be a shifting of structure and emphases. As one of the original members of the European Community and one of the largest economies in the world, Italy had justifiable grounds for seeking to strengthen its policymaking voice and its standing within the organization. As a result of the fall of the Berlusconi government, however, it has now lost the initiative. Just when it seemed that progress could be made toward cementing Italy's status as a member of the EU's core, it has effectively been relegated to the periphery. Its continuation of the revolving door pattern of government calls into question who can speak effectively for Italy within EU councils, especially when it comes to making long-term policy commitments.

Governmental instability undermined foreign policy initiatives in 1994. If Italy has more stable, longer-lived governments, it will have a greater probability of enhancing its diplomatic standing. Until such time, however, there is likely to be nothing substantively "new" with lasting effect in its foreign policy.

Many thanks to Richard W. Harper, Jr. for his diligent research assistance in the preparation of this article.

10

The Uncertain Path of Privatization

Filippo Cavazzuti

The Legislative Picture

In the course of 1994, first with the Ciampi government and later with the Berlusconi government, a complex set of legislation (initiated by the Amato government) was almost completed. As a necessary but not sufficient condition, this legislation could allow a rapid course of privatization of banks and public enterprises (primarily utilities) in Italy.

In the first place, we must recall the Amato law which, since 1990 (legislative decree 20.12.90, n. 356), has allowed for the transformation of the publicly owned banks whose legal nature as a public agencies did not allow their sale on the market, nor even mergers and concentration among themselves, into joint stock corporations. As an effect of this body of legislation and its related tax incentives, at the end of 1993 fully 132 publicly owned banks out of 142 potentially included in the corporate transformation had gone private.[1] Thus, we can consider this process substantially concluded if we exclude the unique case of *Monte dei Paschi di Siena*, which has not yet decided what to do, and which so far retains its nature as a public institution.

Then we must recall the July 11 decree law n. 333 (August 8, 1992, n. 359—also of the Amato government) which forced the privatization of other public companies and institutes: IRI (investment banking), ENI (gas and oil), INA (insurance), and ENEL (electricity). Each of these companies' capital stock value issuing from the privatization has been established by the Minister of the Treasury on the basis of the net assets shown on their latest balance sheets. The resulting shares have been awarded to the Treasury, which is then legally able to proceed with the sale of these shares and to collect the proceeds. Finally, we must recall four more provisions.

a) Legislative decree n. 124/1993, which introduced a new institutional investor (pension funds) onto the Italian scene and which should play a rather important role in the underwriting of the stocks and bonds of enterprises to be privatized. This law foresaw that pension funds could be formed: 1) by means of collective bargaining (or, failing this, through corporate regulation); 2) by people authorized to sell and manage shares (like the SIM, *Società di investimento mobiliare*), either companies selling common funds, or investment enterprises, or, finally, insurance companies.

The law guarantees to the individual worker the freedom at least to subscribe to the joint fund. However, once the worker has entered the work force, that worker can no longer get out of the pension fund until the employment that initiated participation in the fund is terminated. This arrangement may have quite serious consequences for the competition that might develop among the various funds.

For its part, the pension fund cannot directly administer the sums entrusted to it by the workers; it must rely on intermediaries authorized for the management of shares (bank and SIM activities), or on the insurance companies or on bond investment firms. In short, the pension fund limits itself to receiving contributions and functioning as a "super client" of the banks, SIM, and insurance companies.

Finally, it must be underlined that the development of this institutional investor is potentially able to have a very significant impact on the growth of the stock market, especially if the stocks came from the privatization of public enterprises.

b) The new banking law in force since January 1, 1994 (legislative decree n. 385, September 1993, which replaces the 1936 banking law), where ownership of registered bank stock by financial and non-financial enterprises is regulated. In fact, for those who do not carry out banking or financial activity, the law places a 15 percent limit on ownership of a bank's registered stock, and it bars them from assuming control of the bank itself. Even with the prohibitions placed on stock ownership allowed to non-financial enterprises, the new body of legislation could permit the privatization of public banks, particularly the savings banks, to which we will return later in this chapter.

c) Bankitalia's circular (released June 1993), which restricts bank ownership of business capital in accordance with legislative decree n. 481/14.12.1992 (which, with notable delay, was in accordance with EEC directive n. 646/1989). In this case as well, the new body of legislation aimed at maintaining a certain degree of "separation" between banking and industry. In order to avoid control of a business by banking interests, it limited bank ownership of an industrial corporation's capital to 15 percent. On this point, however, we can observe that the ability to hold stock in industrial enterprises conceded to the banks is leading to an expansion of the demand for shares. Likewise, if it is carried out, the privatization of public enterprises will lead to an expansion of shares being offered. The two expansions—supply of and demand for shares—could then be a determining factor in the development of the Italian stock market.

d) The definitive conversion to law of the May 31, 1994 law decree n. 332 (law n. 334, July 30, 1994), invoking rules for the acceleration of procedures for the transfer of State and other public enterprises. This decree introduced new legislative conditions to proceed more quickly to the privatization of public enterprises. With this provision, it was arranged that the transfer of control by the State can take place either through direct transfer to one or more private entities, or through a public sale aimed at a large number of stockholders. For privatizing companies operating in the sectors of defense, transportation, telecommunications, energy resources, and other public banking and insurance services, the companies can introduce a maximum limit to individual share holding that cannot be modified for a period of three years into their corporate bylaws.

This last decree has introduced innovations (for the companies to be privatized) that should satisfy the need for the protection of general stockholders: the reservation of seats on the board of directors and the requirement of the presence of an auditor representing the minority stockholders in the board of auditors; the possibility of introducing into the by-laws maximum limits of stock possessions (limits which drop in the case of the launching of a public offering of acquisition—OPA—for the acquisition of control of the "objective concern"); the postal vote, which allows shareholders (especially small ones) the possibility of voting "from home" without having to confront the difficulties of participating in a shareholders' meeting.

It is worthwhile, finally, to recall that with this last law, the government will be able to reserve certain special powers similar to those reserved by the British golden share or to the French *action spécifique*.[2] These powers, however, unlike the French and the English cases, are assigned directly to the Treasury Minister and, thus, separated from stock ownership by the State. We can also note that even if in the Italian case these special powers appear aimed at blocking an eventual hostile takeover on the part of foreign concerns, unlike other national experiences, the Italian law also allows the possibility of using these special powers for political ends. How one would manage to reach these ends is not stated in the law and so remains vague.

The 1994 Privatizations

Given this regulatory picture, it must be underlined that in the course of 1994, the most important privatizations that took place, with a mixture of public sales and private placements, have been the following:

a) *Banca Commerciale Italiana* (COMIT), already listed on the stock exchange. This transfer was accompanied by the introduction of a by-law limiting the maximum amount of registered stock held by an individual shareholder to 3 percent. Because of accords among those stockholders holding close to 3 percent, COMIT today is in the hands of a group of banks and enterprises that hold about 15 percent of its stock. Because of these accords, COMIT has definitively entered the sphere of influence of the Mediobanca,[3] together with three new large stockholders (Generali, Paribas, Commerzbank). Income to IRI (a public holding company) has been about 3,000 billion *lire*.

b) *Credito Italiano* (CREDIT), already listed on the stock exchange. In this case as well there is a 3 percent limit on stockholding. As a result of accords with the most important stockholders, this bank also is today in the hands of a group of about ten partners who operate through Mediobanca. They include: Gruppo Presenti, Ras, Commercial Union, Nippon Life, Luxottica, Benetton. IRI earnings have been about 1,800 billion *lire*.

c) *Istituto Mobiliare Italiano* (IMI), previously unlisted. In this case the stockholding limit is equal to 10 percent of registered stock. About 37 percent of capital has been subscribed. Income to the Treasury (which is the proprietor) has been about 2,200 billion *lire*.

d) *Istituto Nazionale delle Assicurazioni* (INA), previously unlisted, with a limit of 5 percent on stockholding. About 54 percent of registered stock has been sold, for Treasury earnings of about 5,150 billion *lire*.

On these four transfers, only in the case of the two banks, COMIT and CREDIT, did control of the companies change hands from IRI to private holders. The IMI and INA sales, instead, involved "false privatization," intended for now only to generate revenue for the depleted Italian treasury. In these last sales, in fact, control still lies solidly in the hands of the Italian Treasury.

The privatizations of COMIT and CREDIT merit particular attention. When then-owner IRI announced the public sale of stock still in its possession, it also expressed the desire that these banks become publicly held companies, with widely diffuse stock holdings. To reach this goal, greatly reduced limits were placed on stockholding, just as subscribers were offered incentives to hold the stock for the medium term. In reality, right after public offering, COMIT and CREDIT stock was scooped up on the market, sending its quoted price way up. In the face of such a rapid increase in market value, small Italian savers preferred to sell, taking the increased value in cash. In this way, the public offering of the two Italian banks formally controlled by IRI ended with the passage of those banks into the control of *Mediobanca*.

The final privatization of the two IRI banks, together with the above-mentioned regulations which have lowered a whole series of legal barriers blocking every attempt at acquisition or merger among the banks, has produced an important effect on the market of Italian banks. These banks have gone from an absence of competition to a situation in which every rapid competitive move is allowed and where the law on public offerings allows takeovers, including hostile ones. Examples of this are CREDIT's offer for *Credito Romagnolo* (ROLO) and COMIT's for *Ambroveneto*. While the offer for *Ambroveneto* seems to have fallen apart, the one for *Credito Romagnolo* (by CREDIT) was followed by a "counter-offer" (this time defined as "friendly") by the *Cassa di Risparmio delle province lombarde* (CARIPLO). Credit's next proposal led to ROLO's eventual acquisition.

Resistance to Privatization

In the face of all that might happen within the banking system, some parties and movements within the Berlusconi government (National Alliance and some sectors of *Forza Italia*) have lamented the times in which the banking system, dominated by certain public banks (COMIT and CREDIT and the savings bank system), never changed, year after year. The existing laws placed the effective ownership of the banks into the hands of the public and, whenever anything changed, it was easy to identify the "political" (or rather, party) group responsible.

In those days it was said that the parties made the banking system's "regulatory plan." Along with this "regulatory plan" was the power of the Treasury Minister to name the heads of the savings banks and pawnshops (*monti di pegno*). In exercising that power, the minister gave rise to what has become known as *lottizzazione* (allotment) of banking nominations.

The legal rule that assigned this power to the Minister of the Treasury has been abrogated by popular referendum. Today, the power to nominate has been returned to the general meeting of each institute, and the party system has lost an important tool for influencing the banking system.

Old habits, such as those mentioned here, die hard if we consider the efforts with which, towards the end of 1994, the Berlusconi government's Minister of Transportation, former Christian Democrat Publio Fiori, tried with every means possible to keep the BNC-*Banca Nazionale delle Comunicazioni* (belonging to the state railways) within the sphere of influence of the former Roman DC, opposing the "foreigners" of the *Banco San Paolo di Torino* who had already received the go ahead from the *Banca d'Italia* to acquire the BNC.

Related to the desire to revive this regulatory plan and to keep it in the hands of the parties are the issues of the iron bond between the government and the *Banca d'Italia* over the naming of the director general to succeed Lamberto Dini (who had been named Minister of the Treasury in the Berlusconi government) and of the attempt to take the function of industry "watchdog" away Bankitalia and bring that function back under the domain of the Treasury Minister.

It is obvious that if this watchdog role were made dependent again upon the Treasury Minister (as it was under Fascism), the arrangement of the banking system would be directed by the parties in power. In the face of this assault, Franco Modigliani (Nobel prize winner for economics) stated that Berlusconi needed to "publicly disassociate himself from certain stances made by the Fascists who are a part of his coalition. Or disavow the furious attacks being launched against the *Banca d'Italia*, against former premier Carlo Azeglio Ciampi, and against a number of decent, well-known persons abroad... at whom the Right has taken aim".[4] In this context even the governor of the *Banca d'Italia* has been forced to confirm that "in Italy, in the other countries of the European Union, in most of the economically developed States, the functions of monetary policy and of vigilance over the intermediaries are always joined together, to a greater or lesser extent".[5]

In light of the actions and attitudes of the Berlusconi government, Italy's support of Europe, which strongly induced the Amato and Ciampi governments to remove many obstacles to the privatization of the banking system, must be appreciated even more. Now that the restraints on "state-owned bank property" have fallen away (including the one that required the savings banks to be the exclusive property of a public company), the banking system is reorganizing itself on the basis of business strategies and the tools offered by the financial market and aimed at increasing the average size of the credit institutions through concentration and mergers of the banks. All that must be viewed favorably for its potential to overcome a structural weakness in our banking system: its excessive fragmentation, resulting in its inefficiency in responding to company demands.[6]

In the context of private banks competing among themselves, it has become normal for the most powerful banks, like CREDIT and COMIT, or financial and industrial groups, like the Mediobanca group (FIAT, Pirelli, Olivetti, Generali, etc.) eventually to attempt to increase their own power in the relevant markets. It is in this light that we must judge the surely hostile take-over attempts—which we have already discussed— that the two banks have made to acquire ROLO (by CREDIT) and *Ambroveneto* (by COMIT).

It is however obvious that if all movement within the banking system resulted in the eventual increase of power of the Mediobanca group, the new legislation's success would be greatly reduced: to go from the parties' monopoly over the banks to a monopoly of private enterprises over the same banks increases neither economic democracy in Italy nor the level of competition in the banking sector. If these movements led instead to the formation and competition among themselves of "grand alliances" in banking that would mean that the direction chosen is the correct one. Not because in that way local demands are better satisfied, and the historic roots of the institutions are better respected, but because competition among the "many and great" is the best guarantee for economic democracy and for efficiency. In the years to come, we will have to see whether the Italian banking system will be able to assemble itself into a few alliances, or if it will continue to be fragmented in myriad small credit institutions.

We must not believe that the privatization of the large public banks alone will resolve some of the historic problems of the Italian banking system: weak capitalization; inability to operate on the German model as a regional or national bank; an inability to assist business in its growth and in the inevitable generational shift; entrenched opposition to the construction of a venture capital market; modest entrepreneurial capacities of public sector management not subject to market restraints. As is known, in fact, aside from for the large public banks (now privatized), efficiency in the banking system depends crucially on the set of banking corporations created by the Amato law.

The fact that in the course of 1994 the last legislative barriers to privatization of the savings banks fell favors the evolution toward the formation of a few grand banking alliances. As we have mentioned, as a result of the Amato law, the old savings banks (which existed in the form of public foundations) have transferred their banking operations to special joint stock corporations (SpA's). For their part, the foundations have maintained ownership of 100 percent of the stock of the banking companies organized as SpA's. Thus the foundations are at the same time enterprises pursuing the public interest and, with restraints, enterprises administering a bank holding company.[7]

There is no doubt, in fact, that in the new regime of public control introduced by the Amato law, elements of hostility towards the market and mobility of capital and property rights can be traced. In fact, the anti-free market elements which were still protected under the new rules were quite strong. Consider the requirement for the Treasury

Minister's authorization (article 19, paragraph 3 of the decree implementing the Amato law) for the transfer by the foundations of stock with voting rights (including those transfers not involving a loss of control); or the provision (article 20, paragraph 1) through which majority public participation is ensured through the rule that stocks with voting rights in the annual stockholders' meeting, can only be distributed (or even from released) with a majority of half-plus-one of the votes; or the supervision which the Council of Ministers exercises (article 21) over the transfer of stock resulting in a loss of control.

Four years later, with the final approval of the July 30, 1994 law n. 474, the opportunity to eliminate these "traps and snares" (which take the form of a genuine special right for the government of the banking sector) has been taken, and we have arrived at the abrogation of articles 19, 20, and 21 of November 20, 1990 legislative decree n. 356, implementing the Amato law.

In November 1994, Treasury Minister Dini made new arrangements by ministerial decree for the foundations to sell off the controlled banks completely.

The road chosen is one of tax incentive to sell bank shares. In particular, the Minister's directive provides for a reduction in the capital gains tax on the sale of shares. If the foundations decided to take advantage of the tax incentive, total earnings could vary between 15,000 and 35,000 billion *lire* in the course of five years, including the private earnings arising from the alliances formed among the various credit institutes.[8] Since foundation-controlled banks in general offer a rather low profitability, their privatization should entail an increase in capital remuneration. Profitability, then, should be the basic criterion of management decisions.[9]

The Position of the Parties

In spite of the new legislative picture, the privatizations have stopped, except for those first mentioned above. In particular the following privatizations are not taking place: a) fixed assets (1992 law n. 35); b) the public utilities (ENEL, STET, etc.); c) the *Banca Nazionale del Lavoro* (BNL), even though its new president's duty is to privatize; d) the savings banks, as we have mentioned. The reasons for the delays are almost always political in nature rather than technical.

The Berlusconi government, in fact, has met with enormous difficulties in its attempt to carry out the privatizations. The three components of the governing coalition (*Forza Italia*, the *Lega, Alleanza Nazionale*) have shown quite different attitudes in the face of this issue.

On the one hand there is the *Lega*, which, on the basis of its own lib-ertarian credo, would like to proceed as quickly as possible with privatization. But even in Milan, where for two years a *Lega* member has governed as mayor, no privatization plan has been carried out in full, although that was a deciding factor for the winning mayoral program.

For its part, the National Alliance has lined up decidedly in defense of ownership by the state, in whose command posts the party has long tried to inject its own men.

Forza Italia, Prime Minister Berlusconi's party, has been more concerned in its war with the RAI, with the magistracy, and in defense of Berlusconi's entrepreneurial interests than with privatization.

On the whole, in addition to the stances of the different governing political parties, it should be observed that one still faces certain sometimes contradictory approaches over privatization. Simplifying, we can note that:

a) The Treasury Minister would like to accelerate those privatizations that have an effect on the reduction of public debt (which, in Italy, is on the order of 115 percent of GNP). With that goal in mind, the Minister is pressing for the transfer of the IMI and of the ENEL (*Ente Nazionale per l'Energia Elettrica*), whose return would flow directly to state coffers. To this end, in order to make the market value of the ENEL as high as possible, the Treasury Minister would prefer to maintain ENEL in the form of a vertically integrated enterprise with monopolistic tendencies and endowed with long-lasting, exclusive franchises.

b) The IRI, for its part, is pressing for the transfer of certain of its holdings (like those in the telecommunications sector) in order to reduce its own enormous debt. It is obvious that the transfer of IRI's companies will not satisfy the demands of the Treasury to "pay up." But that's not all. Given the modest depth of the Italian market for private capital investment, there is the obvious risk that the market will not be able to absorb the interests of both the Treasury Minister and the IRI at the same time. This presents the delicate problem of priority in the sales on the stock exchange of various public enterprises. If these priorities are not clearly resolved, a substantial paralysis of the privatization process must be expected.

c) The Minister of Industry, for his part, considers privatization of certain public utilities (ENEL, first of all) an important chance to increase the level of competition within the Italian economy. For that reason he harbors an interest in breaking the ENEL monopoly (reducing its market value) and in introducing competition at least for the production of electric energy.

d) The bureaucracy of the ministries (especially those of the Ministry of Posts and Telecommunications and of the Ministry of Industry) looks on the process of privatizing the public utilities with great suspicion, seeing in it the danger of losing the important measure of power which it has exercised through regulation by the ministries themselves. In fact, if the process of privatizing the public utilities were to be established, Italy to would have to introduce independent authorities for the regulation of the privatized enterprises. That, obviously, would bring about the redesign of some powers (especially those connected to the granting of franchises and to the regulation of rates) now exercised by the ministries, and their transfer to independent agencies. We will return to this matter later.

e) The position of big industry in Italy is very uncertain. At the level of rhetoric, and it could not be otherwise, their representatives are calling loudly for the privatization process to be accelerated. But in reality, it, is not so simple. Above all, the large private corporations which supply the public corporations look on the changes that could take place at the top of these corporations with some suspicion. It is not certain, in fact, that in changing the proprietary arrangements, the various supply connections of the new enterprises would remain unaltered. And we cannot forget the historic preference of Italian corporations to act as interlocutor for public corporations rather than assuming the risk of managing the corporations themselves, unless the suppliers assume command positions in the corporations to be privatized. But that would have to be prohibited either by law or by the decision of the independent authorities named to regulate the public utility sector. One could then ask how many private corporations existing today could survive after the disappearance of many public corporations that have been privatized.

Privatizations and Competition

Some of the questions outlined here show how in Italy the problem of privatizations goes hand in hand with the problem of competition. In fact, the large public corporations that could be privatized are in the electric energy, telecommunications, transportation, and network service sectors, where there also exist situations of natural monopoly and legal monopoly due to the concession of exclusive licenses which do not allow any form of competition.

After the privatization of some public banks carried out by the Ciampi government and the stalled privatization of the savings banks, the issue of restructuring of the public utilities (not limited to the privatization of ownership, but extended to include a reordering of competition) of the public utilities is posed: telecommunications, transportation, energy, gas, and water.

The ENEL case precisely illustrates the difficulties to which we have just alluded, and the debate among the various political forces is still as lively as it is undecided.

Whatever the motivations underlying the ENEL privatization, everyone notes one obvious fact: with the privatization of this corporation the power of command passes from the hands of the political party system to those of the entrepreneurs. So it is obvious that every privatization proposal is accompanied by a surge in acute conflicts of interest between the existing administrative powers (which, let us not forget, includes the network of distributors and labor relations) and the powers yet to come (which do not necessarily leave the business arrangements unchanged).

Obviously (and naturally), from the moment ENEL was formed (1962), a gigantic knot of entrepreneurial, political, and labor interests was formed around it. These interests often exist separately from the restraints of international competition, and will be cause for debate upon the privatization of ENEL itself. In addition, although ENEL is a giant in Italy, it is practically nonexistent abroad. It is obvious, however, that when the privatization of ENEL is proposed, no one is talking about going from a public monopoly to a private one. What many people are proposing is that the public monopoly remain the only network (a genuine natural monopoly) for carrying electric energy, and that production and distribution of electric power be entrusted to a multitude of corporations in competition among themselves.

In Italy, this choice is displeasing for some: for those ENEL suppliers not yet equipped to confront a multitude of corporations that want to produce electric energy at competitive prices; for those labor leaders who would see diminished the "special relations" they enjoy today with the politically nominated management and that tomorrow might no longer be that way; for the ministry bureaucracies that also risk finding themselves deprived of some powers.

The Role of the Regulatory Authorities

The solution to the problems associated with the privatizations depends also on how the government intends to move on a related issue: the institution of independent authorities for the regulation of public utility corporations, about which an important debate has been raging for some time.[10]

In Italy the debate also concerns whether the current regulator (the Ministry concerned and the CIPE—the Interministerial Economic Planning Committee) should be replaced by a new regulator whose powers would be derived from legislation and would not be limited to offering suggestions. From this stems the urgency to endow the independent authority with strong powers in the fields of rates and competition for the regulation of public services. In the case of Italy, in fact, it is a matter of passing from a public corporation regulated through its direct relationship with the political system, to other private enterprises regulated by a "third" authority whose duties (technical and not political) must be to promote competition, to safeguard the interests of the consumers by assuring technical standards that are consistent with the definition of the standards of quality of services offered to the consumers, to regulate rates at a level that makes the internal efficiency of the corporation compatible with the maximization of economic activity, and to set prices for access to existing networks would not constitute barriers to the entry of new firms.

In truth, the Ciampi government moved in the direction of forming independent agencies to regulate public utilities. December 24, 1993 law n. 537 (which accompanied the 1994 budget act) contains authorization for the government to enact both direct rules to establish independent bodies endowed with the function of regulating services relevant to the public interest, and other rules meant to give those independent bodies functions currently exercised by ministries or by other agencies. It is obvious, in fact, that in order to avoid useless and inefficient duplication, the formation of the independent agencies by the executive power must be accompanied by the reorganization (and perhaps elimination) of the offices that carry out analogous functions within the ministries. It may actually have been the resistance of the bureaucracies with the ministries struck by the privatizations that has not allowed this authority to be used. In fact, it lapsed mid-way through November 1994.

For its part the Berlusconi government has introduced a rule into the law on privatization (July 30, 1994, law n. 474) that directs the withdrawal of the State from ownership of public utilities is to be subordinated to the creation of independent bodies to regulate rates and control quality of service (article 1 bis). But the Berlusconi government, because of internal dissent in the governing coalition, let drop the authorization to introduce those authorities by legislative decree. The unrealized formation of those authorities makes up the largest obstacle to the achievement of privatization of the public utilities.

The Senate has moved with greater speed and determination than the government. In fact, the Senate Industry Commission unanimously approved a legislative proposal at the end of November (which must now be examined by the full Senate) instituting three independent authorities for the regulation of telecommunications, transportation, and electric energy.[11]

Analogous to the English experience (the Office of Electricity Regulation, for example) and in North America (the Independent Regulatory Commissions, for example) are the functions of these authorities foreseen in the legislative proposal: a) increasing the level of competition in those sectors where legal monopolies or near monopolies operate. This function involves permitting market access to new businesses through the review of franchises. This may be the case of secondary providers in the cellular telephone industry; b) reviewing cases in which technological progress has introduced new possibilities, so that the conditions of natural monopoly that are the prerequisite of public monopoly no longer exist, and the presence of more companies in the same market becomes possible. This may be the case of the production of electric energy by private concerns or of a multitude of companies in telecommunications.; c) to ascertain whether technical conditions instead exist that would not allow any form of regulation except for the extreme regulation of the totally public corporation that operates under conditions of absolute monopoly. This may be the case of the railroad and electric networks where it is difficult to imagine competing networks, but where regular access by more companies offering the service to the final user is necessary; d) adopting adequate politics of deregulation and re-regulation for the purpose of promoting competition or, where this cannot be shown effectively in the market, introducing conditions and incentives of potential competition through the market. This may involve recourse to competitive auction for allotting franchises for a fixed period. It is obvious that at the end of the period, these franchises will have to be auctioned again.

Since the realization of a competitive atmosphere like the one summarized here does not preclude the opportunity of regulatory interventions concerning quality and the price of goods and services offered, the bill approved by the Senate commission foresees that the independent authorities will at least assure that: a) the drawing up of technical regulations is consistent with the definition of standards of quality of services offered to consumers; b) the regulation of rates is carried out through mechanisms (like the price-cap) that render the objective of efficiency within the corporation compatible with maximization of market exchange.

In order to accomplish all this the three independent authorities would have to be endowed with strong public powers: the power to grant franchises, the power to issue directives to corporations subject to regulation and sanction, and the power to resolve controversies between corporations and consumers.

The political crisis that struck the Berlusconi government at the end of 1994 has interrupted the dialogue which was taking shape between

Parliament and government on the necessity and the urgency of introducing the above-mentioned regulatory authority. However, spring of 1995 might see independent authorities of regulation born even in Italy and, in this way, the privatization of important public utilities like ENEL (in electricity) or STET (in telecommunications).

Translated by Sara L. Brann

Notes

1. T. Padoa-Schioppa, "Profili di diversità nel sistema bancario italiano," in Banca d'Italia, *Bollettino economico*, n. 22, February 1994, p. 30.

2. Both the English experience (golden share) and the French one (*action spécifique*) involved the insertion into the registered stock of a company to be privatized, stock possessed by the government or by one of its representatives endowed with special powers permitting the government itself to impede unwanted corporate raids on the part of foreign entities or unwanted changes in company control, or to protect national interests and national independence.

3. Mediobanca is the only merchant bank operating in Italy. Thus, Mediobanca is a monopoly. It carries out functions of industrial credit, of financial consulting for the stock exchange, of control of ownership equilibrium of client enterprises. Because it has participated actively, since the Second World War, in determining the control of the principal private Italian corporations, Mediobanca's role has often been identified with that of guardian of the interests of existing controlling groups and, thus, with the interests of the industrial families of northern Italy. See M. de Cecco, G. Ferri, "Origini e natura speciale dell'attività di banca d'affari in Italia," Banca d'Italia, *Temi di discussione* of the Servizio Studi, December 1994, n. 242.

4. Cf. interview with F. Modigliani, *La Repubblica*, November 3, 1994, p. 8.

5. Cf. A. Fazio, "La tutela del risparmio," a speech given by the governor of the Banca d'Italia on the 70th World Day of Savings, Associazione fra le Casse di risparmio italiane, Rome, October 31, 1994, p. 9.

6. See "Le banche e l'efficienza. La sfida possibile," Fondazione Rosselli, first report on the Italian finance system, Edibank, Milan, 1994.

7. Cf. F. Cavazzuti, R. Costi, "Le banche ai privati, le fondazioni alla società civile," in *Delta*, July-August 1994, n. 63, p. 15.

8. Cf. C. Demattè, "Fondazioni, ritorno all'origine," in the *Corriere della Sera*, November 29, 1994, p. 17.

9. Cf. A. Penati, "Fondazioni sulla strada del mercato," in *Il Sole-24 Ore*, November 27, 1994, p. 21.

10. Cf. F. Cavazzuti, G. Moglia, "Regolazione, controllo e privatizzazione nei servizi di pubblica utilità in Italia," in *Economia Italiana*, 1994, n. 1, pp. 9-30.

11. Cf. Senate Act n. 359 (Twelfth Legislature), Cavazzuti et al., "Norme per la concorrenza e la regolazione dei servizi di pubblica utilità. Istituzione delle Autorità di regolazione dei servizi di pubblica utilità."

11

Politics and Karaoke

Edmondo Berselli

Forza Italia and Its "Hymn"

On February 6, 1994, at the *Fiera di Roma*, Silvio Berlusconi at last officiated at his own "entry in the field," as he likes to put it in his own special vocabulary. In the audience there was a crowd of small business people, advertising sales people, and mid-range professionals: the Italy of *Forza Italia* (Go Italy), to be precise. They are a sociological sample of a country that already considers itself *azzurro* ("blue," color associated with Italy's national sports teams) down to its bones, the "People" upon whom the leader will anxiously call in his most difficult moments. They are the "People" who, upon finding themselves "participating" together, feel grow and intensify within themselves what they had begun to experience when the *Biscione*'s party made its first sinuous moves: come on, no one ever said that the road out of the First Republic and its debts must be paved with tears and blood.

In fact, Berlusconi promised that no prices would have to be paid. As soon as the kits to establish the party clubs were distributed and the ad campaign for *Forza Italia* was launched,[1] and the children had learned the movement's jingle and sung it to their parents, something caught on in the minds of the Italian middle class. First, an indistinct sensation, then a certainty: we don't have to pay. It was worlds away from Ciampi's rigor and Amato's inhumanity, from the cold Lenten days to come. The resurrection was under way. Silvio Berlusconi recites, with a hypnotic and persuasive slow rap, that "a new/a great/an extraordinary/Italian miracle" is on its way, and entire swaths of the population understand that the hour of sacrifice can be dodged with an unexpected move from the Right. Who will pay the famous two million billion *lire*? But it's obvious: the economic cycle, the new expansion, miraculous growth,

Keynes reinterpreted by the Right—even a child can understand it. Anyone who says it isn't true is illiberal, a bastard son of Brezhnev, who dreams of the old days of *consociativismo* (cronyism). Italy is ready to make her big leap. Anyone who doesn't jump is a Communist. And so the song goes: "And Go Italy, to be free..." (*E Forza Italia, per essere liberi!...*)

But on February 6, 1994, something else happened. Toward the end of his speech (and what a speech: the "doctor" paced back and forth over the stage with a microphone in his hand, like an intimate singer, and continually returned to the anaphoric way of speaking that lends relentless rhythmic density to his sentences, using his two great ideals of good sense and moderation), right in his final lines, Berlusconi was moved almost to tears, his voice caught in his throat and broke with emotion. It is so natural, one feels that the miracle of charisma has arrived, that il Palaeur has become the mystic crucible of his political movement. It is warm fusion, between a people who have found a leader and a leader who has found his people. And it is because of this that Berlusconi can allow himself to close by saying, "And now, let us sing our hymn."

Yes, take it away. Even his bard Emilio Fede, on *Retequattro*, hesitates a moment as the television cameras are modestly focused away from il Palaeur's maxi-screen. But then for just a few seconds we can see Berlusconi singing the "hymn," and we also get a furtive look at the maxi-screen: the words to "Forza Italia" are rolling across the bottom of the screen. Here we are. The circle is complete. It is the year of karaoke.

Is Karaoke an Instrument of the Right?

After the debacle of the March 27-28 vote, the Left, for lack of anything else to do, naturally "searched its heart." The realization that the "joyous war machine," as Achille Occhetto had defined the Progressive electoral alliance, was in fact a wreck with flat tires came out in the formally irreproachable tones: "and now *Il Cavaliere* has the right/duty to govern; let him govern and we will see what he can do." But the defeat was too catastrophic to be digested with a haughty reference to political science texts on the logic of the plurality system.

In these situations it is never convenient to confront problems: it is much more comfortable to commit wholeheartedly to *the* problem. And what, for goodness sake, is the essential problem? But, television, of course. Better yet, the television *system*. And that's not all: TV's reactionary and manipulative essence. Norberto Bobbio, Giancarlo Bosetti, and Gianni Vattimo have condensed one of their conversations into a small volume enclosed in the magazine *Reset* (one of the fora of the Left) and the need is met. The title: *La sinistra nell'era del karaoke (The Left in the Karaoke Era).*[2]

The central point of this brochure, in which karaoke is hardly mentioned (it is only an image, a semantic synthesis describing a civilization dazed by television), there is a reflection by Bobbio that merits repeating here in its entirety.

> Berlusconi, making use of the impact of his economic power in all of Italy, has managed in three months to become the key-player in the elections—to win, and win hands down. If there exists today a government of the Right, it is because Berlusconi has managed to put together two voting blocks that might have seemed absolutely incompatible: the *Lega*, which wants the division of Italy, and the Fascists, who are ultra-nationalists. How has all this happened? I believe that television has been a determining factor, not in the sense that Berlusconi has appeared on the screen many more times than the others, but rather because the society created by television is a society by nature (*naturaliter*) on the Right. It is the society of the Festival of Sanremo, of sports, of ads, of Pippo Baudo, Mike Bongiorno, The Bold and the Beautiful, and the like. I say that it is a society on the Right by nature because its interests are not those of the Left; the Left exists on grand principles, it identifies itself with human suffering. Berlusconi did not win the election so much as win the society that his media empire and his advertising created. A society that enjoys seeing insipid little families gathered around a table glorifying this or that product. For this reason, I nurture great pessimism: in a society of this ilk, the Left, with its traditional values, hasn't a chance.

On the Right by nature. After that, good night. The only possible response could be withdrawal from all worldly things, retirement to monastic solitude, the foundation of communities closed to the world of mass civilization, in which it would probably be nice to use silver plows pulled by steaming bulls to forge furrows thoughtfully in the dark earth that promises honest harvests. And not to have to deal with that vulgar Berlusconi who won the election in spite of the natural cultural superiority of the Left.[3] All the more so since Berlusconi is surely vulgar (his "Notice that tonight we risk increasing our progeny," (*aumentare la prole*) directed at Bill Clinton on the *Notte della Luna* in the gardens of the Caserta Palace during the G7 summit in Naples was unforgettable), but he knows how to use the TV. And consequently, if the others don't want to use it, if they ban it, if they refuse it, fine—he will just go right on using it.

The Left, meanwhile, makes sure to show its hard face, and its hard line: without giving in and with a stringent chain of deductive reasoning. If television means Right, and karaoke means Fiorello—the chameleon-like and notably talented entertainer with the ponytail who fills the squares by getting amateurs to sing—then let's make war on Fiorello. They arrive at an exact, binding, implacable equivalence of Berlusconism with Fiorellism, that is, of the Right and entertainment. "Do not ever forget that the world is divided into the players and the instruments," and to confuse the roles is a reactionary plot. When a grand finale karaoke show was announced for Saturday September 3, 1994, at Rome's Church of San Giovanni in Laterano, the Progressive mayor of Rome, Francesco Rutelli, was imprudent enough to announce his participation in the singing party, and pandemonium immediately broke out. Never let it be said that the burning red heart of the capital, the piazza of May Day and site of the great workers' demonstrations, was handed over to the triumphal choruses of a show so objectively favorable to the government, the direct expression by nature of the *Forza Italia* compulsion to happiness.

Listening to the disapproving tones of Renato Nicolini, the ideologue on behalf of the Communist Refoundation's ephemeral past, we even suspect that the "progressive" horror for Fininvest-sponsored mass performances derives also, or rather above all, from the fact that Fiorello, in spite of the good taste and aesthetic sense of the Left is without a doubt a "popular" phenomenon.

And so we can easily imagine the intellectual disorientation of those who realize that the People love things that are not of the Left, or at least things that the Left has repudiated. Do they now want, as Brecht ironically remarked in the case of the workers who went on strike against socialism, to fire the People?

Already this need to reduce the opposition in order to exorcize it showed that the Left was in sad shape. The Left has been presented with two choices. On one hand, karaoke is an insignificant product of the show factory (as can legitimately be maintained), and so there is no reason to do battle with it, no reason why it must be transformed into an enemy, and the banner of the grand saint unfurled against it. Or on the other hand, Fiorello in effect represents something important and consistent beneath the sociological and social profile of the country, and it would be worthwhile to try to understand what lies behind the success of karaoke. Is it really just the manipulation of television, a trick for temporarily transforming the underlings into key-players, "the instruments into players"—the new opiate of the people, in which pop music rises to the rank of a new and vulgarized religion of the masses?[4]

Perhaps it would be better to keep the two sectors separate, to leave songs to the singers and politics to the politicians. Otherwise—thanks to this Marcusian-style conception in which, in the flight to the demonic logic of power, everything is a capitalist conspiracy—one loses all proportion and at the same time one is resigned to a vision of the world that replaces ethics with aesthetics and proposes a superficial disgust in the place of a rational form of political opposition. It is among the oldest of vices—a disdain for the physical ugliness of the governing class, for the hunchbacks and the potbellies, for Fanfani's stature and Andreotti's hunchback. The same vices are immediately reproduced with strict punctuality with regard to Berlusconi, guilty of blackening his thinning hair and of wearing shoes with lifts: a "bald" dwarf, the masses wrote on the posters in the great August demonstrations against the finance act. It was in those same demonstrations that Gianni Vattimo, a philosopher dedicated to studying Heidegger, protested against the Right by reciting rhyming verses ending in "Berlusconi" and "*coglioni*" (balls).

But in the case of the doctrinaire hate for karaoke there is also an additional factor. The insult of a political adversary is at least inscribed in the sphere of immediate political confrontation; but in railing against karaoke, the Left believes it is indirectly striking at the Center-Right. It attacks Fiorello with the intention of ruining Berlusconi: with the result of proposing by contrast a sullen and fussy image of itself, anything but sober and reasonable, anything but enlightened and liberal.

There is no reason, really, to think that karaoke can automatically convert refrains into votes, that is, to think that musical diversion is of the same essence as the Freedom Alliance and its ideology. It may be that Fiorello has disseminated models of entertainment, styles of behavior, illusions and dreams that the more thoughtful Left objectively judges to be integrated into a hedonistic-consumerist vision of the world. But if so, analogous models have always been proposed even at the *feste dell'Unità*, between the dances and the songs, without scandals and perhaps following precious meditations on popular music by progressive songwriters.

That the progressive mayor of Rome agreed to stand on Fiorello's stage, together with the tone-deaf Vittorio Sgarbi (who was there precisely out of hate for the Communist Refoundation), and sing "*Roma nun fa' la stupida stasera*" ("Rome don't be stupid tonight"), signaled neither a yielding to the Fininvest logic nor a betrayal of the Progressives who had voted him mayor.

The Masses, the Music, and the Audience

And in fact in a few months the karaoke craze evaporated practically into the nothing from which it had come, barely leaving a trace. Just replace Fiorello with Fiorellino and *voilà*, a new miracle, this time in reverse: the audience is reduced dramatically, the situation is no longer a situation, politics is no longer the issue. This fact, a "technical" rather than a political element, seems enough after all to show that the excited protests in Milan requesting that Cardinal Martini not concede the Piazza del Duomo to the new pagans of pop music, just like the hubbub against Rutelli in Rome, were much too obviously cynical.

The reason karaoke became a mass phenomenon, at least for a few months, remains to be explained. It is indeed difficult to explain the thousands of people—mothers, fathers and children, grandparents and grandchildren—who have crowded into the piazzas in small towns as well as in big cities. Be patient with the amateur singers, the "instruments" who have become for a few minutes "players": the possibility of appearing on TV is a sufficient reason to take on much more important challenges than the execution of "*Questo piccolo grande amore*"[5] and all the "classics" of popular Italian music of the last thirty years.

Instead it is the others, the spectators, who are more difficult to explain. To say that it is a province mirrored in itself is only a tautology. And it is not even particularly useful to consider karaoke on the same level as other fleeting fashions and mass phenomena like the hula-hoop in its day. If there is a real political dimension to karaoke singing, maybe it lies in that aspect of politics that has been waning in the last years, and that is public participation.

The fact is that, after the long sleep of the First Republic's finale, political re-mobilization has arrived indirectly. The principal factor of the end to political paralysis, the referendum campaign, entailed a certain amount of public involvement, but that involvement has been projected in large measure onto the electoral-institutional apparatus: that is to say, onto a "cold" element of politics. Later, the first plurality electoral campaign took place mostly on the television air waves, in the televised debates: that is to say, filtered by the cathode-ray tube, dispersed into the houses, atomized family by family.

It was necessary to await the great labor demonstrations of autumn to see an all but forgotten actor like the "masses." Before the political rediscovery of the piazzas, karaoke was the only instrument that made collective public presence possible. Closed-in places like stadiums for rock concerts and sports arenas are not fit for demonstrations of political import. In the open, without invitations, entrusted to the collective will alone is most appropriate.

Fiorello's Italy is not necessarily *Forza Italia*'s Italy. The karaoke audience is a rather indistinct social factor, probably more representative of the society as a whole than of any one segment in double breasted suits. And in effect we don't see double breasted suits in the public, nor on the extemporaneous singers who climb onto the stage and risk comparison with Jovanotti and Anna Oxa, with Zucchero Fornaciari and Eros Ramazzotti, with all the heroes of commercial music. Instead we see jackets and jeans, cheeks shaven clean or with a hint of beard à la Mickey Rourke, hair that is very short or very long, moussed or natural, tight-tight pants and micro-mini-skirts, styles akin to grunge, but also jackets befitting a bank teller. We see, that is, a catalogue of normal, everyday, Italian society.

Now, it is also possible that this undefined "mass" represents the best test of the propagation of Berlusconi's philosophy. It is possible, that is, that the karaoke audience can be identified with a condition of Italian society in which *Forza Italia*'s message is multiplied and intensified with a physiological naturalness. But it must be demonstrated that Berlusconi's proposed political model is perfectly aligned with the desires and the needs of the multitudes that sing in the piazzas. It is not at all certain that Fiorello's public appreciates the "good government," "moderation," and "good sense" on which Berlusconi has created his political program. If this public embodies manipulability in its pure state, that is true for everyone, not only for the Fininvest TV channels and the new political personnel recruited by Publitalia.

In its nascent state at least, *Forza Italia*'s program included a mobilization of the middle class that was not too different from neo-conservative efforts of the last ten to fifteen years in other advanced democracies. In spite of abundant nods in the centrists' direction, the intention was to promote radical political confrontation, which in the long run would have allowed an explicit rival dimension vis-a-vis of other sociopolitical sectors to emerge. Instead, the karaoke audience is to a large extent ideologically neutral. It replaces political participation with television participation, but that is it. One could consider it a sort of Lumpenproletariat of the cathode-ray era, but then it is easier to foresee that eventually this lost herd will split between a mythological adhesion to the man of providence on the Right, and adhesion to the provisions of the Left, to the most childish of revolutionary ideas, to the most ill-tempered antagonism; or maybe to a late demand for those processes and instruments of patron-client redistribution which were in force in Andreotti's Italy.

The proof a *contrario* of all this is offered by the authentically dizzying evolution of the Berlusconi movement and, symmetrically, the evolution of the Center-Right government in action. After a few scattered signals that were supposed to announce the start of deregulation, the Berlusconi government rapidly began to propose itself as a government for all (except the "Communists," of course). The objective was the extended identification of the electorate with the television audience. This naturally meant the abandonment of any sort of reformist intent. Moreover, as soon as the intensity of conflict was raised with the battle over pensions (which, not surprisingly, brings pensioners, a group that numbers among the most devoted television watchers, into the game), which promoted division based on interests rather than membership, the *Forza Italia* leader and the head of government chose to step back. And before that, during the tough debate over the Biondi decree, Berlusconi had to reverse himself in the face of a rebellion of public opinion. On that occasion *Il Cavaliere* also found himself before another great communicator, Antonio Di Pietro, who himself turned not so much to individual sectors of the community as to Italian society as a whole. In this case, Di Pietro's televised statement and the protest of the *Mani pulite* investigative team was performed to the tune of a folk song that was much tighter, more dramatic, and more incisive than Berlusconi's, and the opposition against the *salvaladri* ("thief-saving") decree became an extraordinary national karaoke.

With an approximate accuracy and some awkwardness, Berlusconi was playing by ear a ballad meant to sound "liberal." Di Pietro instead was giving voice to all the residual rancor against the thieves who wanted to be saved. Right away the victory in this operatic finale was one of good over evil, and the "people of the fax," probably not too different from Fiorello's people, decisively asserted themselves and won out. But the lesson to be learned was one of method more than of merit. It was clear that it would be no good to divide Italy in half with two different executions. Given a choice between a Vasco Rossi song and a Riccardo Cocciante song, the public would be more or less equally divided. Asked to choose between a neo-conservative political economy and a *solidarista* one, the country would make its choice based on relative interests.

What was needed was not karaoke singing, which, I repeat, is a fundamentally "democratic" activity, which one engages in voluntarily, where one votes without coercion on the basis of personal musical preferences and the ability of the amateur to play the singer on the stage. What was needed at that point was the invention and formation of another kind of karaoke, with only one singer and only one song. Berlusconi, who over the whole electoral campaign had accepted only one television face-off, with Achille Occhetto, for a while wanted no other rivals. All of his public performances, in Parliament and on television, were loose renditions without competition. The sense of it was: my performance is good, believe in me, trust me. If the orchestra is off-key, it is the players' fault. If the concert reviews are negative, it means that those who have not accepted defeat are plotting against me.

It was Berlusconi who bet that Italian society was rightist by nature: he takes his microphone in hand—the many microphones at his disposal

—and doesn't give up. He invents a song and sings it until he has convinced the majority of the public that his song is beautiful. The Progressives mistake the effect for the cause, the background for the main attraction. They criticize karaoke as an emblem of a civilization in the midst of collapse, as a creator of manipulated agreements, and they retire from the game, in a sort of council of wise men against the stupidity of the masses. They should say: oh no, dear pop singer, we want to climb onto the stage to sing our aria, too, so that the public can judge. Perhaps they would realize that the other singers are not particularly attractive and the other show might not be so great.

But instead they do nothing of the sort. Of course, they never miss the chance to condemn the singer; they criticize his inflection and his intonation, his repertory and his voice. But this they do from the sidelines, outside the boundaries of karaoke singing. And without climbing onto the stage, as they should instead insist on doing. So, "anything goes": the idea that someone is swimming against the current, that the government hasn't let it work, the tribal idea that there is a "Judas," a traitor, a thief (of votes), allied to government. Even the idea that the magistrates, who until a few weeks before had been included in the ranks of heroes, are in reality the artifices of a machination: Berlusconi impresses his own half-truths onto the imaginary collective, mixing in flashy and deliberate distortions of the truth itself. And his clan, the Previtis, the Ferraras, the Sgarbis, the Meluzzis, and the whole group sing in chorus with him. For lack of any other singers, the previously silent majority begins to croon along with *Il Cavaliere*, diligently following his warbling.

They Are Just Little Songs

If it were true that karaoke singing is an instrument being used to manipulate minds, it would be true of everything: television, newspapers, radio, film—true, that is to say, of all civilization of our century and of all that produces information and entertainment. There would be no other solution but moral revolt against modernity and the search for a rustic saint to institute a community of peaceable subversives, prepared, as they say, to witness in poverty against the world of Berlusconi and Fiorello. But insurrection in the name of ethics does not seem that meaningful or efficient on the political level. Against the patina of the soap operas, of the commercials, of the talk shows, of the more or less silly variety shows, against the hyper-reality of programs that transform the life lived into fiction and fiction into life experience, one at the very least has recourse to the "clicker." At the very most would be the introduction of a pedagogically minded television dictatorship. Between the two extremes one could also strive to begin to use television, rather than simply denouncing the use and manipulation of the audience.

But a discussion of the technical use of the means of communication would lead us away from the topic at hand. In the meantime it would be of some interest to understand that Italy is not made up only of universities and scholarly journals; and not only of residual party splinter groups and union organizers. Trying to understand the spectacle of karaoke means grasping the chance to observe Italian society: its tastes, its behaviors, its aspirations. That does not mean reproducing for the hundredth time the debate over the Left's aristocratic vice. More than elitism, in this case it is a lack of curiosity, a rigidity of analytical schemes, a certain interpretive fixation. Until relegated once and for all to the semi-clandestine zone of cultural artifacts, karaoke singing, with its rejoicing crowds, offered and perhaps still offers the possibility of casting a glance on Italian society as it really is, and not as one imagines it to be.

But is there anyone who has at least taken the trouble to observe how these Karaoke-singing Italians are dressed and made-up? And, having done that, has anyone found out what these Italians think? Or do we get along by talking yet again about the fragments of standardized society, molded by fashion, the reign of cultural amorphism, and conformism? Watching fifteen minutes of karaoke on Italia 1, one person might see only the power of television, but someone else could perceive a small segment and some symptoms of contemporary Italy. Televised karaoke singing is not an aquarium like Ambra Angiolini's show, *Non è la Rai*, the other mythological target of progressive disdain for television.[6] Crowding around the stage furnished by Italia 1 are thousands of today's Italians, not alien beings rendered light-headed by the atmosphere.

The alternative, after all, is rather simple. Either we live in a re-make of the *Planet of the Apes*, in which *homo televisivus* has taken the place of his authentically human predecessor on the evolutionary ladder (and in this case the die is cast: a growling audience of gorillas and chimpanzees have found in Berlusconi an incarnation of the ideal Ape, the primate "minister of science and defender of the faith," who breaks karaoke bread every day for his followers, who have been rendered dumb by the virtual reality of the videotape). Or instead, Italy descending into the piazza in search of a popular amusement may still be worthy of being fought over and politically sought after by the different political competitors. Even if the first hypothesis were true, we would still need to find a Charlton Heston able to contest the sacred gospels of the Fininvest religion and show that before there were apes there was humanity. But if the second hypothesis is the slightest bit possible, now surely is the time to take television into account, as a "falsehood-fest" (*fiera del falso*), a "hyper-realist machine." But deep down, as one might have said in the past, it may also be time to take the people into account as well.

Translated by Sara L. Brann

Notes

1. "The ad shot through the airwaves with its implicit roots in the reassuring, community-minded, domestic message of the old publicity 'Carousel.' Several decades later—almost the entire lifetime of the First Republic—the piazza/theater curtain was opening up again to the colors of the Fininvest look and to the urban spaces of an Italy of the Nineties." The quote is taken from Alberto Abruzzese, *Elogio del tempo nuovo. Perché Berlusconi ha vinto*, (Genova: Costa & Nolan, 1994), p. 24. Abruzzese's pamphlet, received with bitter criticism by the Left, is in reality one of the few "disenchanted" attempts to interpret the reasons behind Berlusconi's success: "The radicality of the changes could not be manifested without grand charismatic figures. Berlusconi is the one. And not without danger and risk to everyone. But this should not stop us from praising the new age. I do not know if we are living it, or if it awaits us. I believe rather that it has already happened and that it is up to us—friends and enemies—to be able to take advantage of its nature, to know how to discover its territories and travel them. I do not attribute salvational or liberational power to the expression *New Age*. I just believe that it represents a new dimension of the usual conflicts. A socio-anthropological, cognitive, imaginitive, practical dimension—radically different from the past. Through the media. Through Berlusconi" (p. 95).

2. N. Bobbio, G. Bosetti, G. Vattimo, "La sinistra nell'era del karaoke", ed. Francesco Erbani, supplement to number 6 (1994) of *Reset*.

3. Antonio Caronia writes: "The ex-president and owner of Fininvest would not be President today in the post-Christian Democrat era if his television stations had not represented, interpreted (and also contributed in building, it's true) a mentality that later at the election resulted in the majority, or at least determining... [the means of mass communication] register, amplify, and so contribute in building these mentalities, this implicit conceptual image, into which the political action and the search for public approval can be inserted. Berlusconi's television stations are limited to giving voice to the tendencies and processes already at work in the social fabric." Fine, except for the fact that if the society is naturally Berlusconian, that's not to say that it must automatically be Berlusconi who speaks for it, mobilizes it, and gathers its approval. Cf. "Comunicazione," in *La sinistra nel labirinto. Lessico per la seconda repubblica*, ed. Massimo Ilardi, Genova, Costa & Nolan, 1994, p. 28.

4. I happened to mention karaoke in an article on "popular" culture published in the volume edited by Saverio Vertone: *La cultura degli italiani*, (Bolo-

gna: Il Mulino, 1994). I conclude that, as for all forms of show business the success of karaoke can also be observed "from the inside," trying to distinguish and analyze styles and forms, without, that is, limiting oneself to an *a priori* rejection.

5. This historic hit by Claudio Baglioni, the leading singer in Italy for several decades, is cited here as an example of the music that is too successful and too popular to be taken seriously by the politically correct audience on the Left: because it contains something too "easy," perhaps even *interclassista* or vaguely Christian Democrat, in any case excessively unconcerned with the ever engaged inspiration of the most fashionable songwriters, like Fabrizio De Andrè or Francesco De Gregori.

6. Created by director Gianni Boncompagni, an old working companion of showman Renzo Arbore, *Non è la Rai* is shown every weekday on Fininvest's channel, Italia 1. It is a peculiar show in which young girls perform, and in which there exists no division of roles between the cast and the audience: the roles are interchangeable. By turns, at the direction of Ambra Angiolini (who herself is instructed over the radio by Boncompagni), the show's adolescents sing and dance, or applaud and act as chorus. In July 1994, 15,000 girls rushed to Rome to audition for the show's new cast. In an interview with Stefania Rossini for the weekly *L'Espresso* (July 22, 1994), Boncompagni affirmed that he had saved all the audition tapes: "Because I am sure that in twenty years they will be an historic document, a precious artifact." The director's eye finds a social and existential set of samples that is "disquieting": the aspiring actresses all seemed "cloned," "a swath of middle/low-brow culture," "all accessorized, done up in unlikely hair styles... wrapped in the smallest clothing. The more beautiful they were, the tighter their clothes were." On this topic cf. E. Berselli, "Gruppo di famiglia in televisione," *Il Mulino*, n. 4/1994, July-August, pp. 666 ff.

12

RAI and Fininvest in the Year of Berlusconi

Stephen Gundle

If the Italian "democratic revolution" of 1992-93 had proceeded in the way most observers expected, 1994 would have seen further steps towards the reform of public broadcasting. The groundwork also would have been laid for the revision of all legislation governing television and the press and preparatory work would have been initiated on anti-trust legislation designed to restore pluralism and competition to a commercial broadcasting sector that since the mid 1980s had been dominated by Silvio Berlusconi's Fininvest company. In fact events did not unfold in the expected way. Although there was continuing demand for revision of the discredited Mammì law of 1990, which had sanctioned and consolidated the RAI-Fininvest "duopoly" of the 1980s, Berlusconi's entry into politics at the end of 1993 and the victory of the right-wing coalition in the elections of March 27, 1994 rendered all previous plans for reform highly problematic. These developments ensured that, far from gradually being removed from the arena of political controversy, all matters concerning broadcasting and the media were thrust to the very forefront of national debate and were the subject of intense political conflict.

This chapter examines the continuing implementation of the 1993 mini-reform of RAI, the role of Fininvest in the political emergence of Berlusconi, the clash between the right-wing parliamentary majority that emerged from the March 1994 elections and the non-political board of RAI appointed under the Ciampi premiership, and the relationship between the Berlusconi government and the new board that was appointed following the resignation in July 1994 of the previous team. In the second part of the chapter four broader themes will be explored: the conflict of interest question raised by Berlusconi's assumption of office, debate on revision of the Mammì law and proposals for anti-trust legislation, the implications of the involvement of Fininvest and Berlusconi himself in the Milan magistrates anti-corruption investigations, and finally the dismantling of the team running the third RAI network, which from the late 1980s had been the most innovative and dynamic of all national television channels.

The "Mini-Reform" of RAI in Practice

The five members of the RAI board who were appointed in July 1993 by the presidents of the Chamber of Deputies and the Senate were given a very specific mandate.[1] Their task was to improve and reorganise a company that was close to bankruptcy and which had been gravely compromised by years of political colonisation (lottizzazione). Although internal reform was agreed by virtually all to be necessary, its precise interpretation was the subject of widespread interest and controversy. The board was subjected to relentless criticism and allegations of political bias even though all its members were respected professionals with no party affiliation. Particular suspicion emanated from longstanding RAI employees, and journalists first and foremost, who typically owed their positions to political sponsorship. Yet, despite the obvious difficulty of their position, the board members worked together harmoniously and sought to pursue their reforms in a consensual manner. The president, Claudio Demattè, provided leadership jointly with the director general, Gianni Locatelli, while Paolo Murialdi took responsibility for news and current affairs, Tullio Gregory for radio, Feliciano Benvenuti for legal and organisational questions and decentralisation, and Elvira Sellerio for programmes. Consultation with RAI staff was extensive. As the board members had no previous experience of the public broadcasting company, they sought to win the backing of existing employees rather than alienate them by drastically modifying established structures and practices. "We found ourselves faced with a great choice", Murialdi later said; "either to be confrontational or to try and avoid traumas.... We chose to operate by seeking as far as possible to avoid traumas...; there was to be no blood-letting" (Noi ci siamo trovati di fronte a una grande scelta - o andare contro o cercare di vedere di operare senza traumi... abbiamo scelto di operare cercando di evitare al massimo i traumi... evitando spargimenti di sangue).[2]

The overriding priority of the board was financial reorganisation. RAI was a company whose affairs were not conducted according to normal business criteria. It was used to virtually limitless financial resources, there was no system of cost accounting, no proper records were kept of the curricula of employees, and no incentives to productivity were built into salaries. For Demattè, a professor of business economics at Milan's Bocconi University, the main task was to graft on to RAI proper economic rules and new organisational methods. The head of personnel was replaced and new procedures adopted for managing staff, the measurement of productivity and proper budgeting methods were introduced.[3] Together with the more general attack on non-market privileges and wastage, these innovations were intended to establish proper controls and turn RAI from an indulgent "Mamma" ("Mamma RAI") into a more severe "Auntie" on the model of the BBC. All these measures were rendered necessary and urgent by the desperate state of RAI's balance sheet; without cuts the company's debt could have risen, Murialdi wrote in his diary, to 700 billion *lire*.[4] The situation of near bankruptcy forced Demattè and his colleagues to plead with the reluctant Ciampi government for a series of financial concessions and funds to recapitalise the company—which, after a considerable wrangle, were approved with the "save the RAI" decree of December 1993—that provided for a transfusion of 500 billion *lire*. However although this provided an important breath of air it also had the highly undesirable effect of making RAI once more dependent on the government, the very situation the mini-reform had been intended to terminate. Under Ciampi's mainly technical administration this was not a particular problem but after the March elections the consequences became all too apparent.

The second priority was political disinfestation. Under the *partitocrazia* that fell in the anti-corruption investigations in 1992-93, virtually all appointments within RAI were politically motivated. Moreover each of the three RAI networks was controlled by one of the main parties: RAI-1 by the Christian Democrats, RAI-2 by the Socialists and RAI-3, from the mid 1980s, by the Communists and their successors in the PDS. The task of the new board was to replace the old practice of *lottizzazione* with a notion of pluralism that allowed for a diversity of opinion on each network. All news programmes were expected to observe standards of objectivity that Demattè in particular associated with the BBC. By nominating respected, politically non-aligned professionals and drawing in one or two from outside RAI to head the networks and direct the news departments (such as Nadio Delai, director of the research organisation CENSIS at RAI-1 and Paolo Galimberti of *La Repubblica* at RAI-2 news), the board members took their biggest step in this direction. However, once again, this was merely the beginning of a process that would have taken several years to complete. A few, albeit important, changes at the top were insufficient to root out deeply ingrained practices.[5] To complicate matters, a series of local elections, as well as the general election in March 1994 and the European elections in June 1994 rendered depoliticisation difficult. After the victory of the Left in the local elections of November 1993, there was a marked shift towards the PDS, identified by journalists deprived of their conventional political reference points as the force most likely to dominate a renewed political system. Secondly, journalists aligned with the old parties, especially the Socialists, many of whom had been sidelined by Demattè and the new appointees, clubbed together in the "one hundred group" (*gruppo dei cento*), a splinter faction of the broadcasters' union USIGRAI that acted as a lobby group for their interests. To counteract the resurgence of bias, Demattè personally confronted presenters and journalists and publicly criticised programmes which were known for their strong political colouration.[6] He also proposed the institution of mechanisms of control during the general election campaign. Locatelli and Murialdi vetoed his idea of inviting a team of foreign journalists to maintain surveillance over RAI; instead a research team from the University of Pavia was appointed to monitor the coverage of both RAI and Fininvest channels.

Alongside urgent priorities were more strategic considerations. In essence the board aimed to reorganise RAI to render it more efficient and suited to a more diversified broadcasting context than had been the case in the past. One intention was to end the practice whereby the three RAI networks functioned to all intents and purposes as separate, competing companies, often producing quite similar products. To economise and respond to the perceived decline of "generalist" broadcasting, it was intended to differentiate the networks and turn them more into "channels" geared to different tastes and audiences. To a large degree this design succeeded in radio, where the directorates were unified under Livio Zanetti. In television though it broadly failed; as the coordinator of schedules, Franco Iseppi repeatedly encountered obstacles in his efforts to avoid counter-productive clashes and to shift successful programmes from one network to another.[7] The board also aimed to develop RAI's regional vocation, making better use of its numerous outposts in the provinces and to move towards a situation whereby drama (television films, mini-series and so on) was produced outside RAI either by independents or through the creation of consortia with commercial broadcasters.

Fininvest and Berlusconi

The attempt to remove RAI from political colonisation and controversy was seriously jeopardised by Berlusconi's entry into politics. Throughout the 1980s RAI not only competed with Berlusconi for ratings and advertising revenue (although a legally imposed ceiling on

RAI advertising meant that this was never an even contest); it had also fought a stern battle through the courts in an effort to prevent the emergence of national commercial networks (the Constitutional Court's ruling of 1976 only legalised local transmissions).[8] For his part Berlusconi had frequently criticised RAI and expressed his distaste for state broadcasting in any form. For both these reasons it was exceptionally difficult for RAI journalists and presenters to treat him and his movement in a balanced fashion. Indeed it was probably inevitable that benevolence was shown to his opponents, and especially the PDS, which made a point of defending public service television.[9] The problem of even-handedness was exacerbated by Berlusconi's refusal to put himself on the same plane as other politicians: he refused to participate in debates (save a one-off clash with the secretary of the PDS Occhetto, which was broadcast on his own flagship channel, Canale 5) shortly before the election and he disdained interviews unless they were with journalists of whom he approved.[10] Moreover, from the beginning of the campaign, Berlusconi and his allies attacked RAI as a fiefdom of the "communists" whom they identified as their main adversaries.

The political Left and Centre claimed from the outset that the main reason Berlusconi "took to the field"—to use his own soccer metaphor—was to save his own business empire.[11] The evidence suggests that concern over the future of his businesses was indeed a significant factor in Berlusconi's decision. Because signatures were already being collected in support of a referendum to abrogate key clauses of the Mammì law which had sanctioned his dominant position in the commercial broadcasting sector, and because further reform to broadcasting was scheduled for 1995, a victory for the Left would very probably have spelt the beginning of the end for Fininvest as it currently existed. Berlusconi depended upon a favourable political context because he owed his very existence as a national media entrepreneur to the politicians of the First Republic with whom he had established a relationship of complicity. Although the process of concentration which took place in the private television sector in the early 1980s was a genuine result of competition, it was only the absence of adequate regulation and the political protection of Craxi's Socialist Party that allowed him to establish and maintain a monopoly position.[12]

The crowning glory of Berlusconi's career as a lobbyist was passage of the Mammì law as this brought the long period of a-regulation to an end, not with the establishment of a legal and regulatory framework that limited concentration and guaranteed plu-ralism and competition in broadcasting and advertising, but rather with an *escamotage* designed to confirm the existing "duopoly" and prevent the formation of any future "third pole" in the broadcasting sector.[13]

The removal of Craxi and his other political protectors from the scene left Berlusconi in a vulnerable position. This vulnerability was underscored by the fragile state of the Fininvest company, which expanded rapidly in the 1980s on the basis of virtually unlimited bank loans. By late 1993 Fininvest's total debts were estimated to be 6,000 billion lire, although neither this figure nor the company's running losses were revealed in its formal accounts.[14] Two factors necessitated drastic action to redeem the company. First, the recession of the late 1980s and early 1990s caught it by surprise and hit the advertising revenues that were the company's lifeblood. Second, its largest creditors, the COMIT and CREDIT banks, were keen to put their affairs in order prior to undergoing privatisation. These pressures led to the appointment in October 1993 of Franco Tatò as managing director of Fininvest. An experienced trouble-shooter external to the closed circle of long-standing Berlusconi associates who dominated the group's senior management, Tatò was called in to restructure the company and save it from possible bankruptcy. Inevitably his appointment implied the end of Berlusconi's own business doctrine which was to expand at all times regardless of cost and the scale of the debts incurred. Tatò's first moves were to cut costs and to draw up plans for selling off parts of Fininvest and for floating the group on the stock exchange.

The Italian public displayed little interest in either Berlusconi's political connections with the fallen grandees of the First Republic or the perilous situation of his business empire. Unlike the institutional RAI channels, the Fininvest networks were not associated in the public mind with the political parties that had fallen into disgrace. And, in contrast to some of the top names in other leading Italian companies like Montedison and FIAT, Berlusconi remained personally untainted by anti-corruption investigations in the period prior to the March election.

Fininvest contributed to the launch and success of Berlusconi's political project in three main ways. First, the group provided the marketing know-how through its advertising arm Publitalia, whose personnel formed the organisational backbone of the movement. The three Fininvest networks (Canale 5, Rete 4, Italia 1) also provided channels of publicity and mobilisation especially in the period prior to the formal opening of the election campaign when the *Forza Italia* jingle and spot announcements were broadcast repeatedly. Second, they provided means of pressure and persuasion on the electorate of an explicitly political type. While the Canale 5 news broadcasts remained balanced, those of Rete 4 and Italia 1, whose audiences were comprised predominantly of housewives and young people, were geared quite explicitly to the priorities of the campaign. In addition Canale 5's chief editorial commentators, the former Communist Giuliano Ferrara and the art critic turned showman Vittorio Sgarbi, used their daily rubrics to reinforce the themes of the right while two brief programmes consisting of street interviews with apparently random passers-by (*Qui Italia* and *Luogo comune*, both of which were broadcast several times per day) provided limitless opportunities for soap box outbursts in favour of Berlusconi and against his adversaries. As a gesture to the need to preserve balance, Berlusconi's close associate Gianni Letta was given the task of guaranteeing the impartiality of Fininvest's channels during the election campaign; but this move was widely construed as a public relations exercise of no practical consequence. The third and most significant way in which the channels contributed to the election victory of the right was in creating a mood or structure of feeling that was the antithesis of the earnest and often polemical current affairs shows broadcast above all by RAI-3 (*Samarcanda* and its successor *Il rosso e il nero*, and *Milano, Italia*). These had attracted very high audiences in 1992-93 as the party system was collapsing. Programmes such *Non è la Rai* (singing and dancing adolescent girls) and *Karaoke* (singalongs in the public squares of the country's major cities), both flagship shows of the youth-oriented Italia 1 network, dovetailed with longstanding entertainment products that privileged escapism, individualism, optimism, family and conformism to reinforce an atmosphere of hostility to conventional politics of all types on which the right, and in particular *Forza Italia*, built.[15] In case anyone had failed to get the message, popular entertainment personalities including Mike Bongiorno, Raimondo Vianello and Iva Zanicchi appealed for a vote for Berlusconi in the course of their shows in the days prior to the poll.[16]

The Right in Office and the Conflict Over RAI

The anomaly of an immensely powerful businessman and media entrepreneur founding a political party and running for office gave rise to fears at home and abroad for the quality of Italian democracy. This concern was all the greater because Berlusconi's career as a media tycoon had been constructed in a situation that at best could be described as one of semi-legality and he was not reknowned for his sense of constitutional propriety. The debate over the potential conflicts of interest that he would face after becoming prime minister in May is examined in section five below. Suffice to say here that commentators expected that he would at least abstain from intervening directly in the affairs of RAI. Such hopes proved to be vain for reasons that were connected with the nature of the election campaign, the left bias that by all accounts marked the RAI networks, the financial situation of Fininvest, and the concern of *Forza Italia*'s right-wing allies to overcome their exclusion from the *lottizzazione* of the past and counterbalance to some degree the media resources of their partner.

The right coalition established its predominance in parliament by electing its representatives to the presidencies of the chambers and to the chairs of all the established committees including the RAI watchdog commission and the committee on culture. The former was headed by Marco Taradash, a member of Marco Pannella's "Reformist" group elected in the lists of *Forza Italia* who had a long history of opposition to public broadcasting, while the eccentric personality Vittorio Sgarbi became president of the latter. Taradash's first act was to denounce RAI to the magistrature for its record of *lottizzazione*, while his deputy, Francesco Storace of *Alleanza Nazionale*, repeated the campaign call for a purge of the "Communists" who conducted RAI's news and current affairs programmes.

The verbal assault on a series of named journalists was taken up by other right-wing politicians and supplemented by calls for the resignation of Demattè and his colleagues from the RAI board. In early June Berlusconi intervened personally to condemn the antipathy to the new government that allegedly emanated from RAI's news broadcasts and to castigate the company generally for being dependent on the public purse. His comments caused a storm of protest for they appeared to signal the start of an assault on public broadcasting.

Demattè responded by complaining to President Scalfaro about the continuing verbal attacks on RAI. He also publicly defended journalists who had been singled out for special attack and argued that overall RAI had achieved a fair balance in its output. Generally, Demattè and his colleagues believed that they could ride out the storm even though they did not react as expected to Berlusconi's private intimation that he could only defend them from the attacks of *Alleanza Nazionale* if they offered him "some cards" to play with.[17] In fact the reasons for wanting to oust them were sufficiently strong that it is doubtful whether they would have been allowed to stay in any circumstances other than the unlikely one of complete compliance.

Broadly, there were five reasons why the right majority was keen to oust them. First, they were not pliant appointees of the right itself. Second, like the Ciampi government against which the right had campaigned forcefully, they were broadly of a centre left extraction and were out of sympathy with the government.[18] Third, immense bitterness against RAI built up during the election campaign and fuelled demands for revenge. Fourth, the persistence of left Christian Democrats and sympathisers of the PDS in key positions within RAI led to charges that the old practices of *lottizzazione* had not been dismantled but merely modified. Fifth, their overall aim was to turn RAI into a more competitive and commercially dynamic company, something which, from the point of view of Fininvest and its allies, was to be avoided at all costs.

The final point requires some explanation. From the mid 1980s Berlusconi had been able to count on a sort of fifth column within RAI consisting mostly of the Socialists who conventionally filled the post of president and dominated RAI-2 as well as other internal structures and associated companies. These political appointees not only used the company to pursue the interests of their party but also on occasion to advantage Berlusconi to the detriment of RAI.[19] With the eclipse of the Socialists a more openly competitive situation came about which was potentially damaging to Fininvest. The drive to efficiency and rationalisation in RAI also contained risks. In the autumn of 1993 meetings took place between RAI and Fininvest, both companies with substantial financial problems, to establish ways of containing the costs of purchases and production to their mutual advantage. "To this proposal however was linked another: splitting the audience into equal shares of 45 percent on each side", Murialdi has written. "At that time, despite all its problems, RAI's total audience was slightly greater than that of Berlusconi's networks, and a single percentage point of audience share means around 20 billion *lire* of extra advertising revenue. It was clear what was being proposed".[20] The same proposal was advanced by Fininvest representatives after Berlusconi entered politics and again after he became prime minister.[21] On all occasions Demattè rejected the idea of a commercial truce that would have had the practical effect of artificially raising the cost of advertising and the more general consequence of breaking the spirit of the anti-trust law.[22] Fininvest also had reason to be displeased with the renewed dynamism of SIPRA, RAI's advertising collection agency, after the board reshaped its management. After only six months, revenues had increased by 7.5 percent despite a stagnant market, with the result that 60 billion *lire* was subtracted from commercial outlets.[23]

Despite the atmosphere of conflict, the board continued its work and produced a three year plan for the economic recovery of the company. However this plan and the "save the RAI" decree, which was represented at the end of April and placed before parliament in June, provided the government indirectly with the means to oust the board. Although the intervention of President Scalfaro prevented the government from adding a clause to the decree giving the Minister of Posts the right to dismiss the board in the event that he disapproved of the latter's plans for the company (the 1975 reform of RAI had transferred formal control from the executive to parliament), rejection of the plan had the effect of provoking the resignation of Demattè and his colleagues. Faced with a sharp frontal attack by the Minister of Posts, Giuseppe Tatarella, and the Minister for Relations with Parliament, Giuliano Ferrara, who contested

Demattè's figures and the depth of the proposed financial recovery, the RAI president sternly defended his plan before the parliamentary commission and in press interviews.[24] Although he personally was prepared to continue fighting, however, other members of the board including Murialdi felt that their position had become unsustainable.[25] This view prevailed and the members of the board resigned on June 30, just a year after their appointment.

Towards 'RAI-invest'? The Right Takes Control

The nomination of a new five person board was preceded by intense behind-the-scenes wrangling. Although Irene Pivetti of the Northern League and Carlo Scognamiglio of *Forza Italia*, the new presidents respectively of the Chamber of Deputies and the Senate, were supposed to act autonomously in making the appointments, members of the government, including Berlusconi himself, brought pressure to bear on them. This state of affairs was denounced on Canale 5 news by Pivetti, who sternly refused to be influenced.[26] Her veto ensured that the candidature of Giuseppe Malgara, president of UPA, the association of investors in advertising, which had been actively promoted by the prime minister, fell. In the end three board members (Letizia Moratti, an insurance broker who was subsequently chosen as president, Mauro Miccio, head of the ASCA news agency, and Ennio Presutti, president of the association of Lombard industrialists) were chosen by Scognamiglio acting in accord with government, while two (the medioeval historian Franco Cardini and Alfio Marchini, a young businessman with interests in construction and publishing) were the personal choices of Pivetti.[27] None of the board members had any previous experience of television or indeed a public or political profile; it was widely assumed, however, that all save Marchini felt an affinity to the political right.

The first and arguably the only clear indication of policy given by Moratti was her declaration to the parliamentary watchdog commission that RAI, currently the competitor of Fininvest, should, in time, become complementary to it.[28] This remark caused a storm of protest since it implied a reduction in RAI's role and Moratti was obliged to recant. However the atmosphere remained charged and there was scarcely a day between July and November when the activities or pronouncements of members of the RAI board did not feature prominently in the press. The main controversy related not to fundamental issues of organisation, programmes and strategic innovation but to the nominations to key managerial and editorial positions. This emphasis reflected the renewed politicisation of RAI in the election and post-election period.

It was widely expected that the new board would seek to set its stamp on the company by dismissing many of the network directors and other officers appointed in 1993. This expectation was promptly fulfilled. Gianni Locatelli was replaced as director general by Gianni Billia of the Finance Ministry, a manager with a reputation for successful organisational innovation. In September the directors of the three networks and the heads of the news departments were dismissed *en bloc* along with the chiefs of all the main RAI departments. It was announced that their replacements as network directors would be, at RAI-1, Brando Giordani, a journalist and producer, at RAI-2, Franco Iseppi, another producer, and, at RAI-3, the journalist and broadcaster Sergio Zavoli. The following were appointed as directors of the respective news departments: Carlo Rossella of the news magazine *Panorama*, Clemente Mimun, the deputy director of Canale 5 news, and Daniela Brancati, director of news at the pop music channel Videomusic. Piero Vigorelli, Paolo Francia, Claudio Angelini and Giorgio Tosatti were given responsibilty for RAI's regional network, the radio network, radio news and sport.

The polemics to which these appointments gave rise centred on four separate but interconnected issues: the rough treatment accorded to their predecessors (dismissals were communicated by fax), virtually all of whom were respected and were widely thought to have performed well, the professional "level" of their replacements, the association of several appointees with Fininvest, and the political links of some with *Forza Italia* and *Alleanza Nazionale* and, in the recent past, with the Socialist Party. The most uncharitable argued that RAI had been consigned lock, stock and barrel to Berlusconi and Fini with the insertion in key posts of journalists from the Fininvest-Mondadori stable (Rossella, Mimun, Tosatti), from the MSI (Francia) and from Craxi's former circle (Vigorelli).[29] By most accounts a sort of re-politicisation had occurred in which the distinctiveness of RAI with respect to Fininvest was eroded and the two companies were, on a notional level, merged. This view appeared to be confirmed when *La Stampa* reported that Berlusconi's chief collaborator on questions concerning RAI, the former television journalist and *Forza Italia* deputy Fabrizio Del Noce, had claimed that his party had succeeded in securing posts for four out of five of its desired nominees.[30] On this basis the opposition called for the resignation of the board while USIGRAI proclaimed a strike in protest at the method and the substance of the nominations.

The loudest protests emanated neither from the opposition parties nor from within RAI but from the Northern League. Although it was the largest of the right-wing parties sustaining the government, the League obtained nothing from the round of appointments. There were two reasons for this. First, in government Berlusconi preferred to sideline the League as far as possible in favour of a privileged axis with the more dependable AN. Second, because Pivetti did not follow League indications in appointing board members, the party had no direct means of making its voice heard in RAI's decision-making councils. Bossi vented his fury by threatening an anti-trust law that would force Berlusconi to give up his networks; he also spoke of sabotaging the "save the RAI" decree. He claimed the League had no interest in the spoils system but only in ensuring acceptance of a "federalist" approach in broadcasting; this was the basis on which the *lottizzazione* of others was condemned. In fact the League was not so high-minded. When several of the original nominees opted not to accept their designated posts (Zavoli, Tosatti and a number of those offered minor positions), a reshuffle occurred that resulted in Gabriele La Porta, a journalist viewed with favour by the League, being appointed to direct RAI-2 in place of Iseppi, who preferred not to accept the alternative post in RAI-3 that was offered to him.

In the reshuffle two new posts were created, directors for the late evening slots on RAI-2 and RAI-3, which were entrusted respectively to two journalists closely associated with each network: Giovanni Minoli and Michele Santoro. In addition Luigi Locatelli, a former director of RAI-2, was appointed to head RAI-3 in place of Zavoli. Moratti evidently hoped that by introducing these corrections, the anger of various political forces and broadcasters would diminish. In fact this did not occur. First, the League was scarcely assuaged. It used its influence in parliament, where it joined with the opposition in the watchdog commission to reject the editorial plan that Moratti presented in early October and, by its strategic absence, ensured that a vote of censure was passed on the board in the Senate in early November. Second, the adjustments antagonised media professionals for they betrayed a lack of both resolution and strategic vision (Minoli, for example, was initially sacked as director of RAI-2 and then described as essential to the network when he was offered the joint directorship). Finally the appointment of Luigi Locatelli was seen as a death blow to the unconventional and creative spirit of RAI-3. As a response the veteran journalist Enzo Biagi and the writer and academic Umberto Eco circulated a petition to the head of state among Italian intellectuals in which they called for action to defend RAI from the attack that was being launched on it from inside and outside the company.[31]

At no point did the RAI board acquire the authority and serenity that were necessary for it to be able to function properly. The responsibility for this situation lay squarely with Moratti. Unlike Demattè, she neither formed a close working relationship with her director general (Billia was in fact ousted in early November allegedly for excessive "company loyalism" and appointed, courtesy of the government, to the presidency of the pensions agency INPS)[32] nor did she adopt a collegial approach in her relations with fellow board members. Responsibilities were not shared out as they had been previously and there was so little consultation over the nominations that Cardini and Marchini in fact voted against them. Unease over Moratti's dictatorial style reached a high point in mid-November, when Marchini resigned and Cardini and Presutti were reported to be thinking of following suit.[33]

Two issues concerning the Moratti board remain to be addressed. Did it proceed with or abandon the organisational reforms and rationalisation of the Demattè administration? How far was the board in fact a pliant servant of the government? The first question can be answered relatively simply. The internal reforms set in place by Demattè remained in force and some additional cost-cutting measures were applied. However in general the urgent prioritisation of financial questions and business efficiency that marked the previous administration was displaced by an emphasis on political questions and specifically on the allocation of posts. The "industrial plan" presented by Moratti in mid-October, which, in contrast to Demattè's was accepted immediately by Tatarella, represented an implausibly optimistic picture of a short-order return to fiscal rectitude. It was pledged to eliminate RAI's debts, pay back the recapitalisation funds of the "save the RAI" decree, raise advertising income and increase investment—all by 1996. The main sacrifices were to be 3,000 voluntary redundancies and sale of some of the company's assets, including possibly its headquarters in Rome's Viale Mazzini. While press comment was sceptical, the response of television journalists was to proclaim a one day strike.

The second question is more complex. In essence it may be said that the new council, and especially Moratti and her close ally Miccio, were dependent on the government because they were weak and out of their depth, they lacked support inside and outside RAI, they had no clear vision or purpose of their own, and they were divided between themselves. In consequence they were not well-positioned to assert or defend the autonomy of decision which the law accorded them. But this does not mean that the board was the best servant that *Forza Italia* and AN could have hoped for. A series of gaffes and highly public divisions brought discredit not only to Moratti but also to those who sustained her in her post. Moreover her lack of attention to fundamental broadcasting policies and programmes confirmed the impression of the right's adversaries that the latter's primary concern was to undermine or dismantle RAI. There were two further complaints. First, news and current affairs were not brought to heel as firmly as was desired. Press commentators noted that a big change of tone occurred in the news programmes of RAI-1 and RAI-2 under their new editors. The amount of attention dedicated to politics, and therefore, in the climate of the Autumn and Winter of 1994, to the unease of the League and social discontent, was greatly scaled down in favour of increased coverage of human interest stories (*cronaca*) and the entertainment world. It became customary once again, as it had been before 1975, for the views of figures of authority to be reported without seeking alternative opinion. Moreover Berlusconi was personally accorded much coverage. However the situation was by no means perfect. Several anti-governmental journalists and presenters remained at their posts and the news output of the third network remained firmly anti-governmental. Particular consternation was caused in the right-wing majority by the several hours of live coverage that the network gave on November 14 to the massive union-sponsored protest demonstration in Rome against the government's proposed cutbacks to pensions and health care. Even the first two networks were criticised for giving inadequate attention to the much smaller demonstrations which took place the following month in support of the government.

Some, if not all, members of the majority were also disturbed by the way that Moratti was quite happy to bring once more to the fore personalities who had been marginalised under Demattè on account of their close links with the Socialist Party. Vigorelli was one such person; another was Giuliana Del Bufalo, a former deputy editor of RAI-2 news and chief organiser of the "100 group" who became Moratti's personal adviser. For the League, but also for Taradash and Storace, the presence of these individuals signalled a regrettable restoration, an inability to break with the personnel as well as the practices of the old regime.[34] It may be said that this situation was the direct outgrowth of the need of the board, and especially Moratti, to find allies within RAI at a time when a majority of the staff was hostile to them.

There are four broader issues which require treatment in order to complete the analysis of the broadcasting sector. These are: the conflict of interest question arising from Berlusconi's political role, debate over a possible anti-trust law and reform of the Mammì law, the involvement of Fininvest in the anti-corruption investigations, and the moves towards "normalisation" of RAI-3.

The "Conflict-of-Interest Issue"

Berlusconi's entry into politics gave rise to opposition for two reasons. First, there was concern that his assumption of a political role would distort the democratic process since he commanded massive media resources that were not available to the other contenders for power. This issue has been dealt with above in section two and will be considered further in section six. The second reason was the fear that, should he assume office, he would face conflicts of interest because he would continually be called upon to take decisions on issues and formulate policies in areas affecting his business interests. This matter was not at all an easy one to solve for there was no constitutional provision for such eventualities and, unlike the US, Germany, Spain and a number of other countries, there was no legislation setting down clear procedures either.

Berlusconi himself did not appear to regard the issue as one of importance. His whole career as a businessman bore witness to his disregard for formal rules and proprieties. Most recently this was demonstrated by the way he intervened heavy-handedly to force the resignation of the founding editor of *Il Giornale*, Indro Montanelli, when the latter refused to back his entry into politics.[35] Suggestions that pluralism was threatened by his control over commercial television and potential influence over RAI were dismissed by reference to the pluralism that allegedly existed within Fininvest and Mondadori, between its different news programmes and magazines. Berlusconi claimed that he could be trusted not to confuse personal and public interests, but on other occasions it was clear that he saw a perfect compatibility between his own business interests and the good of the collectivity.

In response to public criticism, Berlusconi made two concessions which he considered to be gestures of magnanimity, generous nods to the formalities of the political game. In January he announced his resignation as president of his company and the appointment in his place of his long-standing friend and collaborator, Fedele Confalonieri. Then in May, on being appointed prime minister, he pledged to President Scalfaro to appoint a commission of "wise men" to study possible ways whereby his detachment from the management of Fininvest could be made even clearer. In the event neither the solution that Antonio La Pergola, Agostino Gambino and Giorgio Crisci announced in September nor the one Berlusconi himself proposed at the end of July was deemed by commentators and jurists to be satisfactory. The prime minister's solution was an "Italian-style blind trust" which would have involved the appointment of a commission by the President jointly with the presidents of the chambers of parliament to superintend the management of the Fininvest group during Berlusconi's term of office. This plan was rejected by Scalfaro on the grounds that there was no provision in the Constitution for him to play such a role. It also failed to address the key question since Fininvest would still have belonged to Berlusconi and therefore could be favoured by him. It did not seem to be appreciated that in the United States, where notion of the blind trust originated, it refers to property and share holdings not operative companies. The problem was not solved either by Berlusconi's "wise men", who conveniently concluded that the management of the company should be put in the hands of a trustee to be nominated by Berlusconi himself and approved by Parliament.

Although it was announced that the government would present a bill to turn the latter proposal into law, dissatisfaction probably contributed to Berlusconi suddenly announcing in November that he had decided to sell all his business holdings. Ostensibly this was exactly what his critics had been demanding, but there were doubts as to whether he meant it and the extent to which such a procedure was praticable given the size and complexity of an empire that was the third largest industrial group in the country. It was estimated that it could take two years merely to compile an inventory and even then the value of parts of the empire, including the TV networks, was dependent upon clarification of the legislative situation.[36] For some this whole idea was a bluff or a strategy to gain time and put off the evil day. What was not pointed out was that this declaration allowed Berlusconi to present as a token of his good intentions the sale of parts of his group, such as the distribution company Euromercato, which Tatò was planning to sell off anyway as part of his drastic restructuring of Fininvest. Many of Berlusconi's opponents remained firmly convinced that the only way to overcome the anomaly was for the prime minister to be ousted from office.

Overall what was striking was the extent to which Berlusconi was able to retain control of all decisions concerning an issue that was precisely a conflict of interest. By the time he was constrained to resign, nothing of substance had been achieved in this crucial area. Perhaps more than anything else this demonstrated the gravity of the lacuna in Italian legislation.

Anti-Trust Legislation and Revision of the Mammì Law

Even before it was passed in 1990 the Mammì law gave rise to unusual controversy. It was the outcome of an immensely long deliberative process and its passage provoked the resignation from government of all ministers belonging to the DC's left-wing faction, which had historically been most attached to RAI and hostile to Berlusconi. However only following the *tangentopoli* scandal, the fall of the parties and the poltical rise of Berlusconi was the question treated with the urgency.

For the League the issue was at first a tactical one, a question that it brought up whenever it felt it needed to gain leverage or to render Berlusconi more compliant. It was dropped whenever concessions were obtained. By the autumn though Bossi shared with the PPI and the PDS the view that measures were needed to combat the risks of a televisual dictatorship. All three parties formulated draft bills that differed significantly on specific matters but which nonetheless had certain points in common. These included measures to limit concentration in the television sector, restricting ownership to one network, and to guarantee competition within the advertising market and pluralism in news and information. They all also agreed on the need to redefine public service television and reduce the number of RAI channels. The likelihood of these being turned into law depended on the degree to which the three parties succeeded in coordinating their actions after the League withdrew its support from Berlusconi and provoked the fall of his administration.

Two further factors rendered the question of an overall redefinition of regulation of the broadcasting sector urgent. The first of these was the prospect of a series of referenda for which the promoters were gathering signatures. Mario Segni, the PDS and others campaigning for the abrogation of specific clauses of the Mammì law received the go-ahead for the collection of signatures from the Court of Cassation in July. However parallel to this was the campaign of the Radicals for a referendum to abolish advertising on RAI networks. Whereas the first was directed against Berlusconi, the second was a direct threat to the public broadcasting company. Although there was some talk of the promoters of the two sets of referenda reaching an accord, the diversity of their proposals revealed just how polarised the debate over the future shape of television had become.

The second factor concerned the abrogation by the Constitutional Court in December of the key section of Mammì, that dealing with the assignment of frequencies to private broadcasters. Invited by the administrative court (TAR) of the Lazio region to rule whether the allocation of frequencies broke the constitutional clauses which guaranteed the equality of all citizens and on freedom of expression and freedom of economic initiative, the Court ruled that it did. The case was brought by a range of small broadcasting companies—Videomusic, Tele Monte-Carlo, Elefante TV—which had always been Fininvest's most determined opponents; they argued that the law favoured Fininvest. The Court decided that Mammì had sanctioned the prior formation of a dominant position in the sector by setting the upper limit at 25 percent or three networks, a stipulation that was less rigorous than that adopted for the press, where the ceiling was 20 percent. In this sense parliament had failed to guarantee pluralism and prevented new entrants into the field.[37] The Court ruled that no one should be allowed to hold more than two networks. To avoid chaos in the sector the Court ruled that the existing law could remain in force until the end of 1996, longer than the deadline of 1995 by which parliament was obliged under the RAI mini-reform to approve new legislation. The Court's ruling effectively sounded the death knell for Fininvest's monopoly, but given the turbulent political situation in the country it should not be assumed that deadlines for legislation will necessarily be respected. Further developments on this question above all are related to broader political developments.

Fininvest and the Anti-Corruption Investigations

On November 21 Berlusconi received three notifications from the Milan magistrates that he had been placed under investigation and would be required to appear before them to undergo questioning. This event, Berlusconi's subsequent seven hour interrogation three weeks later, and his stubborn refusal to resign attracted massive coverage in the domestic and foreign media. For the first time since the *Mani pulite* investigations began in February 1992, a serving prime minister was drawn into the anti-corruption inquiry. That it was Berlusconi was especially shocking because it dramatically undermined his claim to be a new man, untainted with the past, capable of leading the Italians to a new and prosperous and corruption-free future. This claim had been central to his appeal in March 1994.

The notifications were delivered to the Prime Minister in connection with an on-going investigation into corruption within Milan's financial police but they could equally have arisen in connection with any one of the several investigations that were going on into various aspects of Fininvest's business operations. These began in 1993 and resulted in the course of 1994 in the incrimination of several senior officials of the group, including the head of Publitalia, Marcello Dell'Utri, on a charge of false accounting. So numerous and diverse were the various investigations that government figures, many of them former Fininvest employees or associates of Berlusconi, vigorously denounced the magistrature for conspiring to bring down the Prime Minister. Berlusconi himself did not refrain from advancing this argument, while Confalonieri remarked, in singularly poor taste, that he and his colleagues were being "persecuted like the Jews".[38] It is quite possible that company interests informed the timing and content of the government's ill-fated decree in July that was designed to end preventive detention for bribery related offences. This is so because it was issued just prior to the arrest of Berlusconi's younger brother, Paolo, on charges of corruption.

The main question for the investigating magistrates was whether Berlusconi was aware of the bribes that were paid by Finivest's financial director to the financial police between 1989 and 1991. The Prime Minister responded that he did not know and that in any case the payments did not constitute bribes but extortion on the part of the police.[39] However this question led to others concerning the reasons for the payments that led the magistrates to look at the origins and control of three subscription TV channels in which Berlusconi had an interest. An additional issue revolved around the nature and possible legal implications of the offers which Berlusconi was alleged to have made to the RAI board and director general at the time of Demattè and Locatelli for a mutually convenient division of audiences and advertising revenues.

Potentially the most damaging issue for Berlusconi was the investigation into the three Tele + channels in order to discover who the real proprietors were. The investigations were still going on at the end of the year, but if it should be found that Berlusconi owns more than 10 percent of them (the maximum limit for those who own a network permitted to broadcast via the airwaves) it would have grave consequences because the statutory penalty is revocation of permission to broadcast.

The Dismantling of RAI-3

One of the central developments of the whole period was the dismantling of the team that since 1987 had turned the third RAI network into the most creative and original in the whole of Italian television and the alteration in the status of the network. Assigned to the Communists in the middle of the decade in order to ensure their complicity in the wider share out of posts and channels within public broadcasting, RAI-3 had been a little-watched channel with few resources whose signal did not even cover the whole country. From the appointment of literary critic Angelo Guglielmi as director in 1987, the network reinvented itself and became a supplier of new and innovative broadcasts especially in the area of current affairs and "reality television" (court cases, missing persons etc.). Under Sandro Curzi, also appointed in 1987, the news programmes of the network took a pro-Communist (and later PDS) line as a typical product of the spoils system but they also sought to break free of the predominantly institutional style of reporting to give voice to previously excluded social and political actors.[40]

With its unconventional and often polemical programmes, RAI-3 acted in a crucial role between 1990 and 1993 in shaping public opinion in a way that was hostile to the dominant parties. As such it aroused the hostility of those in power within RAI and their party sponsors who tried on numerous occasions but ultimately failed to suppress key programmes and remove the network's managers. With the fall of the parties, RAI-3's staff felt vindicated but in 1993-94 they faced further and more successful attempts to downgrade and change the orientation of the network.

Demattè and his colleagues confirmed Guglielmi in his post in recognition of the quality of the network's programmes but they insisted that Curzi resign like the other news editors. As they saw it a pro-Left TG3 only made sense when the old TG1 and 2 were biased towards the DC and PSI. They were determined to remove the "party imprinting" (*impronta di partito*) from news, stop TG3 being a "party bulletin" (*bollettino di partito*) and generally combat polemical television in name of a more detached BBC-style ideal.[41] In June 1994, as virtually their last act, they vetoed Guglielmi's schedules and insisted that the third network should not compete with RAI-1 and 2 by offering a late evening news show but instead should offer a regionally oriented product. On this point Sellerio resigned in protest.

Under Moratti the changes to news were less brutal than had been feared but overall the process of "normalisation" was unambiguous. The most significant move was undoubtedly the ousting of Guglielmi, the channel's founder and inventor. This was an unequivocal sign of change. His nominated replacement Sergio Zavoli was a company loyalist (and former RAI president) but an exponent of an utterly orderly and conventional televison, as was the eventual director, Locatelli, also a Socialist. This move was reinforced by the design, presented in the editorial plan that was rejected by the watchdog commission, which envisaged the third network as a channel mainly for women and children.[42] Although the channel's schedules for the autumn-winter 1994/95 bore signs of continuity it was widely expected that some celebrated shows would be dropped before long and that all rough edges would soon be smoothed. RAI-3's editors, journalists and presenters did not respond to the challenge passively. A sustained campaign was waged against the "suppression" and "dismemberment" of the network. Stern resistance however was unlikely to result in anything other than a slower, more protracted modification of RAI-3's rebellious profile.

Conclusion

It is too soon to say whether the reform of public broadcasting was interrupted temporarily in 1994 or whether the board headed by Demattè was merely a brief interruption in a long and continuing history of political control of state broadcasting. Those who believe in the merits of public service television clearly hope that reform will continue. Crippled by debt, years of mismanagement, subservience to outside interests, stalled production and a destructive ratings war that had lowered the quality of its output, by 1993 RAI had lost its sense of purpose and was widely held in disrepute. It had no strategy and was ill-placed to respond to innovations in communications technology, broadcasting practices and audience demands. There was some sign that old problems were being overcome and that consideration was being given to new challenges, but the overwhelming attention that was devoted in the second half of 1994 to operative appointments within the company offered an illistration of the extent to which RAI is still regarded as a terrain of conquest. The nature of the appointments moreover raised the question of how far the new masters of RAI were committed to a dynamic future for the company.

If on balance 1994 was an unhappy year for RAI, it was ostensibly a triumphant one for Fininvest. The election of Berlusconi offered proof that its networks, unlike those of RAI, held the trust of Italians and had a purchase on their collective and individual aspirations. But in other respects the picture was less rosy. Regardless of any regulatory framework, the commercial survival of the Fininvest group was dependent upon the extent to which an outside manager would succeed in reversing the headlong expansion of the preceding period and implementing wholesale retrenchment. Moreover Forza Italia's electoral success was insufficient to forestall the demand for strict anti-monopoly legislation in the media sector. The ruling of the Constitutional Court in effect placed Fininvest in a situation of illegality while Berlusconi's high profile role fuelled fear and envy that extended even to his own alliance and ultimately contributed to his resignation. If the issue of anti-trust legislation had become topical earlier, Berlusconi's rise to power and the record of his government ensured that it rose to the very top of the political agenda. Whether legislation is finally implemented or not will depend ultimately on the unity of Berlusconi's adversaries, their determination and whether they succeed in the difficult task of mobilising public opinion on an issue that failed to rouse any passion in the March 1994 election campaign.

Notes

1. For details, see G. Mazzoleni,"RAI tra riforma e ristrutturazione", in C. Mershon and G. Pasquino (eds.), *Politica in Italia*, (Bologna: Il Mulino 1994).

2. Interview with Paolo Murialdi, September 20, 1994.

3. Ibid.

4. P. Murialdi, *Maledetti "professori": diario di un anno alla Rai*, (Milan: Rizzoli, 1994), p. 67.

5. Murialdi reports that Gianni Pasquarelli, RAI director-general until 1992, told him that *lottizzazione* was "in the blood" of RAI. "I fear it is true", was his diary annotation. See *Maledetti "professori"*, p. 11 (*ce l'ha nel sangue; temo che sia vero*).

6. Interview with the author, September 20, 1994.

7. Murialdi, *Maledetti "professori"*, p. 137.

8. On the battles between RAI and Berlusconi in the 1980s, see G. Ruggeri and M. Guarino, *Berlusconi: inchiesta sul signor TV*, (Rome: Editori Riuniti 1987), chapters X and XI.

9. Murialdi, *Maledetti "professori"*, pp. 98-99.

10. Carlo Freccero, formerly the director of programmes at Fininvest, argued that Berlusconi's communication strategy was to present himself to Italians as though he was already their president. See "Il presidente virtuale", *Micromega*, 2, 1994.

11. This was not of course the justification that Berlusconi offered the Italian people, to whom he supplied a more general explanation cast in terms of the need to preserve business freedom from an illiberal and "state-loving" left. However the point was readily conceded in an interview with an American magazine. See Judy Bachrach, "Arrivederci Berlusconi?", *Vanity Fair*, January 1995, p. 80.

12. Berlusconi's Canale 5 began broadcasting in 1979; in 1982 he acquired Italia 1 from Rusconi and in 1984 Rete 4 from Mondadori. On Berlusconi's political connections, see Ruggeri and Guarino, *Berlusconi*, chapter IX and P. Martini, "Molti affari, molta politica: nei rapporti con i partiti il lato forte di Berlusconi", *Problemi dell'informazione*, 4, 1990, 513-27.

13. F. Monteleone, *Storia della radio e della televisione in Italia*, (Venice: Marsilio 1992), p. 469.

14. *L'Espresso*, October 17, 1993, p. 40. See also the issue of October 10, 1993, pp. 168-73.

15. For a fuller discussion of this and other aspects of the role of the media in the period between 1989 and 1994, see S. Gundle and N. O'Sullivan, "The Mass Media and the Political Crisis" in S. Gundle and S. Parker (eds.), *The New Italian Republic: from the Fall of the Berlin Wall to the Rise of Berlusconi* (London: Routledge, 1995). On the contribution of Berlusconi to Italian modernisation in the 1980s, see S. Gundle, *I comunisti italiani fra Hollywood e Mosca: la sfida della cultura di massa 1943-1991* (Florence: Giunti, 1995), chapter six.

16. In December 1994 the five hundred million Lira fine which the press and media ombudsman levied on Fininvest for a series of grave breaches of the rules governing the behaviour of television during election campaigns was confirmed on appeal by the Pretore of Milan. See *La Repubblica*, December 7, 1994, p. 13. Among the episodes cited were the appeals of Bongiorno and company and the appearance of Berlusconi on two sports programmes.

17. Berlusconi had a brief conversation with Demattè and the director general Locatelli on June 10, when he arrived at Saxa Rubra to record the prime minister's traditional address to the country prior to the European elections. Murialdi was informed of the conversation and wrote in his diary that "the first cards he would like to receive, we think, are Deaglio's head and softer news

broadcasts" (le prime carte che gradirebbe, pensiamo, sarebbero la testa di Deaglio e Tg morbidi), *Maledetti "professori"*, p. 155.

18.In particular Murialdi, a former partisan, doubted whether he would be able to work with the Alleanza Nazionale Minister of Posts, Giuseppe Tatarella.

19.See Ruggeri and Guarini, *Berlusconi*, chapter XI.

20.Murialdi, *Maledetti "professori"*, p. 178.

21.Ibid., p. 173.

22.Interview with Dematte.

23.Ousted from his post at RAI, the former head of SIPRA immediately was appointed second in command at Publitalia. Demattè described this situation to me as "highly suspicious" (*più che sospetta*).

24.Ferrara's critique, it transpired several days later, was based on a Fininvest critique of Demattè's plan. This document was reproduced in *L'Espresso*, July 15, 1994, pp. 16-22. For the right's view of the record of the Demattè board and its resignation, see *Panorama*, July 9, 1994, pp. 18-21. Included in these pages is an interview with Ferrara.

25.Demattè told me that he was perfectly prepared to stay but that for other board members it had become "unbearable to be in the firing line" (*insopportabile stare sotto il fuoco*).

26.*La Repubblica*, July 10, 1994, p. 11.

27.Cardini was chosen by the President of the Chamber because, like her, he was "Catholic, conservative and federalist", *La Repubblica*, July 9, 1994, p. 7. It was less clear why Marchini, whose grandfather was a well-known Communist businessman, encountered her favours. Three explanations were advanced in the press: first, that both were young (Pivetti is 31 and Marchini 29), second, that their families were acquainted and, third, that Marchini was mistakenly assumed to be a Catholic conservative because in 1993 he had attempted to save the weekly *Il Sabato* from liquidation. It is possible though that Pivetti was aware that he was not aligned with the parties of government and appointed him to preserve balance.

28.*La Repubblica*, July 22, 1994, p. 17.

29.Giampaolo Pansa produced the most vitriolic attack on the nominations in *L'Espresso*, September 30, 1994, pp. 32-35.

30.*La Stampa*, September 19, 1994, p. 3.

31.*La Repubblica*, November 1, 1994.

32.This "promotion" was later deferred until the end of the year.

33.*La Repubblica*, November 14, 1994, p. 5.

34.*La Repubblica*, September 19, 1994, p. 4 and September 20, 1994, p. 6.

35.Berlusconi had formally divested himself of ownership of the paper—by selling it to his brother—in deference to the clause of the Mammì law which barred owners of more than two television networks from also owning newspapers.

36.*La Repubblica "Affari e Finanza"*, November 28, 1994, p. 2.

37.*La Repubblica*, December 7, 1994, p. 13.

38.Cited in *La Repubblica*, October 5, 1994, p. 11.

39.There were of course a series of other, related questions which were put to Berlusconi. See *La Repubblica*, December 13, 1994, p. 3. Numerous Milanese businessmen argued that they had been victims of extortion but this did not prevent them from being incriminated on charges of corruption. It was the view of the investigating magistrates that a businessman could not plausibly claim to be a victim of extortion when he paid off a public official. This was because his interests (to save on taxes, fines etc.) were perfectly compatible with those of the officials who received the pay-off. For this reason the "extortion" was almost never reported to the police and therefore could not be considered such.

40. See A. Curzi and C. Mineo, *Giù le mani dalla TV* (Milan: Sperling & Kupfer), 1994.

41. Interview with Demattè.

42. *La Repubblica*, September 24, 1994, p. 5.

Documentary Appendix

compiled by Marzia Zannini

Each edition of *Italian Politics* contains a documentary appendix which reports some of the more significant indicators of Italian political and social life.

In addition to the traditional data series we have included a further table which presents the trend of marriages and births, during the last ten years, because of their cultural centrality and in order to analyze the meaning of their changes.

As usual, the documentary appendix is organized in three sections: background data on the population and economic structure, elections, party membership and budget.

The first section (Tables A1-A7) presents data on the population, labor force, marriages and birth rates, crime and selected indicators pertaining to the economy and public finance.

The second section (Tables B1-12) summarizes the results of elections held during 1994. This year has seen many electoral events, political and European elections along with two waves of municipal elections.

In particular, the section reports data, disaggregated by region, for the political elections held on March 27 under the new electoral law, distinguishing between majority and proportional vote. European election results, held on June 12, are also presented. In both cases absolute and percentage figures are reported. The final part of this section reports the results of municipal elections held in the provincial capitals in June and November 1994.

The last section (Tables C1-C3) provides data on party budget and membership for the year 1993.

TABLE A1 Resident Population by Age Group and by Sex (in Thousands)[a]

| | Age Groups | | | |
	0-14	15-64	65 and over	Total Population
	Both Sexes			
1983	11,777	37,568	7,396	56,742
1984	11,497	38,159	7,272	56,929
1985	11,177	38,632	7,270	57,080
1986	10,877	38,854	7,470	57,202
1987	10,541	39,085	7,664	57,290
1988	10,218	39,293	7,887	57,399
1989	9,924	39,467	8,112	57,504
1990	9,620	39,620	8,335	57,576
1991	9,385	39,804	8,558	57,746
1992[b]	8,846	39,164	8,950	56,960
	Men Only			
1983	6,039	18,538	3,011	27,589
1984	5,896	18,837	2,941	27,674
1985	5,732	19,080	2,927	27,740
1986	5,578	19,209	3,003	27,791
1987	5,408	19,348	3,076	27,833
1988	5,245	19,482	3,162	27,889
1989	5,096	19,586	3,255	27,938
1990	4,941	19,678	3,349	27,968
1991	4,825	19,802	3,445	28,072
1992[c]	4,547	19,472	3,635	27,654

[a] Rounded figures.
[b] 1993 data not available.
[c] 1992 data to be published.

Source: Istat, *Popolazione e movimento anagrafico dei comuni*, (Rome 1982-1992).

TABLE A2 Present Population by Position on the Labor Market (in Thousands)

	Labor Forces			Total
Employed	Seeking Job			
	Unemployed	Seeking First Job	Other People Seeking Job	

Both Sexes

1984	20,647	466	1,136	703	22,952
1985	20,742	468	1,215	698	23,123
1986	20,856	501	1,296	814	23,467
1987	20,836	547	1,354	932	23,669
1988	21,103	537	1,412	937	23,989
1989	21,004	507	1,405	954	23,870
1990	21,396	483	1,357	912	24,148
1991	21,592	469	1,285	898	24,244
1992	21,459	551	1,370	878	24,258
1993	20,427	846	1,031	483	22,787

Men Only

1984	13,972	267	533	187	14,959
1985	13,986	269	580	174	15,009
1986	13,953	289	617	209	15,068
1987	13,845	313	665	251	15,074
1988	13,990	305	687	248	15,230
1989	13,851	286	676	257	15,070
1990	14,015	264	667	246	15,192
1991	14,102	256	645	241	15,244
1992	13,945	297	692	238	15,172
1993[a]	13,246	493	533	90	14,363

[a] 1993 data are drawn from Istat, *Indagine sulle forze di lavoro*, (Rome 1993). Starting from 1993 new definitions of «active population» and «people seeking job» have been introduced. The definitions now apply to people who are at least 15 years old, whereas the prior definitions applied to 14-year-olds as well. In particular people who lose their job for reasons different from dismissal (resignation or end of temporary employement) are excluded from «other people seeking job».

Source: Istat, «Annuario statistico italiano», (Rome, 1984-1993).

TABLE A3   Labor Conflicts: Number and Impact of Contractual and Non-Contractual Disputes (i.e. Political) (in Thousands)

	Conflicts	Participants	Number of Hours Lost
		Contractual Disputes	
1984	1,759	3,540	31,786
1985	1,166	1,224	11,036
1986	1,462	2,940	36,742
1987	1,146	1,473	20,147
1988	1,767	1,609	17,086
1989	1,295	2,108	21,001
1990	1,094	1,634	36,269
1991	784	750	11,573
1992	895	621	5,605
1993[a]	1,047	848	8,796
		Non-Contractual Disputes	
1984	57	3,816	29,137
1985	5	3,619	15,779
1986	7	667	2,764
1987	3	2,800	12,093
1988	2	1,103	6,120
1989	2	2,344	10,052
1990	-	-	-
1991	7	2,202	9,322
1992	8	2,557	13,905
1993[a]	7	3,536	15,084

[a] 1993 data are drawn from Istat, «Bollettino mensile di statistica», (Rome, October 1994).

Source: Istat, «Annuario statistico italiano», (Rome, 1984-1993).

TABLE A4 Births and Marriages

	Births		Marriages			
	Total Births	% Variation	Total Marriages	% Variation	Religious	% Variation
1984	587,871	-2.06	300,889	0.01	259,621	0.62
1985	577,345	-1.79	298,523	-0.79	256,911	-1.04
1986	555,445	-3.79	297,540	-0.33	255,407	-0.59
1987	551,539	-0.70	306,264	2.93	261,847	2.52
1988	569,698	3.29	318,296	3.93	266,534	1.79
1989	560,688	-1.58	321,272	0.93	267,617	0.41
1990	569,255	1.53	319,711	-0.49	266,084	-0.57
1991	562,787	-1.14	312,061	-2.39	257,555	-3.21
1992[a]	560,768	-0.36	303,785	-2.65	249,204	-3.24
1993[a]	538,168	-4.03	292,632	-3.67	239,711	-3.81

[a] 1992 and 1993 data are drawn from Istat, «Bollettino mensile di statistica», (Rome, October 1994).

Source: Istat, Statistiche demografiche, matrimoni, separazioni e divorzi, (Rome, 1984-1991).

TABLE A5   Classification of Officially Recorded Crimes[a]

	Against Persons	Against the Family or Morality	Against Property	Against the Economy or Public Trust	Against the State	Other	Total
1984	126,729	12,652	1,457,093	291,409	33,675	56,781	1,978,339
1985	125,940	13,559	1,369,325	385,691	37,831	68,090	2,000,436
1986	125,192	14,118	1,355,507	410,934	41,734	82,688	2,030,173
1987	138,272	14,826	1,507,040	394,360	47,093	103,395	2,204,986
1988	136,685	14,228	1,529,876	416,387	46,158	90,597	2,233,931
1989	125,769	13,073	1,573,805	422,166	41,968	97,314	2,274,095
1990	103,039	7,363	1,575,016	223,740	21,550	67,366	1,998,074
1991	121,881	10,256	2,255,918	326,584	35,590	66,834	2,817,063
1992	202,149	11,552	2,032,579	378,331	43,297	72,983	2,740,891
1993[b]	183,054	12,694	1,980,606	373,129	54,224	76,174	2,679,881

[a] For 1990 and subsequent years, the data are no longer fully comparable with those for earlier years. For criminal accusations against a person already subjected to investigations, the new Code of Criminal Procedure (Article 405) identifies the start of judicial action as the moment at which the person is formally charged with a crime. Unlike previous years, then, the statistics no longer include cases closed without trial for lack of evidence or other causes. In comparing 1990 and 1991 data, it should be kept in mind that organizational difficulties linked to the implementation of the new Code have caused delays in judicial action and in the transmittal of information to Istat. Thus, for most classifications above, the Istat data register decreases in 1990 and then increases in 1991.

[b] 1993 data are drawn from Istat, «Bollettino mensile di statistica», (Rome, October 1994).

Source: Istat, «Annuario statistico italiano», (Rome, 1984-1993).

TABLE A6 Gross Domestic Product (in Market Prices) and the Consumer Price Index: Yearly Values and Percentage Variations Figures Over the Previous Year

	Gross Domestic Product				Consumer Price Index (1990 = 100)	
	In Current Prices[a]	% Variation	In 1985 Prices	% Variation	Index	% Variation
1984	725,760	14.58	790,036	2.69	69.50	10.85
1985	810,580	11.69	810,580	2.60	75.90	9.21
1986	899,903	11.02	834,262	2.92	80.30	5.80
1987	983,803	9.32	860,422	3.14	84.10	4.73
1988	1,091,837	10.98	895,397	4.06	88.40	5.11
1989	1,193,462	9.31	921,714	2.94	93.90	6.22
1990	1,312,066	9.94	941,387	2.13	100.00	6.50
1991	1,426,580	8.73	953,181	1.25	106.30	6.30
1992	1,507,190	5.65	962,037	0.93	111.70	5.08
1993[b]	1,560,114	3.51	953,446	-0.89	116.70	4.48

[a] In billions of lire.
[b] 1993 data to be published.

Source: Istat, «Annuario statistico italiano», (Rome, 1984-1993).

TABLE A7   The National Debt and the Annual Budgetary Deficit, in Absolute
Terms and as a Percentage of the Gross Domestic Product

	National Debt			Budget Deficit		
	Absolute Figures[a]	% Variation	% of GDP	Absolute Figures[a]	% Variation	% of GDP
1984	561,489	23.13	77.37	77,100	30.42	10.62
1985	683,044	21.65	84.27	107,702	39.69	13.29
1986	793,583	16.18	88.19	116,826	8.47	12.98
1987	910,542	14.74	92.55	128,226	9.76	13.03
1988[b]	1,035,812	13.76	94.87	124,986	-2.53	11.45
1989	1,168,361	12.80	97.90	119,466	-4.42	10.01
1990	1,318,936	12.89	100.52	122,471	2.52	9.33
1991	1,485,742	12.65	103.94	118,620	-3.14	8.30
1992	1,675,276	12.76	111.36	107,189	-9.64	7.13
1993	1,862,937	11.20	119.41	149,128	39.13	9.56

[a] In billions of lire.
[b] Some methodological innovations in banking statistics determine a discontinuity in the data series, starting from December 31, 1988.

Source: Bank of Italy, Relazione annuale, (Rome, 1994).

TABLE B1 Elections to the Chamber of Deputies, March 27, 1994, Majoritarian ballots. Regional and National Returns (Absolute Number of Votes Cast)

Lists	Valle d'Aosta	Piemonte	Lombardia	Liguria	Trentino A.A.	Veneto	Friuli V.G.
Progressisti	-	898,616	1,544,270	447,618	57,925	713,083	214,186
Patto per l'Italia	-	456,407	890,550	173,271	70,346	606,338	134,880
Lista Pannella	-	43,510	81,706	24,790	-	-	13,009
Polo della Libertà	-	1,367,241	3,573,096	458,578	127,847	1,535,055	398,904
Polo del Buon Governo	-	-	-	-	-	-	-
Alleanza Nazionale	-	274,622	432,665	106,123	62,022	259,057	111,674
Others [a]	80,805	37,158	3,587	1,037	110,417	96,578	6,347
Svp	-	-	-	-	188,017	-	-
Lega d'Azione Meridionale	-	-	-	-	-	-	-
Total valid votes	80,805	3,077,554	6,525,874	1,211,417	616,574	3,210,111	879,000
Invalid votes	8,051	219,892	343,351	80,847	58,096	191,500	49,956
of which blank ballots	3,964	109,105	197,335	40,509	35,007	109,061	24,898
Voters [b]	88,861	3,298,740	6,872,644	1,293,270	674,984	3,404,938	929,199
Non-voters	11,311	377,699	594,455	193,326	69,466	327,443	142,785
Entitled to vote	100,172	3,676,439	7,467,099	1,486,596	744,450	3,732,381	1,071,984

(continues)

TABLE B1 *(continued)*

Lists	Emilia Romagna	Toscana	Umbria	Marche	Lazio	Abruzzo	Molise
Progressisti	1,460,888	1,273,338	279,203	426,374	1,356,154	282,488	63,837
Patto per l'Italia	425,816	363,804	90,571	217,899	447,634	146,077	28,747
Lista Pannella	51,555	56,614	-	-	45,254	-	-
Polo della Libertà	791,589	515,410	-	-	-	-	-
Polo del Buon Governo	-	-	209,288	358,543	1,725,817	187,348	65,651
Alleanza Nazionale	269,342	319,344	-	-	-	202,517	-
Others [a]	3,140	40,094	-	-	36,746	23,149	45,200
Svp	-	-	-	-	-	-	-
Lega d'Azione Meridionale	-	-	-	-	-	-	-
Total valid votes	3,002,330	2,568,604	579,062	1,002,816	3,611,605	841,579	203,435
Invalid votes	160,782	183,524	47,631	81,068	245,081	72,267	25,177
of which blank ballots	102,086	110,149	26,865	49,311	118,064	38,542	13,280
Voters [b]	3,163,676	2,752,870	626,845	1,087,020	3,859,789	914,064	229,099
Non-voters	233,677	269,987	76,158	145,216	516,056	227,473	85,242
Entitled to vote	3,397,353	3,022,857	703,003	1,232,236	4,375,845	1,141,537	314,341

(continues)

TABLE B1 *(continued)*

Lists	Campania	Puglia	Basilicata	Calabria	Sicilia	Sardegna	National Total
Progressisti	1,115,181	787,459	138,784	384,445	954,865	305,395	12,704,109
Patto per l'Italia	524,569	449,536	85,930	223,195	452,106	231,362	6,019,038
Lista Pannella	65,697	38,718	-	-	3,421	8,392	432,666
Polo della Libertà	-	-	-	-	-	-	8,767,720
Polo del Buon Governo	967,278	930,019	114,237	374,929	1,297,074	36211-	6,794,811
Alleanza Nazionale c	343,930	-	-	-	-	-	2,178,779
Others a	302,649	176,386	6,130	127,316	152,394	123,065	1,372,198
Svp	-	-	-	188,017	-	-	
Lega d'Azione Meridionale	-	46,820	-	-	-	-	46,820
Total valid votes	3,319,304	2,428,938	345,081	1,109,885	2,859,860	1,030,324	38,504,158
Invalid votes	298,674	262,603	64,653	155,498	361,256	90,911	3,000,818
of which blank ballots	150,544	119,815	30,510	76,038	144,205	44,635	1,543,923
Voters b	3,624,488	2,694,923	410,076	1,266,793	3,225,271	1,121,914	41,539,464
Non-voters	930,885	589,782	104,470	480,977	1,080,230	239,111	6,695,749
Entitled to vote	4,555,373	3,284,705	514,546	1,747,770	4,305,501	1,361,025	48,235,213

a «Others» includes the lists which have obtained no seats in Parliament.
b «Valid votes» plus «invalid votes» differs from voters because of a negligible amount of contested votes.
c In the electoral constituency Campania2 Alleanza Nazionale presented an autonomous list.

Source: Calculated from data provided by Ministero dell'Interno-Direzione centrale per i servizi elettorali.

TABLE B2 Elections to the Chamber of Deputies, March 27, 1994, Majoritarian Ballots. Regional and National Returns (Percentage of Votes Cast)

Lists	Valle d'Aosta	Piemonte	Lombardia	Liguria	Trentino A.A.	Veneto	Friuli V.G.
Progressisti	-	29.20	23.66	36.95	9.39	22.21	24.37
Patto per l'Italia	-	14.83	13.65	14.30	11.41	18.89	15.34
Lista Pannella	-	1.41	1.25	2.05	-	-	1.48
Polo della Libertà	-	44.43	54.75	37.85	20.74	47.82	45.38
Polo del Buon Governo	-	-	-	-	-	-	
Alleanza Nazionale	-	8.92	6.63	8.76	10.06	8.07	12.70
Svp	-	-	-	-	30.49	-	-
Lega d'Azione Meridionale	-	-	-	-	-	-	-
Others [a]	100.00	1.21	0.05	0.09	17.91	3.01	0.72
Total	100.00	100.00	100.00	100.00	100.00	100.00	100.00
% of invalid votes/voters	9.06	6.67	5.00	6.25	8.61	5.62	5.38
% of voters/entitled to vote	88.71	89.73	92.04	87.00	90.67	91.23	86.68
% of unexpressed votes/ entitled to vote [b]	19.33	16.25	12.56	18.44	17.14	13.90	17.98

(continues)

TABLE B2 (continued)

Lists	Emilia Romagna	Toscana	Umbria	Marche	Lazio	Abruzzo	Molise
Progressisti	48.66	49.57	48.22	42.52	37.55	33.57	31.38
Patto per l'Italia	14.18	14.16	15.64	21.73	12.39	17.36	14.13
Lista Pannella	1.72	2.20	-	-	1.25	-	-
Polo della Libertà	26.37	20.07	-	-	-	-	-
Polo del Buon Governo	-	-	36.14	35.75	47.79	46.33	32.27
Alleanza Nazionale	8.97	12.43	-	-	-	-	-
Svp	-	-	-	-	-	-	-
Lega d'Azione Meridionale	-	-	-	-	-	-	-
Others [a]	0.10	1.56	-	-	1.02	2.75	22.22
Total	100.00	100.00	100.00	100.00	100.00	100.00	100.00
% of invalid votes/voters	5.08	6.67	7.60	7.46	6.35	7.91	10.99
% of voters/entitled to vote	93.12	91.07	89.17	88.22	88.21	80.07	72.88
% of unexpressed votes/ entitled to vote [b]	11.61	15.00	17.61	18.36	17.39	26.26	35.13

(continues)

TABLE B2 (*continued*)

Lists	Campania	Puglia	Basilicata	Calabria	Sicilia	Sardegna	National Total
Progressisti	33.60	32.42	40.22	34.64	33.39	29.64	32.99
Patto per l'Italia	15.80	18.51	24.90	20.11	15.81	22.46	15.63
Lista Pannella	1.98	1.59	-	-	0.12	0.81	1.12
Polo della Libertà	-	-	-	-	-	-	22.77
Polo del Buon Governo	29.14	38.29	33.10	33.78	45.35	35.15	17.65
Alleanza Nazionale	10.36	-	-	-	-	-	5.66
Svp	-	-	-	-	-	-	0.49
Lega d'Azione Meridionale	-	1.93	-	-	-	-	0.12
Others [a]	9.12	7.26	1.78	11.47	5.33	11.94	3.56
Total	100.00	100.00	100.00	100.00	100.00	100.00	100.00
% of invalid votes/voters	8.24	9.74	15.77	12.27	11.20	8.10	7.22
% of voters/entitled to vote	79.57	82.04	79.70	72.48	74.91	82.43	86.12
% of unexpressed votes/ entitled to vote [b]	26.99	25.95	32.87	36.42	33.48	24.25	20.10

[a] «Others» includes the lists which have obtained no seats in Parliament.
[b] Unexpressed votes= non-voters+invalid votes

Source: Calculated from data provided by Ministero dell'Interno-Direzione centrale per i servizi elettorali.

TABLE B3 Elections to the Chamber of Deputies, March 27, 1994, Proportional Ballots. Regional and National Returns (Absolute Number of Votes Cast)

Lists	Piemonte	Lombardia	Veneto	Trentino A.A	Friuli V.G.	Liguria	Emilia Romagna	Toscana	Umbria	Marche	Lazio
Forza Italia	820,662	1,716,612	767,266	98,246	215,604	276,814	503,561	430,596	90,853	200,571	751,976
Alleanza Nazionale	255,632	379,392	251,064	56,615	125,972	98,722	274,362	285,854	98,325	159,629	926,295
Lega Nord	484,737	1,460,844	701,801	47,572	150,272	140,132	195,192	56,476	-	-	-
Lista Pannella	157,305	300,612	-	-	39,360	68,782	117,176	98,830	-	-	148,510
Pds	515,015	858,088	395,004	41,617	106,847	273,820	1,116,210	883,087	211,775	294,340	854,273
Rifond.Comunista	180,559	336,875	144,059	14,391	53,478	100,151	201,310	265,412	52,668	88,571	241,923
Psi	51,189	90,332	54,123	5,644	15,673	21,208	52,098	66,242	15,879	24,115	63,817
Rete Mov. Dem.	70,001	87,682	-	15,934	-	11,764	25,145	35,195	4,591	15,915	23,355
Green Federation	83,795	143,012	124,178	28,233	35,982	32,571	81,375	61,989	14,051	37,041	94,660
Alleanza Democratica	51,115	63,383	25,378	-	-	17,369	35,190	35,676	8,206	22,311	63,870
Patto Segni	-	274,567	152,339	-	-	73,011	177,235	156,043	34,997	-	153,257
Ppi	369,415	737,939	505,656	73,256	138,690	98,592	253,569	217,884	58,814	174,908	310,009
Socialdemocrazia	-	-	-	-	-	-	13,542	18,676	3,750	-	9,368
Lega Alpina Lumbarda	-	135,954	-	-	-	-	-	-	-	-	-
Svp	-	-	-	231,826	-	-	-	-	-	-	-
Others [a]	53,003	15,296	123,594	17,124	6,195	15,552	7,678	10,278	-	-	22,668
Total valid votes	3,092,428	6,600,588	3,244,462	630,458	888,073	1,228,488	3,053,643	2,622,238	593,909	1,017,401	3,663,981
Invalid votes	202,672	265,928	157,632	44,112	48,194	63,900	110,209	131,661	33,073	69,259	191,451
of which blank ballots	98,115	134,814	79,148	26,355	18,569	27,493	56,235	62,049	15,084	37,682	79,013
Voters [b]	3,298,749	6,872,166	3,405,508	674,718	936,368	1,293,425	3,164,509	2,754,561	627,054	1,087,016	3,859,485
Non-voters	377,690	594,933	326,873	69,732	135,616	193,171	232,844	268,296	75,949	145,220	516,360
Entitled to vote	3,676,439	7,467,099	3,732,381	744,450	1,071,984	1,486,596	3,397,353	3,022,857	703,003	1,232,236	4,375,845

(continues)

TABLE B3   (continued)

Lists	Abruzzo	Molise	Campania	Puglia	Basilicata	Calabria	Sicilia	Sardegna	National Total
Forza Italia	149,956	31,011	649,824	-	40,759	206,956	942,719	225,301	8,119,287
Alleanza Nazionale	175,852	38,602	661,387	649,235	59,273	187,728	393,643	125,116	5,202,698
Lega Nord	-	-	-	-	-	-	-	-	3,237,026
Lista Pannella	71,915	-	117,090	110,254	-	-	95,832	30,073	1,355,739
Pds	170,361	35,241	643,415	471,317	81,070	242,255	462,538	199,337	7,855,610
Rifond.Comunista	62,327	11,102	226,561	165,267	26,134	101,551	79,193	61,690	2,334,029
Psi	29,146	5,174	97,934	65,296	29,991	42,893	-	31,792	841,739
Rete Mov. Dem.	17,880	4,452	21,719	29,526	12,159	15,565	320,553	6,967	718,403
Green Federation	25,538	5,345	128,471	72,480	11,142	20,736	20,512	21,385	1,042,496
Alleanza Democratica	-	2,949	45,050	32,038	-	14,470	12,010	23,381	452,396
Patto Segni	-	10,235	186,802	165,091	-	72,343	154,028	185,322	1,795,270
Ppi	129,730	31,929	314,573	326,988	68,406	130,140	233,234	95,208	4,268,940
Socialdemocrazia	4,870	9,229	21,852	39,091	10,004	25,276	23,709	-	179,367
Lega Alpina Lumbarda	-	-	-	-	-	-	-	-	135,954
Svp	-	-	-	-	-	-	-	-	231,826
Others [a]	7,426	16,496	149,356	237,413	10,373	31,616	70,844	28,785	823,697
Total valid votes	845,001	201,765	3,264,034	2,363,996	349,311	1,091,529	2,808,815	1,034,357	38,594,477
Invalid votes	69,227	26,826	354,684	329,560	60,694	173,818	412,562	87,464	2,832,926
of which blank ballots	36,698	15,981	195,934	178,181	27,016	90,633	196,329	46,571	1,421,900
Voters [b]	914,272	229,098	3,624,819	2,694,922	410,090	1,266,849	3,225,374	1,122,277	41,461,260
Non-voters	227,265	85,243	930,554	589,783	104,456	480,921	1,080,127	238,748	6,673,781
Entitled to vote	1,141,537	314,341	4,555,373	3,284,705	514,546	1,747,770	4,305,501	1,361,025	48,135,041

[a] «Others» includes the lists which have obtained less than 100,000 votes. Valle d'Aosta constituency elects just one deputy with the majoritarian system.

[b] «Valid votes» plus «invalid votes» differs from voters because of a negligible amount of contested votes.

Source: Calculated from data provided by Ministero dell'Interno-Direzione centrale per i servizi elettorali

TABLE B4 Elections to the Chamber of Deputies, March 27, 1994, Proportional Ballots. Regional and National Returns (Percentage of Votes Cast)

Lists	Piemonte	Lombardia	Veneto	Trentino A.A	Friuli V.G.	Liguria	Emilia Romagna	Toscana	Umbria	Marche	Lazio
Forza Italia	26.54	26.01	23.65	15.58	24.28	22.53	16.49	16.42	15.30	19.71	20.52
Alleanza Nazionale	8.27	5.75	7.74	8.98	14.18	8.04	8.98	10.90	16.56	15.69	25.28
Lega Nord	15.67	22.13	21.63	7.55	16.92	11.41	6.39	2.15	-	-	-
Lista Pannella	5.09	4.55	-	-	4.43	5.60	3.84	3.77	-	-	4.05
Pds	16.65	13.00	12.17	6.60	12.03	22.29	36.55	33.68	35.66	28.93	23.32
Rifond. Comunista	5.84	5.10	4.44	2.28	6.02	8.15	6.59	10.12	8.87	8.71	6.60
Psi	1.66	1.37	1.67	0.90	1.76	1.73	1.71	2.53	2.67	2.37	1.74
Rete Mov. Dem.	2.26	1.33	-	2.53	-	0.96	0.82	1.34	0.77	1.56	0.64
Green Federation	2.71	2.17	3.83	4.48	4.05	2.65	2.66	2.36	2.37	3.64	2.58
Alleanza Democratica	1.65	0.96	0.78	-	-	1.41	1.15	1.36	1.38	2.19	1.74
Patto Segni	-	4.16	4.70	-	-	5.94	5.80	5.95	5.89	-	4.18
Ppi	11.95	11.18	15.59	11.62	15.62	8.03	8.30	8.31	9.90	17.19	8.46
Socialdemocrazia	-	-	-	-	-	-	-	0.71	0.63	-	0.26
Lega Alpina Lumbarda	-	2.06	-	-	-	-	-	-	-	-	-
Svp	-	-	-	36.77	-	-	-	-	-	-	-
Others [a]	1.71	0.23	3.81	2.72	0.70	1.27	0.25	0.39	-	-	0.62
Total	100.00	100.00	100.00	100.00	100.00	100.00	100.00	100.00	100.00	100.00	100.00
% of invalid votes/voters	6.14	3.87	4.63	6.54	5.15	4.94	3.48	4.78	5.27	6.37	4.96
% of voters/ entitled to vote	89.73	92.03	91.24	90.63	87.35	87.01	93.15	91.12	89.20	88.21	88.20
% of unexpressed votes/ entitled to vote [b]	15.79	11.53	12.98	15.29	17.15	17.29	10.10	13.23	15.51	17.41	16.18

(continues)

TABLE B4 (continued)

Lists	Abruzzo	Molise	Campania	Puglia	Basilicata	Calabria	Sicilia	Sardegna	National Total
Forza Italia	17.75	15.37	19.91	-	11.67	18.96	33.56	21.78	21.04
Alleanza Nazionale	20.81	19.13	20.26	27.46	16.97	17.20	14.01	12.10	13.48
Lega Nord	-	-	-	-	-	-	-	-	8.39
Lista Pannella	8.51	-	3.59	4.66	-	-	3.41	2.91	3.51
Pds	20.16	17.47	19.71	19.94	23.21	22.19	16.47	19.27	20.35
Rifond. Comunista	7.38	5.50	6.94	6.99	7.48	9.30	-	5.96	6.05
Psi	3.45	2.56	3.00	2.76	8.59	3.93	2.82	3.07	2.18
Rete Mov. Dem.	2.12	2.21	0.67	1.25	3.48	1.43	11.41	0.67	1.86
Green Federation	3.02	2.65	3.94	3.07	3.19	1.90	0.73	2.07	2.70
Alleanza Democratica	-	1.46	1.38	1.36	-	1.33	0.43	2.26	1.17
Patto Segni	-	5.07	5.72	6.98	-	6.63	5.48	17.92	4.65
Ppi	15.35	15.82	9.64	13.83	19.58	11.92	8.30	9.20	11.06
Socialdemocrazia	0.58	4.57	0.67	1.65	2.86	2.32	0.84	-	0.46
Lega Alpina Lumbarda	-	-	-	-	-	-	-	-	0.35
Svp	-	-	-	-	-	-	-	-	0.60
Others [a]	0.88	8.18	4.58	10.04	2.97	2.90	2.52	2.78	2.13
Total	100.00	100.00	100.00	100.00	100.00	100.00	100.00	100.00	100.00
% of invalid votes/voters	7.57	11.71	9.78	12.23	14.80	13.72	12.79	7.79	6.83
% of voters/entitled to vote	80.09	72.88	79.57	82.04	79.70	72.48	74.91	82.46	86.14
% of unexpressed votes/ entitled to vote [b]	25.97	35.65	28.21	27.99	32.10	37.46	34.67	23.97	19.75

[a] «Others» includes lists which have obtained less than 100,000 votes.
[b] Unexpressed votes= non-voters+invalid votes

Source: Calculated from data provided by Ministero dell'Interno–Direzione centrale per i servizi elettorali.

TABLE B5 Elections to the European Parliament, June 12, 1994. Regional and National Returns (Absolute Number of Votes Cast)

Lists	Piemonte	Valle d'Aosta	Lombardia	Liguria	Trentino A.A.	Veneto	Friuli V.G.
Forza Italia	910,319	14,891	2,008,514	324,593	107,967	895,093	253,805
Alleanza Nazionale	205,884	2,852	357,390	83,034	39,923	231,465	84,722
Lega Nord	302,872	3,475	1,013,355	82,432	24,850	443,600	83,894
Liberali	15,150	261	18,820	3,314	-	-	-
Pannella Riformatori	80,570	1,342	153,471	26,121	7,270	54,655	18,342
Pds	406,728	6,142	718,488	240,904	31,016	321,876	89,062
Rifondaz. Comunista	174,244	3,078	295,650	79,235	12,706	123,018	41,052
Psi-Ad	38,205	352	73,358	14,736	4,020	32,126	9,216
Green Federation	98,587	3,107	183,431	34,045	38,928	106,898	30,826
Rete Mov. Dem.	22,069	138	22,171	4,321	5,198	9,141	2,044
Ppi	220,200	3,701	577,805	71,694	53,798	385,829	83,292
Patto Segni	91,779	954	149,155	34,820	9,141	116,609	19,469
Pri	16,364	176	20,609	5,054	1,874	11,491	4,584
Psdi	14,920	186	23,970	10,192	1,766	18,477	5,390
Lega Alpina Lumbarda	10,033	172	50,308	2,219	1,168	14,846	3,747
Lega d'Azione Meridionale	23,481	330	38,987	5,363	2,747	34,269	7,936
Svp	-	-	-	-	189,332	4,354	1,771
Uv	9,258	19,656	7,141	1,524	15,794	35,114	10,550
Solidarietà	-	-	-	-	-	-	-
Total valid votes	2,640,663	60,813	5,712,623	1,023,601	547,498	2,838,861	749,702
Invalid votes	188,376	7,682	284,571	57,757	33,534	163,023	40,927
of which blank ballots	55,026	3,646	79,987	17,701	14,028	44,487	12,202
Voters [a]	2,829,039	68,459	5,997,194	1,081,358	581,032	3,001,884	790,629
Non-voters	822,498	30,343	1,439,425	387,107	150,809	688,737	253,226
Entitled to vote	3,651,537	98,802	7,436,619	1,468,465	731,841	3,690,621	1,043,855

(continues)

TABLE B5 (continued)

Lists	Emilia Romagna	Toscana	Umbria	Marche	Lazio	Abruzzi	Molise
Forza Italia	650,109	542,981	129,828	233,128	829,318	205,448	51,329
Alleanza Nazionale	203,651	231,240	72,784	120,740	728,538	139,115	33,546
Lega Nord	118,682	36,215	3,239	7,223	12,166	4,370	898
Liberali	–	–	–	–	–	–	–
Pannella Riformatori	57,005	47,279	7,393	14,380	71,629	24,294	2,002
Pds	987,497	797,044	173,174	248,939	654,553	138,111	27,490
Rifondaz. Comunista	190,050	224,886	45,340	68,688	206,259	48,590	9,287
Psi-Ad	47,378	46,975	12,701	18,682	53,073	18,151	4,645
Green Federation	84,236	60,796	11,108	26,881	115,007	18,116	4,702
Rete Mov. Dem.	7,470	8,153	1,275	2,912	7,448	5,993	1,457
Ppi	216,716	183,361	41,732	108,811	229,263	81,974	22,641
Patto Segni	76,727	67,636	15,724	27,951	85,310	18,681	4,226
Pri	36,128	18,141	4,502	11,292	33,151	4,821	2,223
Psdi	18,612	24,928	1,923	4,156	22,749	3,234	955
Lega Alpina Lumbarda	5,687	2,566	601	1,143	2,340	1,064	652
Lega d'Azione Meridionale	11,043	4,593	1,077	2,366	5,074	1,808	606
Svp	2,515	–	–	–	–	–	–
Uv	2,987	2,618	620	1,101	2,752	795	268
Solidarietà	–	–	–	–	–	–	–
Total valid votes	2,716,493	2,299,412	523,021	898,393	3,058,630	714,565	166,927
Invalid votes	105,997	118,221	31,802	63,352	175,031	64,409	18,838
of which blank ballots	38,991	44,584	10,959	28,799	46,942	25,188	7,752
Voters [a]	2,822,490	2,417,633	554,823	961,745	3,235,054	778,974	185,765
Non-voters	548,644	587,139	134,669	253,693	1,110,402	337,839	113,236
Entitled to vote	3,371,134	3,004,772	689,492	1,215,438	4,345,456	1,116,813	299,001

(continues)

239

TABLE B5 (continued)

Lists	Campania	Puglia	Basilicata	Calabria	Sicilia	Sardegna	National Total
Forza Italia	804,752	600,431	67,668	261,249	934,126	251,046	10,076,595
Alleanza Nazionale	454,545	439,504	42,189	160,295	389,377	104,685	4,125,479
Lega Nord	8,276	7,386	1,392	5,521	10,726	1,745	2,172,317
Liberali	-	-	-	-	11,739	3,362	52,646
Pannella Riformatori	38,117	33,367	3,266	13,727	36,363	13,558	704,151
Pds	423,695	326,606	57,753	171,410	296,273	168,991	6,285,752
Rifondaz. Comunista	143,383	105,201	19,552	76,373	78,855	49,608	1,995,055
Psi-Ad	78,345	44,425	20,974	33,447	41,181	8,167	600,157
Green Federation	89,480	55,143	6,004	14,408	45,708	20,328	1,047,739
Rete Mov. Dem.	17,560	15,848	4,730	7,129	219,563	1,777	366,397
Ppi	288,237	215,101	62,372	109,675	231,298	101,602	3,289,102
Patto Segni	68,208	54,199	8,314	25,142	65,922	133,457	1,073,424
Pri	25,859	11,791	2,314	11,898	12,570	6,719	241,561
Psdi	29,017	18,899	3,089	7,714	9,266	3,651	223,094
Lega Alpina Lumbarda	3,453	3,020	572	1,452	3,078	691	108,812
Lega d'Azione Meridionale	7,034	60,358	1,603	5,061	7,178	1,380	222,294
Svp	-	-	-	-	-	-	197,972
Uv	3,183	2,315	559	2,832	1,721	5,872	126,660
Solidarietà	-	-	-	-	5,439	9,471	14,910
Total valid votes	2,483,144	1,993,594	302,351	907,333	2,400,383	886,110	32,924,117
Invalid votes	219,768	198,705	42,286	130,290	505,637	133,352	2,583,558
of which blank ballots	71,905	67,871	14,539	57,233	279,608	69,054	990,502
Voters [a]	2,702,912	2,192,299	344,637	1,037,623	2,906,020	1,019,462	35,509,032
Non-voters	1,788,805	1,007,172	149,595	660,512	1,214,537	302,423	11,980,811
Entitled to vote	4,491,717	3,199,471	494,232	1,698,135	4,120,557	1,321,885	47,489,843

[a] «Valid votes» plus «invalid votes» differs from voters because of a negligible amount of contested votes.

Source: Calculated from data provided by Ministero dell'Interno–Direzione centrale per i servizi elettorali.

TABLE B6　Elections to the European Parliament, June 12, 1994. Regional and National Returns (Percentage of Votes Cast)

Lists	Piemonte	Valle d'Aosta	Lombardia	Liguria	Trentino A.A.	Veneto	Friuli V.G.
Forza Italia	34.47	24.49	35.16	31.71	19.72	31.53	33.85
Alleanza Nazionale	7.80	4.69	6.26	8.11	7.29	8.15	11.30
Lega Nord	11.47	5.71	17.74	8.05	4.54	15.63	11.19
Liberali	0.57	0.43	0.33	0.32	-	-	-
Pannella Riformatori	3.05	2.21	2.69	2.55	1.33	1.93	2.45
Pds	15.40	10.10	12.58	23.53	5.67	11.34	11.88
Rifondaz. Comunista	6.60	5.06	5.18	7.74	2.32	4.33	5.48
Psi-Ad	1.45	0.58	1.28	1.44	0.73	1.13	1.23
Green Federation	3.73	5.11	3.21	3.33	7.11	3.77	4.11
Rete Mov. Dem.	0.84	0.23	0.39	0.42	0.95	0.32	0.27
Ppi	8.34	6.09	10.11	7.00	9.83	13.59	11.11
Patto Segni	3.48	1.57	2.61	3.40	1.67	4.11	2.60
Pri	0.62	0.29	0.36	0.49	0.34	0.40	0.61
Psdi	0.57	0.31	0.42	1.00	0.32	0.65	0.72
Lega Alpina Lumbarda	0.38	0.28	0.88	0.22	0.21	0.52	0.50
Lega d'Azione Meridionale	0.89	0.54	0.68	0.52	0.50	1.21	1.06
Svp	-	-	-	-	34.58	0.15	0.24
Uv	0.35	32.32	0.13	0.15	2.88	1.24	1.41
Solidarietà	-	-	-	-	-	-	-
Total	100.00	100.00	100.00	100.00	100.00	100.00	100.00
% of invalid votes/voters	6.66	11.22	4.75	5.34	5.77	5.43	5.18
% of voters/entitled to vote	77.48	69.29	80.64	73.64	79.39	81.34	75.74
Unexpressed votes/ entitled to vote [a]	27.68	38.49	23.18	30.29	25.19	23.08	28.18

(continues)

TABLE B6 *(continued)*

Lists	Emilia Romagna	Toscana	Umbria	Marche	Lazio	Abruzzi	Molise
Forza Italia	23.93	23.61	24.82	25.95	27.11	28.75	30.75
Alleanza Nazionale	7.50	10.06	13.92	13.44	23.82	19.47	20.10
Lega Nord	4.37	1.57	0.62	0.80	0.40	0.61	0.54
Liberali			-	-	-	-	-
Pannella Riformatori	2.10	2.06	1.41	1.60	2.34	3.40	1.20
Pds	36.35	34.66	33.11	27.71	21.40	19.33	16.47
Rifondaz. Comunista	7.00	9.78	8.67	7.65	6.74	6.80	5.56
Psi-Ad	1.74	2.04	2.43	2.08	1.74	2.54	2.78
Green Federation	3.10	2.64	2.12	2.99	3.76	2.54	2.82
Rete Mov. Dem.	0.27	0.35	0.24	0.32	0.24	0.84	0.87
Ppi	7.98	7.97	7.98	12.11	7.50	11.47	13.56
Patto Segni	2.82	2.94	3.01	3.11	2.79	2.61	2.53
Pri	1.33	0.79	0.86	1.26	1.08	0.67	1.33
Psdi	0.69	1.08	0.37	0.46	0.74	0.45	0.57
Lega Alpina Lumbarda	0.21	0.11	0.11	0.13	0.08	0.15	0.39
Lega d'Azione Meridionale	0.41	0.20	0.21	0.26	0.17	0.25	0.36
Svp	0.09	-	-	-	-	-	-
Uv	0.11	0.11	0.12	0.12	0.09	0.11	0.16
Solidarietà	-	-	-	-	-	-	-
Total	100.00	100.00	100.00	100.00	100.00	100.00	100.00
% of invalid votes/voters	3.76	4.89	5.73	6.59	5.41	8.27	10.14
% of voters/entitled to vote	83.73	80.46	80.47	79.13	74.45	69.75	62.13
Unexpressed votes/ entitled to vote[a]	19.42	23.47	24.14	26.08	29.58	36.02	44.17

(continues)

TABLE B6 *(continued)*

Lists	Campania	Puglia	Basilicata	Calabria	Sicilia	Sardegna	National Total
Forza Italia	32.41	30.12	22.38	28.79	38.92	28.33	30.61
Alleanza Nazionale	18.31	22.05	13.95	17.67	16.22	11.81	12.53
Lega Nord	0.33	0.37	0.46	0.61	0.45	0.20	6.60
Liberali	-	-	-	-	0.49	0.38	0.16
Pannella Riformatori	1.54	1.67	1.08	1.51	1.51	1.53	2.14
Pds	17.06	16.38	19.10	18.89	12.34	19.07	19.09
Rifondaz. Comunista	5.77	5.28	6.47	8.42	3.29	5.60	6.06
Psi-Ad	3.16	2.23	6.94	3.69	1.72	0.92	1.82
Green Federation	3.60	2.77	1.99	1.59	1.90	2.29	3.18
Rete Mov. Dem.	0.71	0.79	1.56	0.79	9.15	0.20	1.11
Ppi	11.61	10.79	20.63	12.09	9.64	11.47	9.99
Patto Segni	2.75	2.72	2.75	2.77	2.75	15.06	3.26
Pri	1.04	0.59	0.77	1.31	0.52	0.76	0.73
Psdi	1.17	0.95	1.02	0.85	0.39	0.41	0.68
Lega Alpina Lumbarda	0.14	0.15	0.19	0.16	0.13	0.08	0.33
Lega d'Azione Meridionale	0.28	3.03	0.53	0.56	0.30	0.16	0.68
Svp	-	-	-	-	-	-	0.60
Uv	0.13	0.12	0.18	0.31	0.07	0.66	0.38
Solidarietà	-	-	-	-	0.23	1.07	0.05
Total	100.00	100.00	100.00	100.00	100.00	100.00	100.00
% of invalid votes/voters	8.13	9.06	12.27	12.56	17.40	13.08	7.28
% of voters/entitled to vote	60.18	68.52	69.73	61.10	70.52	77.12	74.77
Unexpressed votes/ entitled to vote [a]	44.72	37.69	38.82	46.57	41.75	32.97	30.67

[a] Unexpressed votes= non-voters + invalid votes

Source: Calculated from data provided by Ministero dell'Interno–Direzione centrale per i servizi elettorali.

TABLE B7   Municipal Elections, June 12, 1994: 90 Municipalities with over 15,000 Inhabitants. Summary of National Returns.

Lists	Valid Votes	%	Seats
Forza Italia	329,349	13.9	299
Alleanza Nazionale	217,090	9.2	189
Lega Nord	132,479	5.6	125
Centro Crist. Dem.	67,857	2.9	46
Unione di Centro	19,783	0.8	12
Liberali	1,814	0.1	1
Lista Pannella	1,319	0.1	0
Pannella-Riformatori	911	0.0	0
Pds	273,020	11.5	379
Rifondazione Comunista	117,517	5.0	109
Psi	22,620	1.0	22
Green Federation	26,446	1.1	11
Alleanza Democratica	1,150	0.0	0
Rete Mov. Dem.	15,768	0.7	10
Ppi	276,788	11.8	198
Patto Segni	37,604	1.6	17
Pri	16,749	0.7	13
Psdi	2,503	0.1	0
Socialdemocrazia	616	0.0	0
Gov. coalition area	138,605	5.9	103
Gov. coalition area-Others	28,245	1.2	29
Progressisti	120,446	5.1	190
Progressisti-Others	50,690	2.1	68
Center mixed	71,069	3.0	56
Other Green Lists	2,390	0.1	2
Other Leagues	4,588	0.2	0
Autonomist Lists	12,362	0.5	2
Right mixed	398	0.0	0
Heterogeneous Lists	18,990	0.8	14
Indipendents	88,847	3.8	80
Civic Lists	234,500	9.9	183
Other Lists	35,009	1.5	30
Total	2,367,522	100.0	2,188

A total of 2,456 seats were assigned; 268 seats are reserved for lists of which the mayoral candidates were not elected.

Entitled to vote	3,419,031
Voters [a]	2,714,194
% of voters	79.4
Invalid votes	196,753
% of invalid votes/voters	7.2
of which blank ballots	69,599
% of blank ballots/invalid votes	35.4

[a] Since people could choose to vote the Mayor alone, the number of voters is not equal to the sum of valid votes and invalid votes. In addition, the Ministry has not corrected its figures on the basis of Prefecture data and this may have increased discrepancies.

Source: Calculated from data provided by Ministero dell'Interno-Direzione centrale per i servizi elettorali.

TABLE B8   Municipal Elections, June 12, 1994: 386 Municipalities with up to 15,000 Inhabitants. Summary of National Returns.

Lists	Valid Votes	%	Seats
Forza Italia	31,560	2.7	101
Alleanza Nazionale	21,790	1.9	48
Lega Nord	68,540	5.9	215
Centro Crist. Dem.	5,412	0.5	16
Pds	20,505	1.8	132
Rifondazione Comunista	7,489	0.6	10
Psi	6,619	0.6	31
Green Federation	198	-	-
Rete Mov. Dem.	2,304	0.2	-
Ppi	73,292	6.3	404
Patto Segni	1,362	0.1	-
Gov. coalition area	150,758	13.0	514
Gov. coalition area-Others	25,321	2.2	82
Progressisti	102,084	8.8	445
Progressisti-Others	80,021	6.9	358
Center mixed	68,210	5.9	229
Verdi-Verdi	34	-	1
Other Lists	398	-	-
Autonomist Lists	174	-	1
Right mixed	118	-	-
Heterogeneous Lists	144,792	12.5	828
Indipendents	49,796	4.3	308
Civic Lists	297,804	25.7	1,639
Other Lists	1,862	0.1	12
Total	1,160,443	100.0	5,374

A total of 5,374 seats were assigned.

Entitled to vote	1,553,379
Voters [a]	1,238,054
% of voters	79.7
Invalid votes	75,822
% of invalid votes/voters	6.1
of which blank ballots	39,179
% of blank ballots/invalid votes	51.7

[a]The number of voters is not equal to the sum of valid votes and invalid votes because the Ministry has not corrected its figures on the basis of Prefecture data.

Source: Calculated from data provided by Ministero dell'Interno-Direzione centrale per i servizi elettorali.

TABLE B9   Municipal Elections, November 20, 1994: 49 Municipalities with over 15,000 Inhabitants. Summary of National Returns.

Lists	Valid Votes	%	Seats
Forza Italia	93,663	8.4	109
Alleanza Nazionale	142,070	12.7	120
Lega Nord	50,318	4.5	83
Centro Crist. Dem.	52,037	4.6	46
Unione di Centro	5,557	0.5	4
Pds	153,705	13.7	199
Rifondaz. Comunista	68,363	6.1	50
Psi	11,748	1.1	17
Green Federation	17,704	1.6	16
Verdi Arcobaleno	213	-	-
Rete Mov. Dem.	425	-	-
Ppi	141,340	12.6	142
Patto Segni	5,537	0.5	2
Pri	2,703	0.2	3
Psdi	1,156	0.1	1
Gov. coalition area	39,898	3.6	24
Gov. coalition area-Others	5,083	0.5	2
Progressisti	34,436	3.1	67
Progressisti-Others	49,075	4.4	89
Center mixed	30,729	2.7	32
Lega Alpina Lumbarda	744	0.1	0
Other Leagues	3,510	0.3	1
Lega d'Azione Meridionale	216	-	-
Autonomist Lists	768	0.1	0
Heterogeneous Lists	10,871	1.0	12
Indipendents	17,177	1.5	3
Civic Lists	169,210	15.1	123
Other Lists	11,482	1.0	5
Total	1,119,738	100.0	1,150

A total of 2,456 seats were assigned; 170 seats are reserved for lists of which the mayoral candidates were not elected.

Entitled to vote	1,612,339
Voters [a]	1,308,175
% of voters	81.1
Invalid votes	73,459
% of invalid votes/voters	5.6
of which blank ballots	18,263
% of blank ballots/invalid votes	24.9

[a] Since people could choose to vote the Mayor alone, the number of voters is not equal to the sum of valid votes and invalid votes. In addition the Ministry has not corrected its figures on the basis of Prefecture data, and this may have increased discrepancies.

Source: Calculated from data provided by Ministero dell'Interno-Direzione centrale per i servizi elettorali.

TABLE B10 Municipal Elections, November 20, 1994: 186 Municipalities with up to 15,000 Inhabitants. Summary of National Returns.

Lists	Valid Votes	%	Seats
Forza Italia	6,324	1.0	23
Alleanza Nazionale	14,598	2.3	27
Lega Nord	25,477	4.0	97
Centro Crist. Dem.	1,470	0.2	3
Pds	5,587	0.9	38
Rifondaz. Comunista	6,738	1.1	18
Green Federation	328	-	4
Ppi	24,592	3.9	108
Patto Segni	75	-	-
Gov. coalition area	102,876	16.2	312
Gov. coalition area-Others	17,697	2.8	50
Progressisti	28,753	4.5	112
Progressisti-Others	49,731	7.8	207
Center mixed	8,247	1.3	45
Verdi-Verdi	28	-	4
Lega d'Azione Meridionale	161	-	-
Heterogeneous Lists	107,339	16.9	478
Indipendent List	32,293	5.1	221
Civic Lists	203,123	32.0	964
Total	635,437	100.0	2,711

A total of 2,711 seats were assigned.

Entitled to vote	839,213
Voters [a]	667,322
% of voters	79.5
Invalid votes	29,475
% of invalid votes/voters	4.4
of which blank ballots	10,310
% of blank ballots/invalid votes	35.0

[a] The number of voters is not equal to the sum of valid votes and invalid votes because the Ministry has not corrected its figures on the basis of Prefecture data.

Source: Calculated from data provided by Ministero dell'Interno-Direzione centrale per i servizi elettorali.

TABLE B11 Mayoral Elections in Provincial Capitals. Second Round, June 26, 1994.

	Candidates	Valid Votes	%	Lists
Asti	Nosenzo Giuseppe	15,850	43.1	Alleanza Nazionale, Coalition gov. area
	Bianchini Alberto	20,892	56.9	Pds, Rifond. Comun., Progressisti
	Total	36,742	100.0	
Como	Botta Alberto	22,461	54.5	Forza Italia, Alleanza Nazionale, Centro Crist. Dem.
	Mantero Maurizio	18,784	45.5	Civic List
	Total	41,245	100.0	
Rovigo	Bellini Paolo	12,652	44.7	Lega Nord, Coalition gov. area-Others
	Baratella Fabio	15,626	55.3	Pds, Rifond. Comun., Ind., Civic List
	Total	45,394	100.0	
Verona	Sironi Mariotti Michela	74,032	61.5	Alleanza Nazionale, Lega Nord, Coalition gov. area, Lista ecologica, Part. legge naturale
	Donella Dario	46,316	38.5	Pds, Rifond. Comun., Green Federation, Civic List
	Total	120,348	100.0	
Gorizia	Valenti Gaetano	12,807	57.7	Forza Italia, Alleanza Nazionale,
	Crocetti Bruno	9,403	42.3	Progressisti, Unione slovena, Citt. per l'Isontino
	Total	73,243	100.0	
Savona	Gervasio Francesco	22,761	52.9	Forza Italia, Lega Nord, P. Popolare Italiano
	Pastore Aldo	20,246	47.1	Rifond. Comun., Progressisti, Part. Pens., Ind., Civic List
	Total	43,007	100.0	
Parma	Busani Angelo	42,650	45.3	Forza Italia, Alleanza Nazionale, Lega Nord, Centro Crist. Dem., Pannella-Riformatori
	Lavagetto Stefano	51,588	54.7	Pds, Progressisti
	Total	94,238	100.0	
Piacenza	Passoni Paolo	29,983	49.0	Alleanza Nazionale, Coalition gov. area
	Vaciago Giacomo	31,259	51.0	Pds, Progressisti, Lista Pens., Civic List
	Total	61,242	100.0	
Pistoia	Forleo Maurizio Aldo	16,485	37.9	Alleanza Nazionale, Coalition gov. area
	Scarpetti Lido	26,963	62.1	Pds, Green Federation, Civic List
	Total	43,448	100.0	

(continues)

TABLE B11 *(continued)*

	Candidates	Valid Votes	%	Lists
Rieti	Cicchetti Antonio	13,601	57.1	Forza Italia, Alleanza Nazionale, Lega Nord., Centro Crist. Dem.
	Lorenzetti Roberto	10,238	42.9	Pds, Center mixed Civic List
	Total	23,839	100.0	
L'Aquila	Volpe Gianfranco	15,101	43.0	Alleanza Nazionale, Lega Nord., Coalition gov. area
	Centi Antonio Carmine	20,029	57.0	Pds, Rete Mov. Dem. Progressisti
	Total	23,839	100.0	
Catanzaro	Lacquaniti Annunziato	16,233	44.9	Forza Italia, Alleanza Nazionale, Ind.
	Gualtieri Benito	19,889	55.1	P. Popolare Italiano, Ind., Civic List
	Total	36,122	100.0	
Matera	Andriulli Domenico	12,124	38.9	Forza Italia, Alleanza Nazionale, Centro Crist. Dem., Unione di Centro
	Manfredi Mario Tommaso	19,080	61.1	Progressisti
	Total	31,204	100.0	
Enna	Alvano Antonio Onofrio	7,696	50.1	Coalition gov. area
	Faraci Claudio Antonio	7,654	49.9	Civic List
	Total	15,350	100.0	
Messina	Carmona Angelo	41,823	39.9	Coalition gov. area
	Providenti Francesco	62,869	60.1	Indipendent
	Total	104,692	100.0	
Ragusa	Malfitano Giuseppe	12,965	40.4	Coalition gov. area
	Chessari Giorgio	19,131	59.6	Progressisti-Others
	Total	32,096	100.0	
Siracusa	Immè Alfredo	19,292	45.9	Coalition gov. area
	Fatuzzo Marco	22,781	54.1	Progressisti-Others
	Total	42,073	100.0	
Trapani	D'Alì Gabriele	11,551	36.9	Coalition gov. area
	Buscaino Mario	19,769	63.1	Civic List
	Total	31,320	100.0	
Oristano	Martinez Marco Pio Giuseppe	7,456	47.1	Forza Italia, Alleanza Nazionale,
	Scarpa Mariano	8,384	52.9	Partito Popolare Italiano, Patto Segni, Progressisti, Center mixed
	Total	15,840	100.0	
Cagliari	Delogu Mariano	47,326	54.5	Forza Italia, Alleanza Nazionale,
	Ciotti Carlo	39,482	45.5	Pds, Rifond. Comun., Green Federation, Civic List
	Total	86,808	100.0	

Source: Calculated from data provided by Ministero dell'Interno-Direzione centrale per i servizi elettorali

TABLE B12 Mayoral Elections in Provincial Capitals. Second Round December 4, 1994.

	Candidates	Valid Votes	%	Lists
Brescia	**Gnutti Vito Martinazzoli**	50,799	43.5	Lega Nord, Coalition gov. area
	Fermo Mino	65,899	56.5	Pds, Partito Popolare Italiano, Lista ecologica, Civic List
	Total	116,698	100.0	
Sondrio	**Camurri Giuseppe**	5,648	42.3	Forza Italia, Lega Nord
	Molteni Alcide	7,702	57.7	Progressisti-Others
	Total	13,350	100.0	
Treviso	**Gentilini Giancarlo**	24,888	54.8	Lega Nord, Center mixed
	Tognana Clarimbaldo	20,506	45.2	Partito Popolare Italiano, Progressisti-Others
	Total	45,394	100.0	
Massa	**Vita Silvio**	11,515	32.6	Forza Italia, Alleanza Nazionale, Centro Crist. Dem., Psdi
	Pucci Roberto	23,779	67.4	Pds, Psi, P. Popolare, Pri, Center mixed, Fed. Laburista
	Total	35,294	100.0	
Pescara	**Pace Carlo**	38,135	52.1	Forza Italia, Alleanza Nazionale, Centro Crist. Dem., Civic List
	Collevecchio Mario	35,108	47.9	Pds, Rifond. Comunista, Psi Green Federation, Civic List
	Total	73,243	100.0	
Brindisi	**De Maria Raffaele**	21,160	48.7	Forza Italia, Alleanza Nazionale, Centro Crist. Dem., Unione di centro, Civic List
	Errico Michele	22,277	51.3	Pds, Partito Popolare Italiano Civic List
	Total	43,437	100.0	

Source: Calculated from data provided by Ministero dell'Interno-Direzione centrale per i servizi elettorali.

TABLE C1   Balance-Sheet of Official Party Budget, 1991-1993.

	Revenues	Expenses	Operating Surplus-Deficit	Accumulated Surplus-Deficit (Including Previous Years)
Dc				
1991	77,713,299,445	76,856,797,809	856,501,636	-12,361,064,050
1992	107,334,589,538	107,325,911,575	8,677,963	-12,352,386,087
1993	23,437,893,107	42,695,276,238	-19,257,383,131	-31,609,769,218
Pds				
1991	103,213,606,672	108,840,933,419	-5,627,326,747	-43,451,614,804
1992	49,815,322,828	50,383,026,259	-567,703,431	-44,019,318,235
1993	31,528,208,101	31,872,581,145	-344,373,044	-44,363,691,279
Rifondazione Comunista [a]				
1991	2,542,774,424	2,550,422,549	-7,648,125	-7,648,125
1992	7,284,206,346	8,518,556,830	-1,234,350,484	-1,234,350,484
1993	11,366,176,679	11,236,146,089	130,030,590	-1,104,319,894
Psi				
1991	60,472,860,418	61,202,845,150	-729,984,732	-26,599,325,426
1992	49,864,149,866	71,134,286,225	-21,270,136,359	-47,869,461,785
1993	13,003,459,631	17,517,850,384	-4,514,390,753	-52,383,852,538
Pri				
1991	7,474,857,200	6,428,781,656	1,046,075,544	-3,287,729,420
1992	11,829,583,353	12,213,332,229	-383,748,876	-3,671,478,296
1993	6,327,233,240	4,831,765,913	1,495,467,327	-2,176,010,969
Psdi				
1991	8,781,955,713	8,282,485,259	499,470,454	-9,398,151,078
1992	9,020,427,741	10,872,465,984	-1,852,038,243	-11,250,189,321
1993	-	-	-	-
Green Federation				
1991	3,859,162,275	4,199,996,261	-340,833,986	132,040,616
1992	5,337,064,972	5,236,323,644	100,741,328	232,781,944
1993	3,995,323,560	3,107,324,694	947,998,866	1,120,780,810
Pli				
1991	4,943,232,180	5,693,821,720	-750,589,540	-9,413,631,089
1992	4,660,754,173	7,845,005,569	-3,184,251,396	-12,597,882,485
1993	-	-	-	-
Lega				
1991	2,190,875,425	2,446,622,815	-255,747,390	194,207,330
1992	12,564,616,843	10,373,661,781	2,190,955,062	2,385,162,392
1993	22,970,666,098	19,430,743,829	3,539,922,269	5,925,084,661
Msi				
1991	7,107,129,667	10,217,444,886	-3,110,315,219	-4,306,491,173
1992	9,656,503,952	10,233,358,795	-576,854,843	-4,883,346,016
1993	11,720,894,589	9,739,438,756	1,981,455,833	-2,901,890,183

[a] The 1991 budget refers to the Movimento per la Rifondazione Comunista which was transformed into the Partito della Rifondazione Comunista on December 15, 1991. The 1992 and the 1993 budgets, referred to the Partito della Rifondazione Comunista, do not include the Movimento's deficit.

TABLE C2   Balance-Sheet of Official Party Budget, 1993

| | Revenues | | | | Expenses | Balance | |
	Membership Dues	State Contributions	Other Revenues	Total Revenues	Total Expenses	Operating Surplus-Deficit	Accumulated Surplus-Deficit (Including Previous Years)
Dc	199,820,000	22,616,020,813	622,052,294	23,437,893,107	42,695,276,238	-19,257,383,131	-31,609,769,218
Pds	8,655,784,000	13,086,282,197	9,786,141,904	31,528,208,101	31,872,581,145	-344,373,044	-44,363,691,279
Rif. Comunista	673,150,950 [a]	5,384,645,963	5,308,379,766	10,693,025,729	11,236,146,089	-543,120,360	-1,104,319,894
Psi	44,525,000	11,095,955,698	1,862,978,933	13,003,459,631	17,517,850,384	-4,514,390,753	-52,383,852,538
Psdi	-	-	-	-	-	-	-
Green Federation	60,000,000	3,102,302,695	833,020,865	3,995,323,560	3,107,324,694	887,998,866	1,120,780,810
Pri	361,781,500	4,325,065,269	1,640,386,471	6,327,233,240	4,831,765,913	1,495,467,327	-2,176,010,969
Lega Nord	3,307,315,444	7,179,572,723	12,483,777,931	22,970,666,098	19,430,743,829	3,539,922,269	5,925,084,661
Pli	-	-	-	-	-	-	-
Msi	156,358,904	5,087,366,974	6,477,168,711	11,720,894,589	9,739,438,756	1,981,455,833	-2,901,890,183

[a] Including differed payments, amounting to L. 221,085,000, for 1992 membership drive, as specified in the 1992 budget report.

TABLE C3   Reported Membership of the Main Parties, 1985-1994

	Rifondaz. Comunista	Pci/Pds	Dc/Ppi	Lega Nord	Forza Italia	Msi/An	Pli	Pri	Pr	Psi
1985	-	1,595,281	1,444,592	-	-	141,623	61,818	-	2,968	583,282
1986	-	1,551,576	1,395,239	-	-	156,520	36,931	-	11,010	589,207
1987	-	1,508,140	1,812,201	-	-	165,427	26,439	117,031	11,822	620,557
1988	-	1,462,281	1,887,615	-	-	151,444	17,768	107,949	5,750	630,692
1989	-	1,417,182	1,862,426	-	-	166,162	19,121	99,386	3,199	635,504
1990	-	1,319,305	2,109,670	-	-	142,347	44,732	83,498	4,287	664,481
1991	112,278	989,708	1,390,918	-	-	150,157	50,327	72,175	4,296	-
1992	119,094	769,944	-	140,000	-	181,243	18,731	71,886	10,474	-
1993	121,055	690,414	813,753	-	-	202,715	-	-	42,676	-
1994	120,000	700,000	233,377	-	300,000	324,344	-	20,916	5,281	-

About the Editors
and Contributors

Edmondo Berselli is assistant editor of the bimonthly review "Il Mulino".

Jack Brand is reader in government in the Department of Government at the University of Strathclyde.

Martin J. Bull is senior lecturer in the Department of Politics and Contemporary History at the University of Salford.

Antonio Carioti is chief editor of the daily "La voce repubblicana".

Filippo Cavazzuti is professor of financial science and financial law in the Faculty of Economic Studies at the University of Bologna.

Stephen Gundle is lecturer in Italian history in the Department of Italian Studies at Royal Holloway at the University of London.

Piero Ignazi is senior lecturer of comparative politics in the Faculty of Political Science at the University of Bologna.

Richard S. Katz is professor and chair of the Political Science Department at the State University of New York at Buffalo.

Tom Mackie is senior lecturer in politics at the University of Strathclyde.

Patrick McCarthy is professor of European studies at the Johns Hopkins University, Bologna Center.

Andrea Manzella is professor of parliamentary law at the Libera University of Social Studies (Luiss) of Roma.

Pernilla N. Neal is director of the Center for European Studies of Dickinson College in Bologna.

Valerio Onida is professor of constitutional law at the University of Milano.

Luca Verzichelli is a PhD student in political science at the University of Florence.

Marzia Zannini participates in research activities at the Istituto Cattaneo.

Index

About the Book

Following the major upheavals of 1993, the Italian political system suffered intense aftershocks tied to the renewal of the political class in 1994. There were shattering changes in the party system—in particular the birth of Berlusconi's Forza Italia—and the first majoritarian parliament was established. In this latest edition of *Italian Politics* all the crucial issues that define Italian political and social life during 1994 are discussed and interpreted by renowned scholars from Italy, the United States, and Britain, who provide an indispensable guide for understanding Italy's transformation.